SHADES OF BLUE

30 YEARS OF (un) ETHICAL POLICING

A novel by

Michael Rudolph

Copyright (TXu 1-776-852) 2012 by Michael Rudolph

All rights reserved. No part of this book may be reproduced, stored in a retrieval system or transmitted in any form or by any means without the prior written permission of the author except by a reviewer who may quote brief passages in a review to be printed in a newspaper, magazine, journal, or on-line publication.

The final approval for this literary material is granted by the author

Second Edition

All characters appearing in this work are fictitious. Any resemblance to real persons, living or dead is purely coincidental.

DEDICATION

This book is dedicated to all those men and women who run toward the things that most people run from. God bless you all.

CONTENTS

PREFACE

CHAPTER 1   TIMING IS EVERYTHING

CHAPTER 2   DEAD MEN TELL NO TALES

CHAPTER 3   THE FOREST OR THE TREES

CHAPTER 4   THE RIGHT STUFF

CHAPTER 5   GUARDIAN ANGELS

CHAPTER 6   YOU CAN'T HANDLE THE TRUTH

CHAPTER 7   SEE, HEAR, AND SPEAK NO EVIL

CHAPTER 8   DRUGONOMICS 101

CHAPTER 9   GOIN' FISHING

CHAPTER 10   ROBIN HOOD AND HIS MERRY MEN

CHAPTER 11   THE BLUE WALL OF SILENCE

CHAPTER 12   HEARTS AND MINDS

CHAPTER 13   STRESS CRACKS

CHAPTER 14   SPECIAL ED

CHAPTER 15   A LOVE-HATE RELATIONSHIP

CHAPTER 16   FUNCTIONAL FICTION

CHAPTER 17   MOON TIDE MAYHEM

CHAPTER 18   PACIPHONIES

CHAPTER 19   BENNY THE BULLY

CHAPTER 20   THE REAL MCCOYS

CHAPTER 21   TRAFFIC JAMS

CHAPTER 22   TRIED BY TWELVE OR CARRIED BY SIX

CHAPTER 23   A DIPLOMATIC FAUX PAS

CHAPTER 24   END GAME

PREFACE

Many years ago I watched an episode of a science fiction TV show in which the antagonist was a genetically engineered super-human. The people who made him could not control him so they placed him in suspended animation for hundreds of years. In typical fashion, instead of dealing with their mistake, they made it a problem for future generations to solve. When he awoke he observed how little humans had changed in all that time. He noted that our technology had improved tremendously, but that "man himself" had not changed.

The notion intrigued me and so I decided to examine some of the oldest texts I could find that had anything to do with human behavior. I looked at *I Ching* (2194 BC), *The Code of Hammurabi* (1780 BC), *The Laws of Manu* (1500 BC), *The Torah* (1280 BC), and *The Book of the Dead* (1240 BC). I also examined *The Republic* by Plato (380 BC) since our western municipal philosophy is based on it.

I concluded that the television character was correct. Although our knowledge of the natural world and our technology has grown by leaps and bounds, mankind has not. We humans are still the same social animals that we were thousands and thousands of years ago. I once read a newspaper story about a wealthy woman who lived on the outskirts of Chicago. She killed her three children in a jealous rage to punish her husband for having had an affair. In Greece, a wealthy woman named Medea did the same thing, as reported by Euripides – in 420 BC!

All you need to do is look at the modern world around us and you will find many examples of how circumstances and events can quickly strip away the veneer of civilization from many people. When this happens, it reveals the same emotionally primitive human beings that first formed into groups for survival and later into communities for efficiency.

Every human community, from the most primitive tribe to the most sophisticated technological nation, asks some community members to perform the function of the police. The reason is simple. There is always someone who does not want to obey the rules of the tribe or the laws of the state.

This tendency we have to violate the rules, or more often to make ourselves exceptions to the rules, (rules are always good for other people) is very natural. It is a manifestation of our survival instinct.

We seek to satisfy our own needs in order to enhance the chances of our survival. The drive to do so is hard wired into our brains by 100,000 years of evolution. Freud called it "the Id," but whatever you want to call it, it is that selfish part of our personality that says I want, what I want, when I want it. I don't want to be told, "No" and I don't want to be told, "You can't do that." In fact it is only through a process called socialization that we learn the elements of self-control. There are three of them. They are morals, ethics, and the fear of consequences.

Morals make up your personal code of behavior. They are your personal ideas of right and wrong and you get your morals from your family, your culture, and your religion. It is hard to find two people with the exact same moral code, even within the same family, because it is personal.

In order to live together in a community, human beings give and take based on their moral codes until they achieve a consensus on a communal issue. That is how an ethic is created. Everyone then agrees that in order to maintain peace in the community, the community's members must forgo their individual moral codes in favor of the communal ethic. No one has ever heard of the Senate Morals Committee because it does not exist. Morals are personal. However, there is a Senate Ethics Committee and unfortunately we hear about it more times than we would want to hear about it.

Ethics are society's expectations of your behavior in whatever role you happen to be playing. We all expect our lawyers to behave the same way. They should keep our secrets and they should work hard for our defense. These universal expectations are examples of a lawyer's ethics. We all expect our police to behave the same way. They should not take bribes, and they should administer the law without bias. Again, these commonly held societal expectations are examples of a police officer's ethics.

Ethics amount to a social contract. They are an agreement you make with society. You say to society, "I want to be a doctor." Society says, "Ok, you can be a doctor. This is what you have to do to become one, and when you do, this is how we expect you to behave." If you agree to abide by the ethics established for doctors, you can be a doctor.

Some ethics become codified. They are turned into laws with criminal and civil punishments for transgressions. Other ethics are not. They remain only societal guidelines in the same way your morals are your personal guidelines.

When your morals (your ideas of right and wrong) are not in agreement with your ethics (society's expectations) you have a dilemma. Some people call it a moral dilemma; others call it an ethical dilemma. It depends on where you feel the problem originates. However, it is really the same thing. We will almost always resolve a dilemma in favor of morality or ethics. One will win and one will lose. The process by which we justify our decision is called rationalization. Rationalization is how we live with ourselves when we violate either our moral code or our ethical code.

The wild card in the self-control game is the fear of consequences. Remember, it takes time to develop morals and it takes time to learn ethics. Little children have neither. They control themselves out of a fear of consequences. A perfect example was a 911 call I responded to early in my career.

There was a little toddler walking around in the kitchen and he saw the pretty blue light on top of the stove under a pot. As many times as his mother said to him, "Don't put your hand in the flame, you are going to get burned," he could not control his urge to reach out and touch that pretty blue light. Well, when he got burned he developed the self-control he needed not to do that again. He developed a fear of consequences. However, what is even more valuable is that the other toddler who watched the first one get burned said to himself, "I'm not doing that." The second toddler developed a fear of consequences without having to get burned.

So which of these three elements of self-control do you think has the greatest influence on your day-to-day behavior as an adult? There is no contest. It is the fear of consequences. No doubt, there are some people who are very moral people. There are certain things that they consider to be wrong and they will never do those things. They would rather die than commit certain acts. No doubt, there are some very ethical people. For them their word is their bond. There might be some legal way to weasel out of a deal they made with you, but they wouldn't take advantage of it. They know what your expectations really were when you entered into it and they will uphold their end of the bargain - even to their detriment.

However, for the vast majority of us in the vast majority of situations the fear of consequences is the most powerful element of self-control. In fact, the fear of consequences often determines whether you rationalize in favor of your morality or your ethics. I can prove it to you with a quick story about a common problem.

One day I was driving back to the station house from the Police Academy after having given a lecture. I was in a business suit and in my private car. My supervisor called me up.

When I answered the phone she said, "Listen Mike, we got a letter from this lady who says that people are running the Stop Sign near her house. Would you go down there and check it out?"

I said, "Sure," and drove directly to the location.

I parked about 50 feet from the corner and watched. Remember, I was in a business suit and in my private car. In a 45-minute period 27 cars passed through the intersection and only two stopped for the sign. Everyone else rolled passed it. So the next day I went to the same location. This time I was in uniform and I brought a big old marked police car. I parked the police car right on the corner where everyone could see it. It was about the same time of day, I stayed there for about the same amount of time, and a miracle happened. Only two cars failed to stop at the Stop Sign.

Now the day before they knew what was expected of them as drivers. They were supposed to stop at the sign (ethics), but I am sure that most of them made a similar moral judgment. Since I can see no vehicles approaching the intersection, what difference does it make if I stop at the sign?

They may have rationalized in favor of their morality, but it was the fear of consequences (me) that motivated them to behave ethically. This is just one of a million possible examples, and as long as the fear of consequences continues to be the most powerful element of self-control, *we all* are going to need someone to police us.

I am a big believer in formal education. Formal education is important if you want to become an expert in a particular subject. The greatest benefit to formal education is that all of the knowledge and research of all the experts from the dawn of history to the present is gathered together and presented to you. It is hard to accomplish that through some self-education process. Still, there is a line from a Bob Dylan song that continues to resonate with me. Dylan wrote, "You don't need a weather man to tell which way the wind is blowing."

Although experts have their value, you don't need them for everything. Some things are just common sense. In common sense situations a layperson's opinion is as good as an expert's opinion. In fact, sometimes "experts" make common sense issues much more complicated than they really are. I suspect it might have something to do with job security, or justifying the expense of their formal education.

I have a lot of formal education in the behavioral sciences, specifically in Sociology, Psychology, and Public Administration. However, I never lost sight of the fact that in the realm of human behavior, and most other things in life, experience is the greatest of teachers. I learned a few things while I was growing up on the streets of New York City that I now call the "Real Facts of Life." They are not taught in school, although they should be. You learn them by paying attention to the world around you. If you paid attention also then you probably know some of them already.

Real Fact of Life # 1: *Herbivores are food for carnivores.*

I realized this as a kid while watching Wild Kingdom on TV, but it applies to people as well. Most people have a herd mentality. They know that the wolves prey on the young, the old, the infirmed, and those who are near the edges of the herd. They protect themselves and their loved ones by trying to spend their lives close to the center of the herd. They play the odds that the wolves will attack someone else, and most of the time they win. Sometimes they develop a false sense of security. They forget what is actually keeping them safe and they venture near the edges of the herd. That is when life gives them a reality check.

Real Fact of Life # 2: *The people with the guns make the rules.*

If it were just money then we would still belong to England, Louie the 16th would still have his head, and Czar Nicholas would not have been shot along with his entire family. It is true that the people with the money do sometimes buy the people with the guns. However, at any moment the people with the guns can shoot the people with the money and take their possessions from them.

This is kind of what happened in Cuba. The wealthy people in Cuba did not treat the military and the police respectfully. They were poorly paid and they were taken for granted. When the communist revolution erupted, the military and the police decided to stop risking their lives for people who did not appreciate them. They stopped fighting Castro's forces, Castro took over the country, and the establishment lost everything. Then, like any good dictator, he took away the people's guns so they could not resist when he took away their rights.

The people who organized our government were very aware of the fact that the people with the guns make the rules. You can debate the Second Amendment until you are blue in the face, but the reason for the Second Amendment is fundamental. As long as "We, the People" keep our guns, "We, the People" will continue to make the rules.

Real Fact of Life # 3: *The meek shall inherit the earth when the bold are done with it.*

The history of human existence bears this out. If you are not bold enough to fight for what you are entitled to or to defend what is yours, expect to lose it. You might be lucky enough to have someone who will do your fighting for you, but just being right has never been enough. Oh, and for the many of you who may choose to exercise your right to defend yourselves and your loved ones, only an idiot brings a knife to a gunfight.

Real Fact of Life # 4: *The true value of any form of life is a function of your emotional involvement.*

      Suppose there is room for only one more in the lifeboat and you get to choose who it is. Someone you love and a stranger come swimming up to the boat. You are not going to toss a coin because you do not actually value their lives equally. If you did, you would toss a coin. Conversely, Adolph Hitler and your dog come swimming up to the boat. You are still not going to toss a coin. You love that trusting furry little guy. You are not going to watch him drown, and Hitler was a genocidal, murderous son-of-a-bitch.

      This fact of life explains some real life conundrums. For example, some people spend a lot of time and money to lobby on both sides of the abortion issue in the United States. Some of those same people do not lift a finger to help the thousands of *actual* human beings who die of preventable causes daily in places like Somalia. The people who lobby are emotionally invested in the abortion issue. Somalia is half a world away. If the Africans were dying in the street outside their homes, these folks would probably become emotionally involved and help them. There is no right or wrong about this. It is simply a fact of life.

Real Fact of Life # 5: *History Repeats Itself.*

      If you are considering a plan that has failed in the past, it will fail again. It will not suddenly start working just because you tweak it a little, re-package it, and call it your idea. In fact, doing the same thing again and again expecting a different result is what Einstein called insanity. To do the right thing you actually have to study the history of the issue and then apply what history teaches. That may require you to abandon your idea. Egomaniacs (narcissists) have a big problem with this one.

Here's a good example. There are occasions when an emotionally disturbed person arms themselves with a deadly weapon and unexpectedly attacks a police officer who is trying to deal with that person. Some people have suggested, that in these situations, the police should shoot to "wound" rather than kill. The only way to reasonably expect that a wound will not be fatal would be to aim for the arms or the legs.

Let us assume that the people who make this suggestion care as much for the officer's life as they do for the emotionally disturbed person. Then the only conclusion is that they did not bother to research the history of this kind of situation. Arms and legs are small moving targets that are hard to hit. History shows that trying to shoot to wound turns out bad for the cop as well as the people who get hit with the bullets that miss the arms and legs.

There are a few other "real" facts of life, but these are the most important ones. People who manage to get power over society and don't accept these truths screw things up for the rest of us. Instead of working in harmony with the things they cannot change they choose to deny the overwhelming body of evidence. They try to create their own reality based on how they would like things, and the world, to be. It never works. Here's a perfect illustration.

Some years back a homicidal mental case boarded a train in New York. He was armed with a loaded 9mm pistol and two back up magazines filled with ammunition. He was in possession of the gun and ammo *illegally.* He then proceeded to kill six people and wound 19 others. The man was eventually subdued by some passengers while he was reloading, but not before he emptied two magazines into people.

Among the dead were the brother and nephew of a woman who was later elected to the New York State Senate. Her campaign had gun control as its centerpiece, and she managed to get a bill passed that increased the mandatory jail time for crimes committed with guns. The bill also made it more difficult for decent, sane, ordinary, citizens to carry guns legally for their own protection.

If this woman accepted Real Fact of Life # 5, she would have researched her idea before trying to implement it.

History would have shown her that mandatory jail sentences for gun possession do not mean much to people who are bent on committing public murders of this type.

The historical record would also have shown her that similar laws across the country have done *nothing* to stem the flow of guns to those who want to possess them illegally. She might have learned that citizens licensed to carry firearms rarely commit crimes with them. Relatively few people are wealthy enough to hire full time professional security personnel, so all she did with her law was ensure that most future victims would be unarmed and unable to defend themselves.

If the Senator accepted Real Fact of Life # 3, she would have realized that, had some of those decent citizens been armed, someone might have shot this maniac before he murdered her brother and nephew.

Government officials do not have to like the Real Facts of Life. Hell, I don't like the Real Facts of Life either, but they are the facts of life. When politicians pretend they do not exist, they pass bad laws. When judges pretend they do not exist, they make bad decisions. It is unethical behavior on their part. Unfortunately, you and I wind up paying the price for their inability to accept, and work in harmony with, the Real Facts of Life.

I once heard a judge tell a defendant that God is the only one above the law. It follows then that playing God can be an overwhelming responsibility. I don't think the judge saw the irony in what he said. Still, we need politicians, and we need judges, and we need police officers.

The character Javert from *Les Miserables* was a very ethical police officer. Everything he did was in accordance with society's rules and laws, but do you think his treatment of Jean Valjean was just?

This book is about the ethical/moral dilemmas that police officers face, partially because of these folks, and partially because of the nature of the job. I have compiled a series of these dilemmas for you to consider. I believe they will challenge your concepts of right and wrong, and make you revisit the issue of whether the end may sometimes justify the means. I hope they will also help you to understand the complex nature of policing and the complicated individuals who do it. Come take a walk in our shoes.

CHAPTER 1
TIMING IS EVERYTHING

It was Sunday at about 7:20 in the morning. I was sitting in the Anti-Crime office with five other guys waiting for Sergeant O'Brian to give us our assignments. My partner Bob still hadn't shown up. We started officially at 0730 hours, but there was no way he was going to get there on time. He went home with a girl he met the night before and typically, he was going to be late. How late? Who knows? I was a little worried about him getting into trouble for not calling in, but Bob leads a charmed life and Sergeant O'Brian is kind of nice that way. He loves to live vicariously through us in terms of picking up women and such. Bob would slide by with a good story for the man.

Bob is former Coast Guard and had 13 years on our job at that time. He has been on the shady side of the line since he was a teenager. I think if it weren't for the military and the police department he would probably be in jail. But he is my partner and has been since I got assigned to anti-crime three months earlier. Don't misunderstand me. Bob is generally honest, knowledgeable, and good-hearted. He is just a wild man doing a wild job. Anyway, he was late.

Sergeant O'Brian was just beginning to give out the assignments when the Reverend walked in. The Reverend, Ronnie Souder, was a real piece of work. He did two tours of duty in Vietnam where he won medals for bravery against the enemy and for saving other soldiers' lives. Over his eight years as a police officer he won many more medals for bravery and lifesaving. He was divorced twice already and about to get married for the third time.

I have no idea what women saw in him. He was about 5-9 and 260 pounds. His face was ruddy and severely pock marked from bad teenage acne. He was balding and he smoked so much that whenever he would run after someone you would think he's going to have a heart attack from how hard he would breathe. He was also nuts in an unpredictable but non-criminal sort of way.

Two years earlier someone told him he could beat the IRS if he became a reverend, so he took a correspondence course from some mail order divinity school and was ordained a bonafide, legal, minister of some sect that sounded generally Christian. I have no idea what religion it actually was. Anyway, he comes walking in with his bible clutched to his chest, and all puffed out like he was walking up the center aisle of some cathedral somewhere. He was dressed in blue jeans, an orange tank top, Converse sneakers, and a wide brimmed pimp hat with a feather on it. His service revolver was strapped to his hip and his belly was hanging over his belt. It was quite a sight.

He didn't look left or right and I only became aware of his presence by the look on Sergeant O'Brian's face when he glanced up from his schedule. Amid an outcry of "oh shits" and "for Christ's sakes not again." Ronnie walked right to the head of the class, jumped up on the desk next to where the Sergeant was sitting, and turned toward us. Everyone pretended to be offended by his antics, but we pretended the same way every Sunday we worked with him. We were all smiling and anxiously waiting for the "sermon" we were about to receive.

"My brethren", he said. "Good morning and Halleluiah."

The Sergeant just put down his clipboard, pushed his chair back, and looked up and to his left to watch the show.

"Thank you for coming this morning to the Divine Church of the Baby Jesus and Discount House of The Lord" the reverend said.

"That's sounds like Imus' church you asshole," one of the guys yelled out.

Ronnie turned toward him and scowled. "Give unto Imus that which is Imus' and give unto the Lord that which is the Lord's. Now shut the fuck up while I minister to my flock."

Don Imus is the original radio shock jock. He has a keen insight into the human condition and an irreverent sense of humor. Every cop I knew at that time listened to "Imus in the Morning." I think Ronnie modeled himself after a character Imus created. Amens and laughter filled the room.

The Reverend continued, "You know my brothers that we work in a world of sin. But how is one to avoid sin if one does not know sin?"

Again there was a round of Amens.

"So I say unto you my brethren, go ye out and sin. Sin that you may know sin. Sin that you may avoid sin."

The reverend continued his sermon telling us about our need to repent and we all enjoyed the irreverence and satire. Then he passed around his hat. It went from man to man until it reached the back of the room and one of the guys threw it out into the hall. Nobody put anything in it. I guess Ron got another tax deduction. When he was finished he jumped down from the desk and walked out of the office with same pomp and clutching his bible just as he did when he walked in. We all clapped and cheered, but I must have laughed louder than most because when I looked back, the Sergeant was glaring at me.

He said, "Hey, FNG (that means *fairly* new guy), I am glad you think he is so funny. I don't see your partner anywhere, so you know what? You got him today."

The smile dropped from my face like a stone and a roar rose from the other guys. You see, they knew as I did, that whoever rode with Ronnie got involved. There was no such thing as a quiet day with him.

Before I even had time to respond, the Sergeant continued, "And I have just the job for you. Homicide-Assault is looking for this guy"

He handed me a picture.

"He is always armed with something, but rumor has it that his latest toy is a MAC 10 machine pistol."

I asked, "How do they know that?"

O'Brian said, "Because that is what he whacked the guy with."

"What guy?" I asked.

"Some guy who cheated him on a Meth deal. He rides a bike with this plate, (he handed me a piece of paper with a plate number on it) and he mules Meth into the City every weekend. They think he might be at his girlfriend's house this morning. Here's the address."

He handed me the intelligence sheet with the details on it.

I asked him sarcastically, "If *they* know he's there why aren't *they* picking him up? Shouldn't the cavalry be involved in this?"

"No" he said, "because they also think he might be at three other places this morning, and you guys are going to sit on this one because it's in our precinct. If you see him, follow him and call for back up before you take him down. Do not engage him without backup."

Now that was a joke. I am trying to imagine the conditions that would have to exist in order for that to work out. Let's see, the guy would come out of the building, not spot us because he's that stupid, and start to stroll down the street with his head in the clouds. Then we would follow him at a discreet distance until back up arrived. Not likely.

I walked out of the office and my mind was occupied with survival issues. There was Ronnie leaning on the Desk rail like he was at a bar and bullshitting and laughing with one of the uniform guys. He was completely oblivious to what he was going to be doing in a few minutes. I knew that to him it didn't matter what job we were given. He approached them all the same way, with no special preparation, and ostensibly counting on life experience and some spiritual power to make things come out OK.

When I told him about our assignment and the fact that I was uncomfortable with our deficiency of weaponry, he put his hand on my shoulder, shook me slightly and said, "My man, as they say in the ghetto, it *bees* that way sometimes. Don't you worry, we'll be fine."

I wasn't going to get any help from him in preparing properly for this. So I'm shitting a brick. I had three years on at that time, and although I had been in some scrapes, I never did battle with a stone killer armed with an automatic weapon. The situation required some special consideration as far as I was concerned. Minute by minute I alternated between telling myself that this was going to be nothing and that this was going to be completely out of control. I decided to hope for it to be nothing, but plan for it to be completely out of control. This meant pulling my shotgun out of my locker and keeping it ready in the back seat.

You have to understand that we are not allowed to carry shotguns. Although we are trained in how to use them, only *special* police officers get to carry shotguns. Our police bosses, and their political bosses, are afraid that ordinary cops with shotguns would scare the public into thinking they were in a police state. The New York State Penal Law allows police officers to be in possession of everything from a peashooter to a nuclear device, but the Department does not. If I took out my shotgun it would mean that I was definitely not buying the program. I would be in violation of the rules and regulations. If I had to use it, I could expect little support from the department, particularly if the political wind was blowing the wrong way.

    O'Brian knew that if this was for real we would be out-gunned. Yet he said what he said. Lord only knows why. So there I was. If I go back in there and tell O'Brian that I am not going to go up against a stone killer, armed with a MAC 10 machine pistol, with only a .38 caliber six shooter, I would probably be out of anti-crime as soon as O'Brian could arrange it. I was expected to handle it one way or the other, without complaining, just as the other guys would.

    I also resented the fact that even though this was a formula for disaster, the bosses covered themselves. After all, Sergeant O'Brian did say not to engage the guy. Obviously, if the guy is there we are going to engage him. How do I know that? I'm with *Ronnie* that's how I know! Here's how I resolved it. I reached into my memory bank of Sci-Fi philosophy and came up with, "Survival overrides programming!" Screw it. I was getting the shotgun and whatever happens - happens.

    As Ronnie and I were getting into the unmarked car, he glanced in and saw my shotgun and a box of extra shells lying there on the back seat.

    In a loud voice he declared, "Oh, my God! My man is looking to get into the shit."

    I glanced over the top of the car at him with a "give me a break" look on my face. Then I got into the car and started it up.

    I turned my head toward Ron in the passenger seat and I said, "I am not looking to get into the shit. That's just in case we *do* to get into the shit. Frankly, I would feel a lot better if you had one too."

    Then, in a booming voice that reminded me of Charlton Heston as Moses, Ron declared in this chastising tone, "The

Lord is my shepherd! I shall not want - for a shotgun! He maketh me to lie down with beautiful women! He leadeth me in the path of Righteousness! Yea, though I walk through the valley of the shadow of death I shall fear no evil, for I am the baddest son-of-a-bitch in the whole goddamn valley!"

As soon as Ron finished his speech I saw a smile come to his face. He was certainly trying to entertain me and he was waiting for my reaction. I just started laughing and shaking my head.

Then, through my laughter I said to him, "Ronnie, you are a mental case. You are the craziest mother-fucker I have ever worked with and I will be lucky to survive the day with you."

His smile widened when I said that and he started laughing with me. I think that was the reaction he was looking for. I continued laughing with an incredulous laugh replaying what he just said in my mind. As we drove off toward the girlfriend's house, I would turn my head to the right periodically, catch his eye, and the two of us would start laughing again. As time went by, I just shook my head in a resigned way and thought to myself, "I'm screwed, so I might as well enjoy the ride."

That is when I realized that actually Ron had my number. I had wrapped myself up pretty tightly as I was preparing for this assignment. Intentionally or unintentionally, Ron pulled the string and loosened me back up for what might be coming down the pike. I wondered if he actually had that in mind or if he was just a whacko. Who the hell knows? Either way I was laughing.

The girlfriend's house was a two-story wooden colonial. It was one of many houses along the street on plots of land that were about 30 feet wide. Each of them had a driveway separating it from the next house in the row. The neighborhood was pretty close to being a slum and was peopled predominantly by poverty level folks.

The guy we were looking for was a white biker who belonged to the Pagan motorcycle gang. When we pulled on to the block everything inside me told me this was for real. There was the bike parked in the driveway. I knew if he would only sleep for another half hour I could have every sort of assistance I needed, but that was not to be. Timing is everything and today our timing sucked.

I had just picked up the microphone to let Central know we had something when the front door opened and a young woman kissed this guy goodbye on the stoop. I glanced at the picture to be sure but I knew it was him. He was carrying saddlebags and he walked straight to his bike. I put the call over while ducking down in a worthless attempt to hide what I was doing. Even though we were in plain clothes and in an unmarked car he saw us immediately but he played it cool. He was probably deciding what to do. You know, fight or flight. He strapped the saddlebags on the bike and left one flap open. I knew why. That's where the gun was.

Ronnie saw it too and asked, "Do you see the flap?"

I said, "Yeah," and I put the call over for assistance, again telling Central in so many proper police terms that I wanted all the help they could send.

Then, we were off.

CHAPTER 2
DEAD MEN TELL NO TALES

The biker gave us the finger and tore off on the bike in the opposite direction so we had to U-turn to follow him. I am thinking to myself, does he know we want him for the homicide? If he does anything can happen. If he doesn't, he might just pull right over thinking we were just going to hassle him. But then I thought if he has a MAC 10 in that bag he isn't going to pull over.

He gunned the bike and it became clear he was planning to lose us. We had about two seconds to decide to chase him or let him go. We literally had about two seconds. I was driving and I decided to chase him, but Ronnie made the choice before I did and hit the lights and siren. We had an unmarked car so the light unit was a flasher on the dashboard. The siren was built in under the hood. Still, the biker knew the chase was on and he took us for a ride.

When you chase someone you are supposed to do the driving while your partner operates the radio. Ron told Central what was going on and about the fact that biker boy was leading us into this industrial area near the airport. It was filled with many warehouses and factories. It had many alleyways wide enough for a bike but not wide enough for a car. It was great place to lose us easily. He obviously knew the area, so I had to ask myself another survival question. Is there something back there among those buildings that he knows about and we don't? Like some sort of trap or something?

The answer came faster then I imagined. As soon as we followed him into this narrow passage between these two buildings, not much wider than a truck body, he reached into his saddlebag and pulled out the MAC 10. He was driving the bike with one hand and reaching back behind himself shooting at us with the other. Many of his poorly aimed bullets ricocheted off the brick walls and some funneled right toward us. Biker boy knew exactly what he was doing. A normal reaction to a hail of bullets whizzing by and glass shattering all around would be to put distance between yourself and the source. It happened so fast that all I could do was hit the brakes and duck.

I am sure you have heard that people who are about to die, or people who are very frightened, sometimes pee in their pants. Ronnie and I did not pee in our pants even though some may say we had good reason to do so at that point in time. I have a theory as to why. I believe that people who pee in their pants when they are in danger are those who are really afraid to die.

Don't misunderstand me. I am not saying that I want to die or that I don't care whether I live or die. In fact, I enjoy life a lot and I would like it to continue. What I am saying is that I am not *afraid* to die. There is a big difference between the two. Hell, to quote Jim Morrison, "No one here gets out alive." It really is just a matter of when, and where, and how right? I like to think that *why* you die is important also. I am actually trying to do something positive for society. I believe the Lord will weigh my good deeds against my bad deeds and on balance; I will make it to heaven, whatever heaven actually is.

I feel sorry for people who don't believe in an afterlife. They have to be very afraid of dying. I'll bet a lot of them pee in their pants when death is near. Think about it. When you die – nothing! It all ends for them. What a drag that must be? This is all they have so I am sure they try to hold on to it desperately. Ah, who am I kidding? They would never become cops to begin with. Anyway, I think that's why we didn't pee in our pants.

While all this was happening I did try to back out of there. I managed to put the car in reverse but I got stuck when the passenger side of the car jammed against the wall of the alley. We couldn't back up any further and who knew what those bullets were doing to the engine. What I did know is that we were going to die if we remained stuck there. I peeked one eye above the steering wheel. I saw that the biker was stationary and in the process of loading another magazine. He had the big ones. They held 20 rounds. While I still had power in the engine, I put the car in drive and stepped on the gas. I was really hoping to run biker boy down.

My move caught him by surprise. He had exited the alleyway and was in a wider parking area behind the buildings just straddling his bike. It was where big 18-wheelers maneuvered to back up to loading docks. He took off on his bike to my left in reaction to my move. He drove about 100 feet and then his bike skidded out from under him and he fell down. I came out of the alleyway and made a sharp left to chase him. I jammed on my brakes as soon as I saw him on the ground to keep some distance between us. Then I threw the car in park and reached into the back seat for my shotgun. I was planning to step out of the car, use the door for cover, and blow this guy to kingdom come.

All of a sudden I realized that there was another unmarked police car behind ours. It managed to stop just as Ron and I were opening the doors. The biker started shooting again. As we were setting up behind the car doors, the biker started running away from us while shooting toward us at the same time. I was just bringing the barrel of the shotgun to bear on him when he suddenly stopped shooting and began examining his gun. I thought either the gun had jammed or he ran out of bullets.

I was taught you never give your opponent a weapon. Even a jammed or empty weapon can be unjammed or reloaded and used against you. But you know what? You have to be pretty stupid to be a drug dealing gang biker in the first place, so it didn't surprise me at all when the asshole dropped the gun, turned, and continued to run away with his back to us.

I didn't fire at him. I glanced to my right to get Ron's attention in anticipation of having to get back in the car and either chase him with the car or chase him on foot. Ron was standing with his revolver in a bladed stance just like we do at the range. He was calmly taking aim at this guy running from us. Then he fired one shot and hit the biker right in the ass.

Ron carried a .357 magnum. The shot knocked the guy off his feet, but the asshole actually got back up and kept going. He was limping badly. It was obvious that he wasn't going to get far, but he kept going. What is it about really bad guys that they never give up easily? Even shot, he was still trying to get away. He was moving much slower now. I knew I could just jog up to him and catch him, but Ron had another idea.

Ron left his position behind the car door and began walking toward the guy with his revolver still pointed at shoulder height. He stopped for a moment, took aim, and then shot him again. This time Ron hit him right in the back. The guy fell to the ground but he still wasn't dead. He cursed and yelled and then his voice became a low moan. I stood there stunned.

Right then I became aware of the guys behind me. One of them was my regular partner Bob. He must have come in late and partnered up with Kevin, another anti-crime guy. They were the first ones to come to back us up. Bob was always cool and collected. I found out later that he was on his way to relieve Ron and sit with me on the biker job. He was close behind us when the pursuit started and he had been there ever since. I was glad he was with us. It gave me a sense of security.

Bob and Kevin exited their car and were moving forward toward us. Obviously, we all had our guns trained on the bad guy lying on the pavement. He still might have another gun on his person. It turned out that he did not. Central was trying to reach us. The radio was crackling with "What is your location?" and "What is your status?" I was still standing behind the driver's door. I put the shotgun back in the car, reached over and picked up the microphone. I was looking at the biker lying on the ground and began to call for an ambulance.

I knew I should have given Central my location first, but the sight of the bleeding man moaning made me hurriedly say, "13 Crime to Central, request an ambulance forth...."

I never completed the sentence. Bob snatched the microphone from my hand, held it up in front of my face, and shook it at me in cadence with these words. "Dead-men-tell-no-tales."

He was staring into my eyes and then he threw the microphone back into the car. There was no confusion on my part. I knew exactly what he meant. If this guy dies, we would be the only ones who knew that Ronnie shot him twice while he was unarmed and trying to flee rather than threatening us. However, Bob was not leaving anything to chance. He walked forward and picked up the MAC 10. Then he continued forward and placed it on the ground near the wounded man, just out of his reach. Central kept on calling, but I just watched, listened, and went with the flow.

I turned and leaned into the car for a moment to secure the shotgun. We didn't need any accidents at this time. During that time I lost track of Ronnie. When I regained my focus on Ron he was kneeling next to the biker's head. He was holding his head up by the hair, and lightly tapping him on the face with his fingers.

I heard Ron saying to the biker, "Open your eyes. Open your eyes. I want you to see who's sending you to hell you prick."

As I got closer, I could see what seemed like a gallon of blood pooling on the concrete around the biker's lower torso. I know that one shot hit him in the back, but I realized then that the first shot didn't hit him in the ass. There was too much blood. We discovered later that the first shot hit him in the upper leg and severed his femoral artery. He was bleeding out as we watched. I screamed at Bob.

"Bob! We have got to call an ambulance and Central is screaming to know where we are."

Kevin pulled Ronnie away from the guy and we all retreated to the cars where Bob said, "Everybody slow down. First, let's get our stories straight."

He looked at Ron and said, "The guy held the gun until after your second shot. He got hit from behind because he was running away as he was shooting."

At one point the biker was doing exactly that, so Bob's story was not too far from the truth. Ron nodded in agreement with a look on his face that told me he had already planned to say something like that. However, I was worried about another issue and I spoke up.

"Bob, your fingerprints are all over the gun."

Bob said, "So what? I picked up the gun and moved it away from the asshole in case he tried to grab for it."

I nodded in agreement with the reasonableness and plausibility of Bob's response.

Then Bob said, "Mike, you tell the detectives that you tried to put the call over for the ambulance and you did give out our location. You have no idea why Central didn't hear you. Maybe you got excited and didn't key the microphone properly the first time. Wait till after the guy dies and then do it again. You know what I mean."

Again, I nodded and did as Bob directed. We knew it would take several minutes for help to arrive and by that time the biker was dead. It seemed to be a long time as I stood there and watched the biker die. The unmarked police cars had to be moved in order to get the ambulance and other police vehicles through. In fact, our car had conked out after being hit with what they later determined were 9 bullets. It was a miracle that Ron and I were not hit, but then miracles are Ronnie's business these days. At that point, the rules of engagement changed from protect your life, to protect your ass. The next stop for us was Homicide Squad, Internal Affairs Division (IAD), and then the Grand Jury.

CHAPTER 3
THE FOREST OR THE TREES

My grandmother was probably one of the luckiest mothers on the planet. She had four sons in WWII and they all came back basically unharmed. The oldest was my Uncle Steve who flew 25 missions in a B24 in the Pacific. My uncle Dave was a top Sergeant in command of one of General Patton's tanks in France. Uncle Lou was in the infantry. He fought in North Africa, Sicily, and Italy. Then he was shipped off to the Pacific. He was preparing to become part of the invasion of Japan, but we dropped the Bomb on the Japanese, and the invasion never took place. That probably saved my uncle's life. The Japanese had sworn to fight an invasion to the death. Based on previous encounters with them throughout the Pacific, the military estimated the invasion would have cost another 50,000 American lives.

My dad, who was the youngest brother, trained to be a fighter pilot. He had just gotten his wings as the war in Europe was winding down. The only action he saw was when he bombed cowboys with grapefruits in the Florida panhandle. The cowboys would shoot at the planes whenever he and his fellow pilots "bombed" them. I think it always bothered my dad that he never got a chance to turn some Nazis into ghosts.

The Army Air Corps grounded my dad because they no longer needed fighter pilots. However, since the military expected a protracted war with Japan, they sent him to bomber pilot training. He began to flight test B29 bombers before the planes were sent across the Pacific to bomb Japan. He claims he actually flight-tested the B29 that was later named Enola Gay, but we have no proof of that. He went down four times in the Gulf of Mexico with defective B29s. My dad used to say that by the time the fourth one went down he could land a B29 on water as though it were on a runway.

Whenever we would have a family event the four of them would get half a load on and it was easy for us kids to get them to tell war stories. When we were young the stories were all funny and heroic. Also, the way they told them made us proud and made us laugh. They were good storytellers and there was never any blood and guts, if you know what I mean. Years later, when we were all adults, I attended a family gathering and my Cousin Steven, Uncle Steve's son, asked my Uncle David a question. In the context of a conversation about the subject, he asked how many prisoners Uncle Dave captured during the war. Uncle Dave's response has everything to do with why Ronnie shot the biker.

My uncle said that he did not take any prisoners during WWII. He said that the only surrender he recognized was a negotiated surrender. You know, where one group of military has another group surrounded and one side says to the other, "Surrender and you will be well treated." That's a negotiated surrender. Uncle Dave said he never had the opportunity to be part of something like that.

My Cousin Steven looked at Uncle Dave with a confused facial expression, but I knew exactly what he meant. My uncle went on to explain to my cousin, in blunt and direct terms, that if one minute ago a man was trying to kill him, and the next minute the man was surrendering simply because he ran out of ammunition or his gun jammed, Uncle David shot him. It didn't matter whether the enemy had his hands in the air, or whether the enemy was running away at the time. I can clearly remember the way he put it.

Uncle Dave said, "Think about it Steve. He's shooting at you and he's trying his hardest to kill you. Given the opportunity, a minute later if he finds another gun, he is going to try to kill you again. You don't owe him anything just because at that moment fate gives you the upper hand."

It was very clear to me that Ronnie felt like uncle Dave did when Ronnie shot the biker. Unfortunately, the New York State Penal Law, Article 35, does not agree with either of them. Among other things, the law says that the police can only use deadly force when we reasonably believe that deadly force is either being used, or is about to be used. In other words, if a guy is clearly trying to kill us and then suddenly stops trying to kill us, we can't shoot at him once he stops trying to kill us. If we do, we can be charged with homicide.

Here's the dilemma. My morality was telling me that Ronnie and Uncle Dave are right. Personally, I believe the biker deserved to die for what he did. My ethic, codified in the Penal Law, tells me that Ronnie and Uncle Dave are wrong, and that Ronnie should be punished for what he did, as prescribed by law. Here's my rationalization of the dilemma.

There are many precedents in history where governments have passed laws that reasonable people in modern times now agree were bad laws. In Germany in the 1930's the government passed laws regarding Jewish people that were obviously bad laws. Some police officers supported those laws others did not. In some southern states they passed laws that African Americans could not drink from the same water fountains, use the same toilets, or sit in the same vicinity as Caucasian Americans. Again, some police officers enforced those laws while others did not.

However, make no mistake about it. If police officers publicly choose not to support a law, or even if they get caught privately not supporting a law, those cops could lose their jobs and could even wind up prosecuted themselves. Police officers swear to uphold the constitution and the law (their ethic). The common thinking is that you can't have police officers picking and choosing which laws to support and which ones not to support. Or can you?

How does one handle a bad law? How should a police officer handle a bad law? Could I have justified herding Jewish folks into a gas chamber by saying I did it because it was the law or because it was my job? Could I justify beating an African American man into submission if he resisted being arrested for drinking from the wrong water fountain? These may be skewed examples but the philosophical issue is exactly the same. It is about picking and choosing which laws to uphold and which ones to ignore. It has always gone on and it will always go on. Only the circumstances, and the degree of a given law's absurdity, are different.

Ronnie is a man who has saved many lives and has served his country and his community faithfully. Yes, he's a little nuts, but he never beat anyone out of meanness. He wasn't bigoted in his thoughts or in his deeds against races or religions. He is the kind of police officer you would want to come and help you when you eventually need one because he is pretty much selfless. I felt we needed more cops like him, not fewer. How could I justify taking away that man's job, or possibly putting him in prison, because he did something that is quite natural and understandable (at least to me) under the circumstances?

I even agree with what he did. Anyone who has ever been in a fight for his or her life can understand what happened. It is unreasonable to expect that every human being can switch the fight response off just like that. I can't help feeling that the people who wrote NYS Penal Law Article 35 never had to fight for their lives. If they did, Article 35 might read quite differently.

I was at a seminar once where I was involved in a group discussion that centered on what justice really means. After some time, the participants established a rapport. We were all talking honestly and philosophically. One member of our group was a criminal defense attorney. I remember asking him this hypothetical question.

"Suppose you know for certain that your client brutally raped and murdered a woman. He shows no signs of remorse and even says he would do it again because he liked it so much. Would you try as hard to get that client off as you would if you really believed the client were innocent of the crime?"

I could not have given the guy a better opportunity to say no. I was shocked when he said, "Yes." I then asked him how he would be able to sleep at night, or look at himself in the mirror every day, knowing that he turned such an animal loose on society, particularly when he was in a position to see justice done. I asked him how he would feel if the guy he helped free went and raped and murdered someone he loved.

He told me that justice is done when the system decides a person's guilt or innocence. He said that a lawyer's job is to use the system any legal way he or she can to get clients off. That was one of his ethics. If I didn't like that, I should change the system and the law to prohibit lawyers from using it that way. I shouldn't blame the lawyer for the system's or the law's shortcomings.

Personally, I think this attorney could not see the forest for the trees. I wonder if the Jewish people who went to the gas chambers, or the southern blacks, would have agreed with his assessment that as long as the system permits it, it is justified. What about right and wrong? What about the lesser of two evils? Which is the greater evil, to lie about what Ronnie did and let him continue to save lives and arrest criminals, or to put a relatively good man in prison just simply because the law says you should? I concluded that, if the lawyer was being honest with me, then he could probably rationalize any behavior that wound up being in his own interest. I wondered if in his heart he ever took personal responsibility for anything he did.

Well, I had some interesting decisions to make. If I wanted to protect Ronnie, I had to lie. I had to lie to the detectives, to Internal Affairs, and I had to lie to the Grand Jury. If I got caught lying I would lose my job and face jail. Hell of a choice right? In truth, the decision to lie was made behind those buildings when we saw justice as something other than what the law said it was. Our fate depended on a number of things. Most important? We all had to stick to the story. I wasn't too worried about that. Everyone who was there knew that, as Ben Franklin said, "If we do not hang together we will surely hang separately."

The next problem? Were there any witnesses? If there were witnesses, and their stories were different from ours, we would certainly get indicted. Conviction is another issue. Conflicting eyewitness testimony usually means no proof beyond a reasonable doubt. Reasonable doubt means a not guilty verdict. I believed that at worst we would have a hung jury.

The biggest problem was the Crime Scene Search Unit (CSSU). If the evidence CSSU came up with, corroborated the witnesses' story, we were all going to jail. Interestingly, the amount of effort put into a CSSU investigation is often triaged. In other words, they work harder on some cases than others. Sometimes these things depend on which way the political wind is blowing. For instance, if the victim is an upstanding citizen, or a member of any minority group, they will pull out all the stops. CSSU realizes that their investigations in these types of cases will be closely scrutinized. This guy happened to be a white, male, career criminal, with a long and sordid rap sheet. Our odds were good that CSSU would choose not to investigate thoroughly enough to cause us a problem.

You can also get a feel for how you are going to fare when you see the players involved. I was relieved to see that the Crime Scene detectives were three cops who had been active and aggressive police officers. I knew one personally and I knew the reputations of the other two. Best of all, there were no witnesses!

Fictional detectives like Sherlock Holmes had a scientific approach to solving crimes. Whenever Sherlock would investigate a crime, he started with a blank slate. Then he would add facts, circumstances, and physical evidence (clues), which he followed to wherever the evidence led him. Eventually he would develop a suspect by linking up motive, means, and opportunity.

Most real detectives don't operate that way. It takes too long. Real detectives usually start out by making someone a suspect. The choice might be based on experience, or statistical inference, or a gut feeling. Then they try to fit the facts and physical evidence to the suspect. They start from the premise that you did what you are suspected of, and work backwards from there. The suspect is considered guilty, until facts and circumstances point to that person's innocence. Internal Affairs works this way also.

Another thing you have to keep in mind is that the Police Department is essentially a Kangaroo Court. A Kangaroo Court is one in which the prosecution can hop from place to place using physical and testimonial evidence without regard to admissibility, continuity of evidence, discovery, and other such constitutional protections. They don't care how the evidence is obtained or introduced as long as it isn't falsified. They want to know whether you really did what you are accused of doing. When investigating its own, the department is actually concerned with getting to the truth.

I have always appreciated the utility of the Kangaroo Court. Ironic, isn't it? My own philosophical beliefs were now biting me in the ass. Just like Scrooge with the ghost of the future, I feared the Department's investigators most of all. One after the other we went through, and cleared, the Homicide detectives' interviews. For the Internal Affairs interviews, our Police Benevolent Association (PBA) representatives, and our individual attorneys, were always there to insure we received our rights, and proper treatment.

Justice isn't blind. However, sometimes it does look the other way. I suspect that our people in CSSU and Homicide did exactly that. With the blessing of CSSU and the Homicide Squad, Internal Affairs chose not to crucify us. Our interviews with them went very smoothly. We cleared IAD, and then we cleared the Grand Jury. Ronnie continued to arrest bad guys and save people for another five years. Finally, a heart attack did what Vietnam and a host of bad guys could not do.   His death gave me a feeling that the world would be worse off for lack of him.

CHAPTER 4
THE RIGHT STUFF

In most parts of our country, the vetting process for police officers is constantly evolving. The evolution is influenced by changes in society's expectations (new ethics). It is also influenced by a growing understanding of how society's treatment of police officers either motivates, or de-motivates, ethical police behavior (See Real fact of Life # 2). Actually, my experience teaching at the FBI National Police Academy has shown me that in some parts of our country the vetting process still leaves much to be desired.

As the result of a poor vetting process some people become police officers without completely understanding what society actually expects of them. Others become police officers with unrealistic expectations of their own. Ethically, when they finally come to understand what society expects, they should either adapt to the ethics, or resign. Unfortunately, rather than do either, some officers simply choose not to fulfill their obligations. They perform at a marginal level and find ways to rationalize their unethical behavior. The public, and sometimes their fellow police officers, get short-changed because of it.

Then there are those people who become police officers through a poor vetting process who simply do not have the right stuff. Some people could not perform the job of a police officer no matter how hard they try. It is just not in their nature. These individuals cannot live up to society's expectations of police officers even if they want to. Over the years many police departments have developed a vetting process that has resulted in a more professional police force. Most police officers today are more ethical than police officers have been in the past. There is no doubt that better compensation and better working conditions have contributed to this. However, it all starts with recruitment, and recruitment starts with "Career Day" presentations at the local high schools.

A good career day presentation should be effective in attracting *only* those individuals who would lend themselves to the ethics society has established for its police. Over the course of my career, I was called upon to do many Career Day presentations. On those occasions, the students would hear something like this:

"Hello everyone, my name is Mike Rudolph, and I am here on Career Day to talk to you about a career in the police department. I am going to begin by making a suggestion. I suggest that you be proud of whatever career you eventually choose. You see, all of our careers are like the pieces of a jigsaw puzzle. They fit together to make something. They make the quality of life we enjoy here in this country. Every career makes a contribution and that is what is important. We all need to give something back and not just be takers. However, with this in mind, it is important to realize that nothing in society functions correctly without the police – Nothing!"

"You can't teach when there are bullets flying through the windows. You can't run a hospital if the local gang lord can send in his thugs to kidnap your doctors and your nurses. You can't grow crops, or raise livestock, if bandits are able to raid your fields and flocks. You certainly can't run a business if people are allowed to steal from you. Societies all over the world give their police the mandate to "protect life and property," because in the places where we don't do it, people have to fight for their own lives and their own property every day."

"This makes policing a very noble profession and certainly one I hope you will consider as a career. However, for those of you who might, there are some things that you absolutely need to know."

"First of all, society has huge expectations of its police. Society expects that with only a moment's notice, a police officer will be willing to take someone's life. That is a very heavy responsibility, but their next expectation is even heavier. People also expect, again with only a moment's notice, that a police officer will be willing to sacrifice his or her own life. This is why when we work we wear body armor and we carry guns."

"I want to be very clear about this. I am talking about being willing to give up everything you have, and everything you are ever going to have, to protect someone that you don't even know. If you are not the kind of person who can do that, then you need to choose a different career. You see, when you take away all of the hype, and all of the TV shows and movies, and all of the mucho macho stuff that surrounds police officers, this is what policing is all about. It is about the willingness to take a life, or to sacrifice your own."

"Another thing you absolutely need to know is that police officers are never compensated appropriately for what they put at risk. When one of you calls 911, your favorite movie star does not show up to risk his or her life for you. Neither does your favorite musical performer, or sports figure, or the president of Nintendo for that matter. Yet, society pays these people millions and millions of dollars a year, and all *they* do for you is provide you with entertainment."

"So you may well ask yourselves, 'Why would anyone want to become a police officer? You put an awful lot at risk, and you can make more money doing something else.' Well, the reason people become police officers is that, most of the time in this world of ours, what goes around comes around. Just as I am willing to risk my life to protect someone I don't know, other police officers are out there, willing to risk their lives to protect my loved ones who, in effect, are people that they don't know. Do you see how what goes around comes around?"

"On the other hand, if you are the kind of person who cares enough about your fellow human beings to stand up against selfish people who take advantage of others, and if you are brave enough to stand up against wicked people who like to hurt others, then this is the job for you. At the end of the day when you look in the mirror it can be very satisfying."

"We don't care if you are a man or a woman. We don't care about the color of your skin. We don't care about your sexual orientation, where you came from, or by what name you call God. If you become a police officer you will become my brother or my sister and we will try to take care of each other as we go through the process of taking care of everyone else."

"The process for becoming a police officer is actually very interesting. First of all, you have to be 20 years old and you have to have 24 college credits. There was a time when all you needed was a high school diploma. Then high schools began giving diplomas to people who could barely read and write and who had trouble with basic math. We discovered that by the time you have 24 college credits (and they can be in underwater basket weaving for all we care) you will have taken the remedial courses necessary for you to be able to read, write, and do basic math."

"The first test you take is a written entrance examination. The exam tests you for these skills (reading, writing, and basic math). It also tests you for some things that really should be taught in school. We call them critical thinking skills. One is the ability to look at a set of facts and circumstances and draw logical, supportable, conclusions from those facts and circumstances. Another is the ability to come up with reasonable solutions to actual daily real life problems, not just those you see in classrooms, laboratories, or textbooks."

"After you pass the entrance exam, you take a medical exam. They want to know that you can see, that you can hear, that you can smell, that you have two arms and two legs, and that your heart works well."

"Then you take a physical exam. The physical exam consists of a series of exercises that mimic the types of physical tasks a police officer has to perform in the line of duty. They are things like chasing people, climbing over things, carrying things, dragging things, etc."

"Next, you take the psychological exam. Obviously, we don't want to give guns to crazy people. However, besides the blatantly crazy, there are four kinds of people who are not crazy, but we still don't want them to become police officers. They are power trippers, bigots, adrenaline junkies, and cowards. We try to weed them out during the psychological exam."

"Power trippers are people who will become bullies if you give them a police officer's powers. Bigots are people who believe that one entire group of people is either superior or inferior to another entire group of people. We don't want them either. Adrenaline junkies are folks who have watched too many cop shows. All they want to do is drive fast and shoot their guns. Finally, there are cowards. Cowards are an interesting group. Many of them are in love with the idea of being police officers, but when the time comes to risk their lives for people they don't know, cowards will chicken out. We don't want them."

"After the psychological exam, you have to submit to a background investigation. The purpose of the background investigation is to find out if you are a criminal who just never got caught. Let's face it. If you are a really good criminal you are not going to get caught. So we send out investigators who talk to your family, your friends, and your neighbors. If you work they speak with your boss and your coworkers. If you are in school they talk with your teachers and your fellow students. All of this is designed to keep criminals from becoming police officers. However, the investigators are also checking to make sure that you are not a power tripper, a bigot, a thrill seeker, or a coward, who just happened to make it through the psychological exam. If they find that you are any of those things your journey ends there."

"When you pass all of these hurdles you go into the Police Academy for eight months. You work five days a week, ten hours a day, and we teach you everything you need to know to be a police officer. All the while you are in the Police Academy your instructors are watching the way you interact with others. They often create secret little tests to try to reveal if any recruits are power trippers, bigots, adrenaline junkies, or cowards who slipped through the net. If they find that you are you won't make it out of the academy."

"When you graduate the police academy you are a police officer. You go on patrol by yourself and you are trained and equipped to handle just about anything that comes your way. However, you are still on probation for an entire year. During that time your supervisors and your co-workers are watching how you interact with the public. Guess what they are looking for? Power trippers, bigots, adrenaline junkies, and cowards."

"Once you are off probation you are good to go for the rest of your career, assuming you don't commit a crime. After 20 years of service you become eligible to retire. Your retirement compensation consists of half your salary each year for the rest of your life. In addition, the Department pays for your medical plan. Not bad right? It is not movie star money, but it could carry you through if you are a frugal person without too much debt."

CHAPTER 5
GUARDIAN ANGELS

There was a time when all police officers on patrol worked "around the clock." His meant that you would work 5 shifts in a row from 8 AM to 4 PM and get two days off. We call them day tours. Next, you would work five shifts from 4 PM to Midnight and get three days off. We call those 4 to 12s. After that you would work five shifts from Midnight to 8 AM and get four days off. We call those late tours or midnights. You needed those four days off after your midnights in order for your body clock to get back to normal.

For those of you who think that is a lot of time off, consider this. Cops have been working around the clock for over 100 years, so we've got some good statistics concerning life expectancy. The life expectancy of cops who work around the clock is about five years shorter than the life expectancy of cops who work steady days. How many days off would you want to compensate you for five years of life?

This particular week I was working my set of midnights and I was on my fifth and last one. It is easy to say the words "sleep during the day," but you can never get good sleep during the day. By the time this last midnight shift came along I was definitely sleep deprived. It was about three in the morning and I started to fall asleep at the wheel. I knew enough to get off the road so I got on the radio and asked to take my meal period.

As soon as radio authorized my meal I drove to the Knights of Columbus hall and parked the police car in the rear of their parking lot. The location allowed me to hide the car from the public. It also provided me a good defensive position where no one could approach the police car without coming at me from the front. I set the alarm on my watch, blew up my neck pillow, opened the windows of the car, and nestled in for a nap.

The police department prohibits cops from sleeping on their meal periods. You can go to the firehouse and watch TV on your meal period. You can run some personal errands if you like. You can practice your religion on your meal period. You can even eat a meal on your meal period, but you can't sleep. Even though it has been proven that a well-rested individual is a more effective employee, perception is everything. The department does not want the public to perceive that their police force is sleeping. The department expected me to stay awake and therefore what I was doing was unethical.

    About 30 minutes into my nap I was awakened by the smell of smoke. At first I thought it was someone's fireplace, but it soon became a very strong smell and I realized that a house was on fire. When I opened my eyes it was as though I was surrounded by fog. My first thought was that the Knights of Columbus hall was on fire. I freaked at the thought that I, the cop on duty, was asleep behind the building while it was burning to the ground. I quickly put the car in gear and drove to the edge of the driveway to assess what was going on. There were voices to my left and when I turned to look I saw that the apartment building at the other end of the block was on fire. I could see the flames setting the clouds aglow, and there were people gathering in the street across from the building.

    The building is a three-story walk up with six apartments. There are two on each floor, one in the front and one in the rear. I turned the police car left and raced down the block shaking the sleep from my mind as I went. I stopped the car in the middle of the road about 75 feet on my side of the building. Then I set it across the roadway to block traffic from coming down to the fire scene. I put the police car's lights on and notified radio. This incident occurred before the proliferation of cell phones and 911 had not yet received a call regarding the fire. Then I opened the trunk, got the oxygen and the first aid kit, and started to jog toward the front of the building.

    In the darkness I could see what appeared to be about 20 people gathered across the street. The fire had burned through the electrical and phone wires, and there were no lights in the apartment building. Flames were leaping out of some of the windows on the third floor. Smoke was coming out of some of the windows on the second and first floors.

    I called out to the crowd, "Is everyone out of the building?"

Two voices answered, "Yes."

A third said, "I think so."

Then a man and a woman said what I dreaded to hear, "No!"

The man said, "Darlene in the front apartment on the second floor isn't here."

The man and woman who said that began walking toward me along with several other people and they gathered around me. It was obvious that they were looking to me, the cop, for guidance about what to do next.

I asked the man if he was sure that Darlene was home tonight. He said yes. He said that she had broken her leg in a skiing accident about two weeks ago. Between the cast on her leg, and having to use crutches on the stairs, she did not go out except to see the doctor. The woman, his wife, said she lived alone, that they were friends, and that she was checking on her every day to help her with the daily chores of life while she recovered. The couple's apartment was the apartment in the rear on the second floor. They had seen her just before bedtime. The wife said that Darlene took a sleeping pill just before the wife said good night. I asked how old she was, and the man said Darlene was about 45.

Then I called out to the crowd, "Is everyone else out of the building? Is everyone else accounted for?"

People started looking at each other, and looking for each other and the response was a resounding "Yes."

Now here's the dilemma. I knew that police department protocol directs the first responder at the scene (me) to disregard someone stuck in the building. My job as the first responder is to insure that other emergency personnel are not blocked from the scene by curiosity-seekers and others. People are notoriously thoughtless in situations like this. They leave their cars blocking streets and our people and equipment are prevented from getting to the scene. Also, cars that innocently turn on to the street wind up blocking the road because they cannot pass through. The logic is that by insuring that emergency personnel can get to the scene, I could be saving more lives in the long run.

Also, the department feels that if I run into the building without the proper equipment, I could become another victim.

Additionally, if the woman I am attempting to rescue gets seriously hurt through my efforts, and the department, can be sued. This is the world we live in. The Good Samaritan law does not apply to professionals who are supposed to know better. The police department's rules and regulations said that if I undertook a police action, and did not use the proper safety equipment, the department was under no obligation to indemnify me against lawsuits or injuries. Most likely they would consider me a hero, but if things went terribly wrong, they had the right to hang me out to dry.

There was also one other "itsy-bitsy" issue. The idea of running into a dark, burning, building, filled with smoke, scared the crap out of me. I did not have air tanks. I did not know what condition the stairs were in, or the floors for that matter. This was not like one of those situations that slowly develop into something life-threatening as you become more and more involved in it. This was a conscious decision to go into a situation that was most definitely life-threatening. I would be doing it without the proper equipment, without any backup, and against the department's guidelines.

So there I was, standing with 20 some odd people looking to me to do something. There was no doubt in my mind that everyone present expected the police officer to run into that building and save the woman (ethics). There is no doubt that, in this situation, the police department was directing me *not* to run into that building and save the woman (conflicting ethics).

My morality was clear on the subject. I knew that running into that building and trying to save that woman was the right thing to do. Hell, it was the kind of thing I knew was possible when I swore my oath as a police officer.

Then there was that all-important and influential "fear of consequences." What did I fear the most? Did I fear getting injured and having to fight for my benefits? Sure I did. Did I fear what those people would think of me and the police in general, if I told them I was going to control traffic while that woman burned to death? Sure I did. Did I fear being burned alive? Damn straight I did!

I cannot even express to you how much I wanted to take refuge in the department's ethics and not go into that building. By that point in my career, I had been shot at in one incident, and in another incident I was forced to fight hand-to-hand for my life. I would have repeated either of those two events rather than run into that dark, smoke filled, and burning building.

    I looked around me desperately hoping to see some volunteer firefighters running toward us with their equipment. Unfortunately, it was three in the morning and I got to the scene so quickly that help was still several minutes away. This cup was not going to pass me by. I had to drink from it one way or the other. In the end my morality won out and I decided to try to save the woman. I knew I could not live with myself if I did otherwise. Apparently, not being able to like what I see in the mirror is what I feared the most.

    I quickly got on the radio and told the dispatcher that there was a woman stuck on the second floor in the front apartment. I also told the dispatcher that I was entering the building to try to pull her out. I concluded that this information would give the people responding after me a clear picture of what was at risk. Hopefully, that would also help them focus their efforts more quickly. I had a feeling I was going to need them to do so. The dispatcher tactfully tried to remind me of the rules by asking if I had equipment and assistance at the scene. I ignored her as though I did not hear her transmission. Then I pulled my flashlight from my belt and headed across the street toward the building.

    The smoke was dense but I could make out the staircase in the hallway just to the left of the vestibule. I took a deep breath of clean air, headed in, and started up the stairs. As I ascended I prayed that the fire had not burned through the stair supports. God I did not want to fall through that staircase. When I got to the top of the stairs I remembered my fire training at the Police Academy. I dropped into a crouch, almost to my knees because of the smoke, and began to crawl/walk quickly toward the door of the front apartment. Once there I took another breath from close to the floor.

    I started to panic when I found that the door was locked. I imagined the occupant was one of these women who lived alone and had four or five locks on the inside of the door. Partially out of anger and partially out of blind fear I stood up and kicked the door as hard as I could. Twice, then three times. On the fourth try the door gave way.

There was no fire in the apartment but it was filling with smoke. I dropped to the floor again and took another breath. There was no truly clean air left and I started to cough. I found the woman lying on her couch. Her right leg was indeed in a cast and she was either unconscious or dead. I did not take the time to find out. I grabbed her under her arms and dragged her off the couch. Her cast made a thump when it hit the floor, but fortunately she was light enough that I could get up some momentum as I dragged her.

Another deep breath and I dragged her out the door into the hallway.

By that time, the walls of the hallway were in flames. I was walking backwards and I felt and smelled my hair starting to burn from the intense heat. I started to feel the urge to vomit from the smell of my burning hair. I guess my adrenaline and the fact that I was holding my breath so tightly kept it from happening.

I made the turn at the top of the stairs still dragging the woman from under her arms and then I collapsed to the floor. I needed to breathe and I did not know where I could get a clean breath of air. Believe it or not, I drew it from the space between my body armor and my chest. It wasn't truly clean but it was better than anything else that surrounded me. My eyes were hurting so much from the smoke that I could not keep them open anymore. Fortunately, I was on the staircase. If it did not collapse beneath us there was only one direction I needed to go – down.

I began edging down the stairs on my side, feet first, thumping my butt from stair to stair as I went. Once the woman was on the incline, her body pressed against mine, and the two of us slid down several steps together. I lost my breath at that point. This time when I took another I breathed in a lot of smoke. I knew that I had only seconds left before I went unconscious. The heat was incredible and my brain screamed at the thought of dying on a stupid staircase in a stupid burning building.

I pulled the woman with me as hard as I could and I attempted to stand up. Then I lost my balance and we both went careening down the rest of the stairs together. When we landed at the bottom we were right next to the vestibule, only about six feet from the front door. Her head was tucked closely into my neck. I had no strength to continue. I rested my head on hers and prayed for a miracle.

Suddenly, a firefighter grabbed me and started to drag me out the front door of the building. Then another firefighter grabbed the woman and did the same for her. I felt like I was flying as the cool night air hit me and I took a breath. As I started to cough, I realized that I had been lifted to my feet and I was being carried by two firefighters, one on each side of me. When the other firefighter emerged from the vestibule doorway with Darlene in tow I heard people clapping and cheering. I guessed that they realized that I had successfully gotten her to the ground floor.

The firefighters took me over to a fire truck and slapped an oxygen mask on me. Not realizing that it was a demand valve mask, I took a deep breath and got an incredibly forceful blast of oxygen into my lungs. I think I nearly died right there. I was seeing bright lights with my eyes closed. I tore the mask from my face and tried to breathe normally. The firefighters kept telling me not to lie down. They held me up on my knees while they forcibly kept the O2 mask on my face.

The next thing I remember I was in the ambulance on my way to the hospital. I felt cold and I realized that the paramedic who was working on me had cut away all my clothing from the waist up. I guess they were anticipating cardiac arrest but it just wasn't my time yet. By the time we got to the hospital I was leaning up on my elbows still sucking on oxygen. I laid back down as they carried me into the emergency room, but I was back up on my elbows as soon as they pushed the trundle against the wall and went off to talk to the ER staff. I was feeling better and better by the second. Just about the time I began to think about the woman from the fire, another ambulance crew burst through the doors of the ER and rolled her in. I immediately looked for her head and I saw that a sheet did not cover her head. They had an oxygen mask on her. Darlene was alive!

They eventually put me into an ER cubicle. The two cops who had accompanied me to the hospital began to compliment me on my nerve, my good luck, and the fact that the people were cheering for me. When my squad supervisor, Sergeant Collins, arrived at the hospital it was another story. Right after thanking God I was unhurt, he began to chastise me in front of the other cops for doing what I did. I know what he was thinking. He was not trying to embarrass me. He was making sure that the other cops present did not get the idea that what I did was Kosher in any way. He quoted chapter and verse from the department protocols and from the rules and regulations.

Then he added, "…and I am telling you, if they don't give you a medal for saving that woman, they are going to burn you for not following the rules."

"Burn" is police jargon for a punishment that involves a fine. I just looked at him and smiled at the irony of possibly getting "burned" by the department for almost getting "burned" to death in the fire. Then I caught a whiff of my own singed hair and threw up. The Sergeant and I both knew that my fate was sort of in the Sergeant's hands. If he recommended me for a medal I would certainly skate. If he didn't, I still might skate, because I did actually save the woman and I wasn't hurt. Some supervisors wait to see which way the political wind is blowing before they commit to a course of action. I was lucky. My Sergeant had balls as big as church bells. God bless him.

I recovered completely. The woman recovered completely. The apartment building nearly burned to the ground. It had to be demolished and has since been rebuilt. This incident is a good example of how morality, ethics, and the fear of consequences play off each other in the real world. I can tell you one thing from my heart. I will never forget the volunteer firefighters who rescued the rescuer that night. They were guardian angels. They lifted me up and flew me to safety. Those people run into burning buildings as a *sideline* and they do it for free! It is a humbling thought considering that I almost had to be shamed into going in there. Firefighters are the bravest people on the planet.

CHAPTER 6
YOU CAN'T HANDLE THE TRUTH

Lying to the public is the most frequent dilemma that police officers encounter. Sometimes we tell lies that are specifically fabricated to deceive. These are called lies of commission. More often, we withhold information from the person or persons we are speaking with. These are called lies of omission. What makes this dilemma so interesting is that, depending on the situation, lying to the public can be both ethical and unethical at the same time. There are actually conflicting ethics within our society and which one dominates the situation depends on a person's perspective.

For instance, in New York State the courts have ruled that once a suspect has been given his or her rights, police officers can tell lies to that person to try to get the person to give up the information that they are looking for. We can also lie to get them to incriminate themselves. The criminal justice system expects this from its police. The practice is ethical from that perspective. The citizen being interrogated most likely does not know this. That person may be under the impression that the police must "play by the rules." To the portion of our population that experiences interrogation lies of commission would be unethical.

Police Officers can easily rationalize telling lies of omission because the media and the public have a long record of doing stupid things with the truth. Media folks have knowingly chosen to ruin ongoing investigations in order to get a headline or a scoop. When it happens, they will usually say something like, "the people deserve to know," but I suspect it is really about furthering their own careers. In some cases they have actually put people's lives at stake by doing so.

As far as the public's handling of the truth, it really depends on the issue. The public has often responded in a manner disproportionate to the threat. That is a nice way of saying that people can panic. Other times they can develop a mob mentality. There have been situations throughout history where people have gone so far as to form mobs in response to certain issues, and as you know from Real Fact of Life # 5, history repeats itself.

During WWII, the public became so incensed with the threat from Japan that decent Japanese Americans had to be interned and guarded for their own protection. The government learned from that experience and withheld tremendous amounts of information from the public after the 9/11 attacks. Several law enforcement agencies thwarted attacks against our country on our own soil shortly after 9/11. If that truth were known at the time, some members of the public might have attacked innocent Arab Americans on the streets.

Since the police officer's first priority is to protect life and property, objectives like preventing panic in the populace or successfully concluding an investigation are ethical goals. Other people, who trust their police to tell the truth, would consider lies of omission to be terribly unethical. The whole situation reminds me of what John Lennon once said out of frustration with the government, "Just give me some truth." The question is what would John Lennon have done with the truth?

I am sure you can recall instances in your own life where your morality tells you that lying is wrong but you do it out of the fear of consequences. Sometimes those consequences may be as small as hurting the feelings of the person you are speaking with, so you tell that person a "white lie." There are also times when self-protection and protecting your loved ones is what will influence your decision to lie. No one knows this better than whistle-blowers. If you blow the whistle on a corporate or government lie of omission or commission you can expect to experience some negative consequences for your actions. It is a rare occasion that a person who bucks the status quo is given a medal.

One of my duties as the precinct Crime Analyst was to attend community meetings and to deal with police-community relations. Often, the public's issues involved complaints about youths causing problems, drugs being sold on the streets, alcohol and tobacco being sold to minors, Vehicle and Traffic Law violations, etc. I also did school presentations and safety lectures. One evening I was addressing a senior citizens group because three members of the senior community had recently become victims of muggers. The general consensus was that the police were not giving the older folks the protection they needed.

An elderly man, who appeared physically frail but mentally alert, stood up and said, "It seems that crime is getting worse and worse each year. We are all older people. You know how criminals pick on older people. (See Real Fact of Life # 1) Are you guys going to be able to protect us or do we have to get guns and protect ourselves?"

I knew what I was expected to say. My bosses would have been very happy if I had said, "Certainly we are able to protect you and guns are not the answer." Truly, there was no way that we could possibly protect these people from crime. According to the census, there are 181, 000 permanent residents in my precinct. There are also hundreds of miles of streets. Each tour of duty starts out with only 24 police officers on patrol.

To make it worse, the number 24 is deceivingly high because it is reduced by a variety of factors. For instance, it takes two officers to process an arrest. Arrest processing can take as long as four hours. It usually takes two officers to handle a motor vehicle accident. Between assisting the ambulance, traffic control, arranging for tow trucks, and report writing, handling accidents can take in excess of an hour. Then there are administrative assignments and mechanical issues that take cars out of service for hours at a time. At any given time during the day the number of officers available to protect 181,000 people and patrol all those miles of streets averages about 12.

If someone is intent on raping you, robbing you, or murdering you, what are the odds that one of us will be passing by at precisely the time that you are becoming a victim? The fact is we would need a very large police force to effectively *protect* citizens from crime. However, we are really good at catching criminals after they commit their crimes. It is actually the fear of eventual apprehension and punishment that really deters the would-be criminals who can be deterred. It is not the fear of being thwarted during the act.

I wrestled with how to respond to the old man's question. My morality told me to tell him the truth. He needed to do whatever he felt was necessary to defend himself. Our right to defend our lives is the most fundamental of rights and the police really could not protect him from a random attack. My ethics were much more confusing. From the crowd's perspective, I was expected to tell the truth. That would have been ethical to them. My bosses expected me to lie, to give the old folks the party line and a false sense of security. For me to tell the truth would have been unethical from the Department's perspective. Very quickly I evaluated what my consequences would be if I told the truth.

Now it just so happened that this was going to be one of my last community presentations. The police department's administration, in their great wisdom, decided that the individual precincts did not need Crime Analysts anymore. We did not need anyone particularly familiar with the area and the players anticipating seasonal crime trends, or evaluating raw data to determine crime patterns to target our limited resources. They made the decision to eliminate the precinct Crime Analysts and to put us back on patrol. Doing so reduced overtime on the street by one officer per precinct, a total of six officers. They then began producing "daily crime reports" containing the raw data from the previous day. The average patrol officer, besides all of his or her other duties, would have to determine for him or herself what to do with the information.

I am sure the average citizen's expectation (ethic) would be that the police, as experts in this field, would try to anticipate criminal issues and would target police efforts as efficiently as they could. Unfortunately, as with many ethics, this one was discarded in favor of saving money. When you think about it, policing with a minimum of expense to the public is an ethic also. Management often justifies cutbacks by saying it saves the public money. Unfortunately, you get what they pay for. Anyway, I determined that my only punishment for not spouting the party line would be getting transferred to another command and being thrown back onto the street doing sector patrol. Well guess what? That was happening to me anyway so I went for it.

I smiled at the old man and said, "You know, you make a very good point sir. With the small number of police officers available to do patrol, the odds are pretty small that we would be able to protect any individual from a personal attack that we did not suspect was about to occur. I believe that every American must decide for himself or herself whether owning a gun is the right answer. You know that the constitution entitles you to do so, but there have been many instances where guns have been taken from their owners. They are then used against the owner by the very criminals that the guns were supposed to thwart. I suggest you think long and hard about the subject and decide what is best for you and your loved ones."

Now wasn't that an innocuous response? I thought it was. I told the truth without being an alarmist. Unfortunately, Nicholas Stolaris, a reporter for the local community newspaper, was in the audience to cover the meeting. This is how the headline read: "OFFICER TELLS SENIOR TO GET A GUN - COPS WON'T PROTECT HIM." Don't you just love the way the press handles information?

The day the article came out I was called to my Commanding Officer's office. I had a union representative present to act as a witness and to insure that my rights, as set forth in our union contract, were respected. The PBA rep would also make sure that the supervisors did not violate the rules and regulations regarding how I should be treated. The Deputy Commanding Officer and the Administrative Lieutenant were also present. I stood at attention as the Commanding Officer (C.O.) read the newspaper article and I prepared to be dressed down (yelled at and possibly disciplined). My C.O. at that time was Inspector Gorman.

You have to understand something. To get promoted in the police department you do not need a Master's Degree or a high IQ. You don't need managerial skills or organizational skills. You don't need a lot of experience, common sense, dedication to duty, or any people skills whatsoever. You don't even have to show any leadership ability at all. The only thing you have to do to get promoted in the police department is memorize more material than the other people taking the promotional examination. That's it!

To show you how dysfunctional the system is listen to this. On promotional exams the department gives the officer taking the test only $1/20^{th}$ of a point extra for each year of experience as a police officer up to 20 years. 20 years of patrol experience equals one measly point! They give you five points extra for having a Bachelor's Degree even if the Bachelor's Degree is not related to criminal justice or law enforcement in any way.   In other words, test scores and other things being equal, a person who has a Bachelor's Degree in Music, and as little as three years employment as a police officer (regardless of assignment), will be promoted to supervise other police officers over someone with 20+ years of actual police patrol experience. You can make Sergeant, Lieutenant, and Captain through this method. Above the rank of Captain it is all about schmoozing, politics, and attrition.

     To be fair, some of the people who get promoted in the police department have all the skills to be excellent managers and leaders. Some of them are also bright, dedicated, ethical, unselfish, and pragmatic. I thank God for them. However, those positive skills, abilities, and personality traits are completely co-incidental. No one is tested for, or has to show evidence of, any of those positive attributes. The current promotional system in the police department is like affirmative action for dilettantes.

     I knew a brilliant guy who was a dedicated leader. He had good organizational skills and a lot of common sense. He made Captain and actually set out to improve some of the police department's more antiquated ways of doing business. Upper management stopped him in his tracks. One day, when he was expressing frustration with the system, I asked him about it.

     He said, "Mike, do you know the mathematical probabilities that I had to beat in order to make Captain on this job? With all these numb skulls memorizing as much as they can it is one hell of a statistical accomplishment. I am way up there on the food chain. Although there is nothing really bad that they can do to hurt me, they will not let me make any significant changes. Even though they can clearly see where an improvement could be made, no is willing to risk their career. They are afraid that if they change anything and it doesn't go right, their chances for further promotion diminish. No one wants to upset the power structure they depend on for promotion. It's scary, but even mediocrity has enough sense to perpetuate itself. I choose not to entertain these idiots any longer."

He received no further promotions. Eventually he retired as a Captain.

Gorman was no ball of fire as a cop. He did the absolute minimum during his first three years as a police officer. He got himself a clerical position inside the stationhouse as soon as he could. Almost as soon as he was off probation, he was off the street. He had no interest in really learning the job of police officer or in protecting the public. He immediately began memorizing (some people call it studying) and taking the promotional tests. As he was promoted through the ranks he sought assignments that kept him as far from danger as he could get and would allow him to continue to study for further promotion.

Gorman's eye twitched when he got stressed. I guess by virtue of that and the fact that he is measurably inept he also developed an inferiority complex. When he came to our precinct as Commanding Officer he had already acquired the nickname "Twitchy," although no one would call him that to his face.

Twitchy resented people with advanced degrees and he showed no particular respect for those officers who had risked their lives and distinguished themselves thereby. He paid dedicated police officers the expected lip service, but it was clear by the way he patronized them that he considered those officers to be beneath him intellectually. After all, they chose career paths other than promotional advancement. How smart is that? If Gorman had a resume it would probably have three entries:

Education:
Degree in BS from What's –A-Matter-U

Police Experience:
Three years' worth over 24 years.

Personal Accomplishments:
Memorizes things well.

The police department is like a well-oiled machine. It is a super well organized bureaucracy and for better or worse it runs just fine unless you do something to screw it up. Despite these institutional safeguards, Twitchy was always at odds with the union because of his poor administrative and organizational skills. He would lie to subordinates in order to manipulate them into achieving his ends and his ends were always selfish. When someone would try to hold him to a commitment he made he would often deny having made the promise. There were also times when he would deny having given an order if that order resulted in a negative outcome.

He thought nothing of violating the union contract. Given his druthers, Gorman used coercion on subordinates and he cheated them whenever it suited his needs to do so. Bosses of his ilk are the very reason why unions evolved and why unions must continue to protect employees. He was the ultimate bad boss and he caused more union grievances to be filed for contract violations than any other supervisor in the history of our department.

As a result of his unethical and immoral behavior, no one respected him but I don't think he cared. All he wanted to do was get promoted. Worst of all, he paid no consequences for his actions. Gorman was always causing problems for his supervisors. Still, for years they did nothing about him.

Gorman inherited me as precinct Crime Analyst when he became the Commanding Officer. He knew me by my reputation as both a thinker and a doer. He resented the respect I had earned from my peers, my supervisors, and even people above his rank. I was dead meat the moment he got assigned to my precinct and he proceeded to make my life as miserable as he could.

It might also have been because Gorman was constantly violating Real Fact of Life # 5. As the precinct Crime Analyst, I was often forced to be the messenger of bad tidings. It was in Gorman's personality to kill the messenger rather than correct the problem. They handed him a great way to get rid of me when they decided to put the Crime Analysts back on patrol.

I was one of those people who chose a different career path than Gorman did. Here are some of the reasons why Twitchy hated me so much:

    Valedictorian of my Police Academy class
    Bachelor's Degree in Sociology
    Master's Degree in Psychology
    Master's Degree in Public Administration
    Adjunct Instructor - FBI National Police Academy
    NYS certified Police Instructor
    NYS certified Crime Prevention Officer
    NYS certified Traffic Safety Officer
    NYS certified Emergency Medical Technician
    NYS certified Recruit Field Training Officer
    Red Cross Certified Counselor for Post-Traumatic Stress Injuries (PTSI)
    Department Commendation (pulled a woman from a burning building)
    Department Lifesaving Award (CPR)
    Three Meritorious Police Duty Awards
    Stork Award (delivered a baby)
    Homeland Security Liaison

I stood at attention in front of this man who was sitting in judgment of me. I guess on a subconscious level I must have wanted this confrontation with him. I knew that what I said at the senior citizen meeting might land me here.

He finished reading the article looked up from the newspaper and said, "What the hell were you thinking? Why in God's name would you tell an old man who can hardly walk to go buy a gun?"

He didn't give me a chance to respond and continued, "You know something? I knew you would eventually step on your own dick. You guys always do"

When he said that, I couldn't help but smile. I had this picture of my dick being so big I could step on it. It was funny.

He said, "Why are you smiling? Do you think this is funny?"

I said, "No sir. I was just imagining having a dick that big."

He continued to rant and when he saw that his rant was not rattling me it pissed him off further. I knew that it would be very difficult for him to do anything more than transfer me. He was going to do that anyway but the heat he would take from his superiors for letting this newspaper incident happen in the first place was worth the aggravation to me.

Eventually he said, "Well what do you have to say about this?"

I said, "I was misquoted sir. I never told the man to go buy a gun."

There was a pause.

Then Gorman said, "That's it? That's all you have to say? Well, what did you tell him exactly?"

I said, "I really don't remember sir. It was last week, and I don't remember things as well as some people do. If I did, I would have been promoted by now."

Then I continued, "However, I know what I did not say. I did not say he should go buy a gun."

I could tell he was already becoming frustrated. He really wanted me to either confirm the newspaper article or say something else that would give him the ammunition he wanted to discipline me beyond a transfer. I noticed his eye starting to twitch and he caught me staring at it.

"What are you looking at?" he asked.

I couldn't resist the opening. I looked him straight in the eyes and said, with distain in my voice, "Nothing much sir."

I was standing at attention, and out of my peripheral vision I could see the administrative Lieutenant and the PBA guy look at each other and smile. Gorman went ballistic.

He said, "That is insubordination. That's going to cost you big time." Charles, I want charges and specifications for this man. Wait and see how many days pay that insult is going to cost you."

Charles was the Administrative Lieutenant. He and I had worked well together for years. He knew in his heart that Gorman was an asshole but I knew he wasn't going to stick his neck out and defend me. They were both supervisors and in situations like this the Lieutenant would just do as he was told. Fortunately, Anthony the PBA guy, spoke up.

He said, "Inspector, you have to give the officer the chance to explain his remark. There are other interpretations of that remark. What exactly did you mean by that Officer Rudolph?"

Anthony was looking at me and pleading with his eyes for me to take the opportunity to get myself out of this situation. Gorman's eye was going crazy now as he waited for me to respond. I knew if I smiled I was dead so with my best effort I faked sincerity.

I said, "Inspector, your eye was twitching and it drew my attention. We all have such things and I know these things have little to do with who we really are. When you asked me what I was looking at this was on my mind. I was thinking that in the grand scheme of things a twitching eye was not a big deal. It was 'nothing much'. That is what I meant by my remark. There was no insubordination intended."

Gorman knew I was full of shit but after my explanation he would be hard pressed to convince the police department trial board of that. He just glared at me and moved on to his next point.

He said, "And what about this business of us not being able to protect the people. Did you say that?"

I responded, "Not exactly sir, I simply pointed out the truth; that there are not enough cops on the street to effectively protect all of the people all of the time. I spoke the truth sir and I was under no orders to lie. You can't punish me for that."

Gorman had steam coming out of his ears. With his eye twitching a mile a minute he started screaming, "I'm the one who determines what you will be punished for. You were representing me! I am the one who determines what my representatives say at community meetings. Those people did not have to hear that. You have enough time on the job to know not to say that. Besides, we protect people every day. What you said was inaccurate. You had no right to tell them we can't protect them."

I asked for permission to speak freely and then I said, "Sir, you know as well as I do that the people we protect *effectively* are those who we know are experiencing some sort of threat. If a previously unidentified mugger decides to choose a victim at random there is no way we can stop that from happening. What I told them was true sir."

Gorman screamed, "Bullshit! If I knew you were going to say something like that I would have replaced you before you ever said it. You did this on purpose to harpoon me. You have been doing things like this ever since I got here."

I said, "Now why would I do that sir? You have always treated me so well."

He knew I was being sarcastic. I could see in his eyes that he recognized that I was paying him back for making my life miserable and for taking such joy in putting me back on patrol. He walked right up to my face. Then he stepped to my side and spoke loudly into my ear.

"I know where you live. I am going to transfer you to a precinct as far as possible from your home. Each day when you make that commute you are going to think of me. Every time you fill your tank with gas you are going to think of me. I am going to talk to the C.O. of whatever precinct you go to and tell him what a fuckup you are. Oh, and any time you try to better your situation, I will be there to stop it. Your career is over. You hear me? – OVER!"

I am not sure what he was expecting me to say. If he guessed that I was going to apologize or beg him not to do it he missed his guess. When I was at the Police Academy, there was an instructor named Sergeant Blevins. Sergeant Blevins concluded that since I resigned from the City Police to become a stockbroker, and then I resigned from the brokerage firm to become a County cop, I must me a quitter. In my early days at the Academy he would make me do incredibly boring and uncomfortable details just to get me to resign.

One day, just to be a prick, he made me guard the flagpole in front of the Academy for an hour in the pouring rain. He walked up to me in his raingear as I stood at attention and got right into my ear.

He said, "Hell of a way to make a living isn't it Rudolph? Why don't you just quit? Isn't that what you do?"

I remember saying to myself if they want to pay me to stand here in the pouring rain doing nothing, I'll just pretend I am a cab driver with the meter running. Then I'll go on sick leave with a cold and take a couple of days off.

Back in Gorman's office I just glanced down at the patch on my shoulder and said, "The patch says County Police sir. You put me anywhere you like."

Gorman glared at me then he walked back to his desk and said, "You're dismissed. Get out of my sight."

I turned, walked out of his office, and waited for Anthony in the hallway. I could hear Anthony arguing with Gorman about what Gorman could and could not do to me. I heard Gorman say, "I want his head on my wall." Yea, like he was some big game hunter or something. If he ever went afield Bambi would probably take his gun away, kick his ass, and throw him on to the highway to get hit by a semi.

At one point Anthony told Gorman, "Officer Rudolph simply told the people the truth Inspector."

To that Gorman responded, "Well they can't handle the truth."

It was right out of a Jack Nicholson movie. I waited in the hallway for about five minutes. Finally Anthony came out of the office.

He walked up to me and said, "I have never seen him so pissed, but it is only going to be a transfer. You can expect it in about a week. It's going to take them about that long to coordinate everything. He would love to cancel your training assignment but I think he is afraid to pull that trigger. Everyone agreed that even interviewing the old folks to see what you actually said might not be definitive. You might have used poor judgment, but you didn't violate any rules."

I thought to myself, poor judgment? I think I judged this perfectly. I had done exactly what I wanted to do. I was leaving my position as Crime Analyst with a bang not a whimper. Someone needed to give Gorman some upward discipline. I hoped that I had caused him at least a little trouble with his bosses. He deserved so much more.

I said to Anthony, "I am sorry that you had to get involved in this but you happened to be the union rep working today."

He said, "Ah don't worry it's all part of the job. Do you know that twice I had to keep from laughing in there?"

I smiled at having entertained him and said, "Sometimes I just get tired of lying to people and this was a good opportunity to tell the truth. Let him put me anywhere he wants. I am more upset that he didn't thank me for saving his life."

Anthony looked at me puzzled and said, "Saving his life? When did you save his life? More important, *why* did you save his life?"

He laughed at his own joke.

I said, "I saved his life a few minutes ago in his office. I decided not to shoot him."

A smile came to Anthony's face and he chuckled. He got the joke.

Then he said, "You know Mike, you really do have a few screws loose."

I responded, "It's the post-traumatic stress. Sometimes it just bubbles over."

We both smiled again because the department was finally beginning to realize that post-traumatic stress is actually responsible for a lot of what had just been thought of as bad behavior. Then Anthony walked away from me down the hall. He was smiling and shaking his head in disbelief at the whole situation that had just transpired.

Anthony had no idea, or maybe he did understand that if it were not for the fear of consequences, I would have had no qualms shooting Gorman to keep him from messing with people in the future. I had no moral problem with it. His continued existence on this planet could not be good for anyone who worked with him. (See Real Fact of Life # 4) I wondered if he treated his friends and family so selfishly.

Ethically there is obviously an issue. I am sure Gorman had the general expectation that, as an Inspector in the police department, he should be allowed to behave selfishly and abuse subordinates without worrying about being shot.

I may have rationalized in favor of my morality but it was definitely the fear of consequences that kept me from doing it. Anyway, fate intervened. The date was September 7, 2001. Tomorrow I was headed to Virginia to teach at the FBI National Police Academy in Quantico. The following Tuesday the world would change forever.

CHAPTER 7
SEE, HEAR, AND SPEAK NO EVIL

In the 1920s and 1930s, gangsters like Baby Face Nelson, John Dillinger, Al Capone, Bonnie and Clyde, and Machine Gun Kelly were running rings around local law enforcement. They were robbing banks and trains, blowing up businesses that did not pay them off, and killing innocent folks along the way. The American people demanded that the representatives they elected to run the government do something about it. So our government hired some experts to handle this challenge to our internal security. Today, these people make up the Federal Bureau of Investigation.

After World War II America needed some people to protect us from communist spies. Our enemies had already acquired the secrets to the atomic bomb and they were seeking to steal other scientific secrets as well. In addition, the Communist Manifesto, as well as the stated Soviet policy, called for communist world domination. America needed experts who would work outside our country to protect our interests and counter the actions of those who would seek to destroy our way of life. The people our government hired to handle this problem make up Central Intelligence Agency.

When the issue became smuggling the government hired experts, Customs Agents and Border Patrol Officers. When the issue became drugs, the government hired experts. They are the members of the Drug Enforcement Agency.

The point is that this country has some excellent experts and bureaucratic systems that have proven to be very effective at keeping us safe. After all, we are still here.

In 1993 when Sheikh Omar Abdel-Rahman and his cohorts tried to blow up the Twin Towers the City decided that it might be a good idea to assess future threats. Since the fate of the City is so closely linked to the surrounding areas, and visa-versa, they decided to invite other law enforcement agencies to participate in the threat assessment. They formed the Metropolitan Area Anti-Terrorism Task Force. They invited all law enforcement agencies in the vicinity of the City to send two officers as liaisons to represent their respective departments or agencies. After 9/11 the Metropolitan Area

Anti-Terrorism Task Force morphed into the Joint Counter Terrorism Task Force.

I was one of the two police officers the County assigned to this task force in 1993. We met once every two months in a conference room in One World Trade Center. We began by assessing the threats to our own jurisdictions and making presentations detailing our Departments' plans to deal with them. It became clear very quickly that all the municipalities involved would do nothing. Our politicians did not care enough to allocate any resources (money) for anti-terrorism planning, target hardening, or tactical training. There was no political will to do anything about anything. Skeikh Rahman was treated like a common criminal not a terrorist. The politicians who oversaw the various federal agencies refused to believe the wickedness of this organization called al-Qacda even existed.

Law enforcement did not drink the Kool Aid. Our counterparts at CIA told us of the growing threat of al-Qaeda abroad. Our counterparts at the FBI told us that al-Qaeda had fellow travelers right here in this country; that they were being organized into terrorist cells that would attack us from within. The *experts* knew trouble was coming. Unfortunately, their bureaucrat superiors, usually appointed by politicians, parroted the government's attitude of see no evil, hear no evil, and speak no evil. So the prevailing law enforcement philosophy was something like, "Father forgive them, for they know not what they do. Oh and Father, please grant us the opportunity to protect them from themselves because they're idiots"

Every two months the Anti-Terrorism Task Force would send a report to whatever agency of government was responsible for that particular part of our homeland security. We told them about the cockpit vulnerability and how all aircraft should be "El-Al'ed." There is a reason why nobody hijacks El-Al aircraft. El-Al became shorthand for hardening the target

We told them that the airline industry's aircrew hijack training, which called for them to cooperate with the hijackers, was outdated. It was designed for a time when the hijackers just wanted money like D. B. Cooper or wanted to be taken to

Havana to become communists. It did not account for people turning planes into flying bombs which, by the way, was right there in the al-Qaeda so-called training manual.

Interestingly enough, while we were attempting to solve the problem of porous airport security checkpoints we came up with a way of solving the carry-on luggage problems at airports in general. First, we suggested that each airline be required to have carry-on sizing boxes at their check-in counters. That way folks would know before entering security lines that their bags were too big to be carried on to the aircraft. Then we found a manufacturer who could produce hard plastic forms that would fit over the entrance to the conveyor belt x-ray machines at security checkpoints. They would have cost only $5.00 each at the time. The cut out for the bag to pass through would limit the bag to the specific size of the sizing boxes at the check-in counters. Any bag that did not fit through the opening of the x-ray machine would have to be checked. Security personnel at the checkpoint would account for the number of bags people carry on. This would force them to scrutinize passengers at the security checkpoint.

We know that when people take the time to check for one thing they often find other things amiss. If our plan was employed, no one would ever get to the gate with too many bags or a bag that was too big. Also, in order to more easily match up suspicious carry-on luggage to passengers once they were on the aircraft, we suggested that passengers be required to use only the space in the overhead luggage bin above their own seat.

How's that for organization? No Good! The FAA refused to mandate that the airline industry institute any of these precautions. That is why you are still dealing with carry-on issues today such as people with too many bags or bags that are too large. It is also why we still have no way of knowing whose luggage is above our heads when we fly.

We reported that the government needed to start screening containerized shipping for dirty bombs, biological weapons, smuggled conventional weapons, and terrorists themselves. Human beings have been smuggled into this country for years in shipping containers. We reported the need for increased border enforcement, increased customs and port enforcement, and the need for increasing airport security procedures in general.

We even explained to them how firing a couple of rounds from a low-tech hunting rifle into a landing plane could stall air travel for hours, if not days. One 50-cent bullet could terrorize the entire air travel industry in America and maybe even around the world. We suggested airport perimeter security procedures that would have addressed this issue. Our suggestions fell on deaf ears.

We reported that our citizens needed a nationwide education program to inform them about the growing threat of terrorism. We suggested that it should be similar in scope to the anti-drug and anti-smoking programs that the federal government had launched. We even gave them a catch phrase: "If you see something, tell somebody." After 9/11, The City of New York took the catch phrase suggestion, but they changed it to "If you see something, say something." Hey, better late than never, right?

Americans needed to start looking out for things like folks buying pallets of fertilizer when they aren't farmers. People who take flying lessons with no goal of obtaining a license to fly. People who buy propane tanks 10 at a pop, and people staking out airports and recording landing schedules. We even suggested that a comprehensive federal law be passed to allow law enforcement to track the activities of terrorist cells right here in America. We reported that the Internet was the up and coming means by which they were communicating. All of this was reported to the proper authorities between 1993 and 1996.

Every two months the governmental agencies responsible for keeping the public safe learned what was coming down the pike from the *experts* and had a chance to do something about it. Nobody did anything but file the reports. The nice politicians and bureaucrats said we were "overly diligent." The not-so-nice ones called us paranoid. Are you paranoid if they really are out to get you?

Our government told the public a huge lie of omission. Think about it. The government brought together all of us, experts in our fields, to give them our expert advice on how best to move forward from the 1993 attack and protect our people. Then they ignored everything we said and made the country think that the first attack was an isolated incident. Even after al-Qaeda attacked the USS Cole and our embassies in Africa the government would not do anything additional to defend our homeland. Is that not a huge lie of omission?

They never gave the American people a chance to evaluate the evidence, debate it, and make informed decisions. Instead, they buried our reports, and us, under a mountain of bureaucracy. The amount of money they would have spent to adopt our suggestions for hardening America as a target would have been microscopic compared to the billions and billions of dollars they have spent, just so far, on wars and other efforts to clean up the mess their apathy and incompetence caused. Over three thousand human beings lost their lives because the people we elected and/or trusted to protect us failed to act on the warnings that their own *experts* gave them. In my mind they committed the most unethical act imaginable when they decided to see no evil, hear no evil, and speak no evil.

Morality didn't keep them from lying. Ethics didn't keep them from lying, and they had no fear of consequences. How many times did they use the phrase, "There's enough blame to go around."? What that phrase means is that they do not intend to hold anyone responsible for our country's lack of preparedness and no one is going to be punished for deceiving the American people.

They even went so far as to deceive the first responders to Ground Zero. I will never forget a government spokesperson telling everyone on TV that the government had tested the air around Ground Zero and found that it was within "acceptable limits." Then the government refused to allow for independent tests to verify that assertion. They cited security concerns as though the professional air testing companies were going to attack us with their testing devices. It was almost as stupid as taking away eyelash curlers from air travelers while letting them keep sharp pens and pencils.

The dedicated people who responded to Ground Zero would not have run from the scene because the air was polluted. They would not have left the bodies of their fellow rescuers and all those innocent people to rot under a pile of steel and concrete. They would have donned the proper safety equipment and continued to work the pile.

Instead of telling the first responders and the recovery workers what they were facing, and making sure they had enough masks and replacement filters, they lied. Instead of insuring safety procedures and work shift limits to keep the workers safe, they lied. Why did they lie? Sure the cleanup would have taken longer if proper safety procedures and work shift limits were imposed, but people would not have gotten sick.

It was not like they were really in any hurry. They let the site remain fallow for years while they decided what to do after we cleaned it up. The federal government wound up having to pass a bill that compensated the first responders and the recovery workers for all the ailments they contracted while they were trying to put the City's downtown back together again. All because people, who were facing no consequences, decided that it would be better somehow to lie than to tell the truth.

The day that the attack came and the towers fell I was in Quantico, Virginia at the FBI National Police Academy teaching Ethics to police officers from all over the country. Obviously everything stopped. First, we went to the scene of the crash at the Pentagon to see if we could help. Don't believe these idiots who claim the Pentagon was hit by a cruise missile. The Pentagon was not hit by a cruise missile. There was airplane debris everywhere and plenty of witnesses cleaning up the mess. As investigators, the guys responsible for that report would not make good pimples on a police detective's ass. Either that or they were just looking for their 15 minutes of fame.

By the time I got to the Pentagon I wasn't needed there so I tried to get home. The government shut down the roads crossing the Hudson River into New York City for almost 48 hours. I thought I would be able to cross into the County north of the City, but with the Indian Point Nuclear Power Plant as a potential target, the bridges north of the City were closed also. Trucks loaded with food and other staples for daily life were backed up for miles on all the roads. I placed my car in a line of trucks and slept in my car while I waited for an opportunity to get through. I correctly determined that they had to let the trucks in soon or 11 million people were going to get awfully hungry, and what is worse, run out of toilet paper. As soon as the opportunity presented itself I identified myself as a police officer and my brother and sister officers let me through to do my job.

After the first days working on the pile I began doing post-traumatic stress (PTS) counseling with the Red Cross. I had to do it on my days off because the County claimed that they did not want to pay someone overtime to replace me while I worked at Ground Zero. They were also too short of personnel to protect the many potential targets that became evident during the early days of the crisis. Remember, just like the military, we in law enforcement were expecting these maggots to crawl out from under their rocks with AK47s. There was no reason to suspect otherwise and we needed to deal with that threat.

There were a few terrorist cells that tried to attack targets within the U.S. in those days following the 9/11 attacks, but we stopped them in their tracks. With the help of HR 3162 (The U. S. A. Patriot Act) we have successfully prevented further attacks on our soil for 10 years now. Thank God, and knock wood. That is one hell of an accomplishment since, as Condoleezza Rice said, "They only have to get it right once to succeed. We have to get it right every time to stop them."

When I began doing PTS counseling I was working out of a building right near Ground Zero. We de-briefed the construction workers and other recovery workers before they left for home each day. Debriefings reduce the severity of PTS. When a person knows ahead of time what their mind is going to do to them, that person is better able to handle the symptoms. When a problem occurs, that person is more likely to seek professional help quicker. At one point it became clear that the building we were working in was going to collapse, so we moved the operation to the hospital ship that was docked along the waterfront. After that, we used a school in the area.

Some counselors moved on to the Javits Center and began doing PTS debriefings with the volunteers who were taking in DNA evidence from the families of the victims. Eventually, I started helping with that task. Talk about messing up your head. Try collecting DNA evidence from person after person whose loved ones have just been incinerated. It damn near blew my mind. I spent a total of 21 days working between Ground Zero and the Javits Center for which I eventually received a congressional award. I would much rather congress had stopped 9/11 from happening.

I made the decision to try to attend as many funerals of firefighters and police officers as I could. I managed to get to 18 before I could not take it anymore. I felt like I was betraying all the rest of them who died at Ground Zero, but I just could not take it anymore. I heard Amazing Grace played by bagpipes too many times. Even now I tear up when I hear that song.

I am a member in good standing of the Emerald Society. Sometime after that, I called the president of the Emerald Society and told him that I did not want Amazing Grace at my funeral. I thank God for having received his grace. Besides, I like the words to *The Minstrel Boy* better. It is an Irish march that an old Irish friend Dennis Murphy taught me years ago when we both were drunk one afternoon after attending a cop's funeral. It goes like this:

> The Minstrel Boy went off to war
> In the ranks of the dead you will find him
> His father's sword he girded on
> And his wild harp he flung behind him
> The Minstrel Boy fought hard and brave
> In the fight they cut him down
> And my heart they buried on the day
> That they laid him in the ground

Everyone says we should never forget what happened on 9/11. I agree, but we should also never forget how the philosophy of "see, hear, and speak no evil" led to 9/11.

There was one positive thing to come out of all this. Gorman could not screw me because the world had been turned upside down. By the time the dust settled Gorman was transferred to another precinct. Yes, he made a mess of things there also. Eventually, in typical fashion, the Department promoted him to Chief. Then they marginalized him so he could not hurt anything or anybody anymore.

    I think Gorman achieved his Nirvana. He had a high rank, great pay, and no responsibility or personal risk. They eventually forced him to retire when they discovered that he was taking days off without deducting them from his personal leave records. I am reminded of an old adage my grandfather used to use, "Much wants more."

    As for me, the people running the department thought it was more important to let me continue my work than to entertain Gorman's vendetta. How about that for ethics! It made me proud of them. Eventually I was put on patrol without being transferred and I set about trying to make the world a little better for those I came in contact with (not the bad guys, of course). After all, that is what we are all about. The side effect of going back on the street was that I got my game back. I had been riding a desk for several years and all that administrative stuff can distort your view of things sometimes. I put my priorities back in order. I was re-born as a police officer. Chairman Mao Zedong would be proud.

CHAPTER 8
DRUGONOMICS 101

Most police officers are willing to cross swords with about 85% of the criminal population. They try to avoid engaging the other 15% because they are emotionally handcuffed by fear for their families and other loved ones. About 15% of the criminal population will not hesitate to use kidnapping, rape, torture, dismemberment, and murder, essentially any type of terrorist act, against officers' loved ones. It works well to dissuade those officers from interfering with their criminal enterprises. They are also willing to use the same tactics against prosecutors, judges, and jurors. The harder law enforcement officials push, the more likely those criminals are to go after their loved ones.

In most cases these individuals are drug dealers who come from, or are based in, countries where this type of coercion is commonplace. Please do not misunderstand me. The officers who only do 85% of the job are very brave people. They would be willing to risk their own lives to combat the remaining 15% of the criminals. However, they are not willing to risk the lives of their families and loved ones to do so. Would you?

In society's effort to protect the innocent from the possible abuses of the government, society created a legal environment that allows criminals of this type to easily get away with such things. The best lawyers money can buy, dream teams if you will, are very successful at limiting the scope of police investigations and interrogations. They are very good at using the legal system to keep juries from examining evidence of guilt. It is one thing for police officers to know, beyond a reasonable doubt, who is guilty of something. It is another thing to be allowed to prove it in the courts.

Additionally, society will not let law enforcement personnel hunt down and kill the people who make such threats, even when those people have the means to carry out those threats. Most police officers are not willing to fight that fight under the current legal system. It is weighted too heavily against the officers. The frightening part is that this 15% of the criminal population are the most vicious criminals. They are the most destructive to our system of law and order.

So how is it that we seem to keep them under relative control in this country? They are kept in check by law enforcement officials who choose to sacrifice their personal dreams and personal desires for society's (our) sake. These officers make some very hard decisions early in their careers. Some decide not to marry because they know that they cannot have spouses and children and still combat the drug dealers. Others decide to fight the 15% for some years and then stop and join the other 85% when they are ready to settle down and have families.

Some officers take severe steps to "harden the target" so that is not as easy for the bad guys to find their loved ones. They may transplant their families to other states. Some make it public that they are single or divorced when in fact they come home to their spouses or significant others after every shift. They arrange for their registrations and drivers licenses to show as post office boxes. They have the FBI use their technology to track anyone who might try to research them via the internet.

Narcotics enforcement officers and their prosecutorial counterparts in the legal system are the tip of society's spear. They are in a constant fight against those who would use any means possible to achieve criminal ends and would control the rest of us in a savage and brutal way. There are many places in the world where 15% of a population controls the other 85%. As I write this, Mexico is trying to decide whether to continue their unsuccessful attempt to eliminate the drug gangs through their legal system or to ask for our help. It would mean going to war against these rebellious groups who have literally taken over parts of Mexico and are ruling those areas with an iron hand. We did it successfully for Panama when we arrested General Noriega and killed most of his cohorts. We did it again for Columbia when we took out Pablo Escobar. (See Real Fact of Life # 5)

There was a very interesting dilemma that challenged a group of narcotics enforcement officers some years ago. I am going to tell their story. However, before I do I need to put the problem in perspective. You see, the people who sat in judgment of the officers involved in this "scandal" were very unethical people. Please bear with me as we go through Drugonomics 101. You need to appreciate the hypocrisy of it all because, whether right or wrong, that hypocrisy contributed to the decisions that the officers made.

Narcotics Enforcement has always been a tough business. It is tough on your emotions. It is tough on your family life and it is tough on your morality and your ethics. The people who do narcotics enforcement are fairly enlightened about the economics of the drug business. They understand it in a way that many lay people do not.

Our government forces law enforcement to practice what we call "supply-side enforcement." The history of supply-side enforcement is murky. I have been unable to pin down exactly whose idea it was. There is some evidence that points toward J. Edgar Hoover, the first director of the Federal Bureau of Investigation. He certainly took credit for it. Although, most of the things he took credit for were, in fact, other people's accomplishments. In any event, the fact that we are still using supply-side enforcement in modern times to counter the drug trade flies in the face of logic.

My research leads me to believe that supply-side enforcement has its roots in the alcohol prohibition era. It was a time before the economics of the issue were ever really known or studied. Back then, the police and the FBI simply applied the same law enforcement methods to the illegal activity of bootlegging that they applied to every other criminal activity. They had no way of knowing that their methods would be ineffective. They had never faced a situation in which an activity like selling alcoholic beverages, which had been legal for centuries, was suddenly illegal. Society's demand for alcohol was enormous because it had always been part of our culture.

The 18th Amendment to our Constitution prohibited the sale of "intoxicating liquor" in the United States. The Volstead Act provided the legal grounds for the federal government to enforce the 18th Amendment. When the 18th Amendment was repealed in 1933, the government and the law enforcement community had the benefit of hindsight to examine their failure. Why did law enforcement fail to stop the flow of liquor to the general public? They learned from their own history why traditional law enforcement methods were not effective in this kind of law enforcement situation.

In today's application of supply-side enforcement you still try to stop the supply of something. During the prohibition era it was alcohol. Nowadays it is drugs. You burn poppy and coca fields, you try to infiltrate cartels by electronic and human means, and you try to arrest drug dealers. You spend millions of dollars on high tech surveillance equipment, on wiretaps, on payoffs to informants, and on payoffs to foreign leaders. There are other costs as well, such as law enforcement man-hours and prosecutions.

Supply-side drug enforcement also has a human cost. Many law enforcement people are killed or injured trying to do border patrol or make arrests. Other law enforcement people lose their lives as undercovers. Even the undercovers who survive are affected by having to become part of that cruel and criminal culture. Because of the money, power, and blackmail associated with the drug business, supply-side drug enforcement can take dedicated and philosophically righteous police officers and seduce them.

Then, after spending millions of dollars, sometimes years to build cases, and um-teen man-hours, you have arrested some higher-level drug dealer. These criminals have tons of money. You still have to get past top-notch lawyers, corrupt politicians, and the government and banking systems of drug-dealer friendly countries. After that, should you get a conviction, you pay more money to incarcerate this one person than some families need to live on for a year.

You can see how supply-side enforcement is already a pretty dismal approach to the problem, but are you ready for the clincher? The cartels are like corporations. If a vice president or middle manager of AT&T leaves to take a job at another company do the phones stop working? Of course they don't. Someone simply replaces that person and the business continues.

Similarly, the individual arrested in supply-side drug enforcement is holding a comparable type of corporate position. If you arrest one, another one takes his or her place. From the top to the bottom the drug manufacture and supply network is a company that runs like a corporation. The organization never stops, and there are several of these organizations (cartels) in operation all the time. Supply-side enforcement is like trying to fill a bottomless pit.

Currently, our society has taken the legalization of certain drugs off the table. That leaves only one other option, but it is a rather good one. The other option is called "demand-side enforcement."

Demand-side law enforcement is much more economical, and yet the people focusing our law enforcement efforts ignore it. It has been proven to be more effective than supply-side enforcement, and it only takes about one-tenth as much money to make it work. However, it takes something our leaders seem to lack, political will.

You begin by enacting stronger laws that would more severely impact drug buyers. Next, you concentrate your enforcement efforts on eliminating the demand for the drug by focusing on arresting the drug buyers and helping the addicts. You can still arrest the sellers as the opportunities arise, but you concentrate your resources on the buyers.

One of the biggest attractions for the people, who are either non-addicted occasional users or potential users, is the fact that getting caught as a buyer is not likely. Getting punished for it is even less likely. Everyone knows that the penalty for possession is less than the penalty for selling. In demand-side enforcement the penalty for possession is greater than the penalty for selling.

Non-addicted occasional users and potential users begin to realize that apprehension and punishment are now likely. They are not junkies, and the fear of consequences will makes them think twice about becoming involved with illegal drugs. The down side is that if people want to get high, they will still gravitate toward alcohol and other legal drugs to do so.

Demand-side enforcement does call for terms of imprisonment, but the laws enacted in other countries leave room for judicial discretion in the same way our laws do for alcoholics and mentally ill people who commit crimes. Addicted persons can be coerced to undergo treatment programs as an alternative to their incarceration. We know that treatment programs are far less expensive to run per person than prisons are.

How do we know demand-side enforcement works? We know it works because it is working successfully in many countries right now. It is tried and true. (See Real Fact of Life # 5). Demand-side enforcement makes sense from another perspective as well. It utilizes the economics of supply and demand in a wonderful way.

Right now, as we proceed with our puny efforts to reduce supply, the result of any supply reduction is that we increase price. Remember, we have done nothing to lower demand. This simply means higher prices per sale. The cartels then reinvest their profits in efforts to secure their own survival just like any other business would do. On the other hand, if we reduce demand by deterring the potential users and helping the addicted users, we will severely impact the profitability of the drug business. Who knows, maybe Ali Baba will go back to growing wheat instead of poppies and Juan Valdez will go back to growing coffee instead of coca.

When the law enforcement community began to seriously address the issue of drugs they had an overwhelming body of evidence to prove that supply-side enforcement would fail. It did exactly that during the prohibition era of the 1920s and 1930s and the result was that organized crime grew bigger than AT & T. The government, which directs the law enforcement community, decided to go with supply-side drug enforcement anyway. They knew it was an extremely poor use of taxpayer money. They saw that happen in the 1920's and 1930s but they did it anyway. It was a truly unethical decision.

Additionally, the government saw the corrupting influences of supply-side enforcement during prohibition. Yet they still set up some generally honest, but very human, law enforcement officers for the fall. Society expects the police to use all their expertise to fight the drug problem and to do it with the least amount of money possible. That is an ethic! Supply-side enforcement is simply unethical. The people who defend it do so, either out of inertia, or with a full understanding of its shortcomings. It is wrong in either case. Is it any wonder that some creative and dedicated officers tried to do an end run around the system? Is it any wonder that the practitioners and supporters of supply-side enforcement would go after them for doing so?

CHAPTER 9
GOIN' FISHING

Once upon a time, in a large eastern city's police department, there existed a street-level Narcotics Enforcement Team whose acronym was NET 104. The cops assigned to NET 104 were very dedicated narcotics enforcement officers who bought our government's argument that we have to fight a war on drugs. They looked at their police duties as more of a calling than a profession. You could not have asked for a more focused, honest, and philosophical cadre.

The team supervisor was a Sergeant named Atwell. George T. Atwell was a heavyset man about 5 feet 10. He spoke with no discernible accent even though he was born and raised in Brooklyn, USA. He is a former Marine Lieutenant whose Japanese wife left him. She was enough in love with him to marry him while he was stationed in Japan after Vietnam, but according to him, years later she got a severe case of the guilts. She went back home to mom and dad. George claimed it was a cultural thing. She and George had two kids before she left. The girl was eight and the boy was ten at the time she split for Japan. For the past four years he had been raising the kids by himself.

Normally, Atwell's team consisted of three men and one woman. I was an add-on. Detective Dennis Murphy was a veteran police officer with 15 years' experience. Some cops stand on a street corner directing traffic for fifteen years. It is like having one year's experience fifteen times. That was not Dennis. He was always eager to learn and Dennis was the first to get involved in whatever was going on. Dennis was Irish and let everyone know it. He actually came from Ireland when he was 17 and spoke with a really cool brogue.

He used to tell us that God invented alcohol to keep the Irish from ruling the world. I think he really believed it. He was never drunk on duty but he never missed a party either. Dennis was a good family man. To my knowledge, he never cheated on his wife and he always provided for his family. He was also a cop's cop. That meant that if your intentions were good he would never sell you out no matter what mistake you might make. Intentions, or heart, were everything to Dennis. Dennis Murphy had terrific technical skills. He was the team's electronic gadget guy. The department sent him to various technical schools to learn about surveillance equipment and Dennis ate it up.

Detective John Caputo was another veteran and one of the undercovers. He had the look of a wise guy and got over pretty easily buying drugs. He was 34 years old and single. John was a thrill seeker in the truest sense of the word. At about six feet tall, he was thin and wiry. He sported a full head of hair and a Fu-man-chu. John lived for the rush of being on the edge and he generated an aura that drew women from everywhere, good-looking women. No matter where he was, no matter how drunk he got, no matter how lame his lines were, they flocked to him. I think it was his sense of humor. He was so outrageous in attracting women that he acquired the nickname "The Blue Magnet."

Detective Roger Thomas was another undercover. He was 28 years old and lived with his girlfriend. He did drug enforcement in the army. When he became a cop, he did the mandatory stint in uniform on patrol but the Narcotics Division snapped him up immediately thereafter. He was also tall and lean and looked like any street dealer. Roger had a chip on his shoulder. He had nothing specific against white people, but he was sensitized by the black experience. One of his favorite analogies had to do with squirrels.

He would say, "Black squirrels are exactly the same as gray squirrels. The reason the black squirrel has an attitude is because people keep trying to run him over and the man is out to get him." Roger clearly understood Real Fact of Life # 2 and Real Fact of Life # 3. Another "Roger-ism" was, "God does not make men equal. The Colt Firearms Company makes men equal."

One thing is for sure, he hated drug dealers. Roger would say it had to do with the fact that they were poisoning their own people, but his actions showed that it didn't matter if they were poisoning blacks or whites or anybody else. He was a very private man and he never let anyone see his soul, except maybe his girlfriend. Mostly we saw was his business side and Roger was always a cop on a mission. Now and then he would laugh and clown around and everyone could trust him. We just never really got to know him deeply because he wouldn't let us.

Detective Nancy Castillo was a pretty Puerto Rican girl raised in Queens, NY. She was very attractive and had particularly beautiful eyes. Nancy played a vital role for the team. She was that person who you could not imagine being a cop. This allowed her to get close to situations that the male team members could not touch. Nancy could get into anywhere she wanted that was guarded by men. Before she was a cop, Nancy was a dancer. She was very physically fit and brave to a fault. I am thoroughly convinced that the reason she was single is that she was too aggressive. She took no shit from guys and could probably kick most of their asses. Nancy was quite an intimidating package all things considered. She didn't scare John Caputo though. He was constantly trying to get her into bed and she refused to give him the satisfaction.

I was an unofficial member of NET 104. I became involved with the unit while I was on limited duty mending three broken ribs. The Department assigned me to Atwell to help him with his clerical work. They had no way of knowing that my organizational skills were excellent. I had that office tuned up and spinning like a top in no time. My efficiency allowed me to kick back and put my feet up. My father used to say that if I owned a company it would be called "Lazy Man Industries." He said I would always find the easiest way of doing something just so I could finish and be lazy. I felt, that with necessity being the mother of invention, I was particularly creative. I worked smart instead of hard.

How I broke my ribs is a story in itself. A 29 year old psychopath, who was doing a 15 year sentence for killing a gas station attendant during a robbery, managed to convince the parole board to let him go after seven years. The first thing he did after getting released was to visit his old girlfriend. She wanted nothing to do with him, and when she closed the door in his face he became enraged. He kicked in the locked door and began dragging her out of the house by her hair. Her mom and brother were there at the time and they called 911. The psycho, realizing that kicking down a door and dragging a woman out by her hair might actually be a violation of his parole, ran away.

    I was by myself in a marked police car doing traffic enforcement when the 911 call came over the radio. Since I was so close to the location, I told Central that I would respond to the call along with the assigned officers. I was the first police officer to arrive at the house and took the guy's pedigree information; things like his name, age, etc., from the girlfriend. She also gave me a great description of him physically and what clothing he was wearing. Based on this, I put all the information over the air in a BOLO (be on the lookout) for the benefit of the other cops assigned to the call and any other police units that might be available to look for this guy. The guy had just left the ex-girlfriend's house so I was in the best position to follow and catch him. I told radio that I was leaving the house to try and find him. Then I began driving around and looking for the guy.

    I spotted him on one of our procinct's major three-lane roads. He was standing at the door of a municipal bus that was stuck in traffic in the center lane. The psycho was trying to pull the doors open so he could get on the bus. I was approaching from a different road and I was caught in traffic also. I could see from my position that the bus driver was on the phone trying to call for help with one hand while he was struggling to hold the manual door handle closed with the other. I heard the psycho scream loudly, "Open the fucking door or when I get in there I'll to kill you." He followed that up with some racial slurs aimed at the African-American bus driver.

    Besides worrying about the people on the bus, I feared that he was about to give up on the bus and would then decide to hijack a car and its occupants instead. Potential targets were all around his location, so I jumped the curb with the police car, grabbed my baton (that is a politically correct night stick), and left the police car locked on the sidewalk. I was dodging between the cars as I was running toward the guy.

    When I got close I yelled, "Police – Don't Move! You are under arrest. Put your hands above your head."

I had a pretty good hunch he wasn't going to comply, but I also knew it would get him away from the bus and diffuse any plan he might have to hijack one of the cars stopped in traffic. When the guy turned and saw me, as I expected, he took off. He was running between the lanes of traffic and I was catching up to him by virtue of some lucky breaks in the way the cars were situated. He eventually ran on to a sidewalk and I was about 30 feet behind him. I had my nightstick in my right hand and the radio in my left. I managed, through my panting, to tell radio that I was in foot pursuit and gave them my location and direction of travel.

Suddenly he stopped short, turned, and started to run directly at me. I was carrying my stick in my strong hand. I was just able to bring my weak hand on to the stick and put it in a defensive position as our bodies collided. I dropped the radio to the ground in the process. There was no time to do anything else with it. My body was in a good defensive stance and he sort of bounced off me. The psycho grabbed the center of my stick with both hands to try and pull it from me. I immediately went into a self-defense maneuver.

I brought the stick to a vertical position, pointed the tip at him, and stepped back pulling the heel of the stick toward me. This broke his grip. God bless those Police Academy tactics instructors. They know their stuff. Then I went into the second part of the maneuver. I brought the heel of the stick up quickly under his chin to break his jaw and terminate the attack. I executed the maneuver perfectly. However, I only grazed the right side of his head because as soon as he lost his grip on my stick, he had immediately lunged for my gun. My reaction was just a little slower than his action and his head was already out of position when I brought the heel of the stick up.

Our holsters are designed to stop someone from pulling our guns out like the psycho was trying to do. He began to tug violently at my holster trying to free my revolver. I had seen the look in his eyes when he turned on me and charged toward me. If you ever see that look and survive, you will never forget it. I knew if he got my gun I was dead. I also knew that the holster would not hold out forever.

I dropped the stick and grabbed for my holster with both hands. In one fluid move I pushed down on his hands forcing the gun down into the holster. Then I twisted my body away from him to break his grip. Again, this was something the Police Academy instructors taught us so many years ago. Now I understand why they drilled us so often. It worked. As I spun away from him, I had every intention of drawing my gun and emptying it into this asshole. Unfortunately, I put so much force into the spin that I lost my balance. I fell to the ground on my gun side.

I tried to stand up quickly, but before I could the psycho began to kick me mercilessly. Each time I tried to stand up he would kick or stomp me back down to the ground. I tried to protect my neck and head with my left arm while I struggled to pull my gun out from underneath me. My body armor had ridden up on my chest and gave me some additional protection around my neck from his kicking. By doing so, it exposed my lower rib cage to his stomping. He cracked the three lower ribs on my left side.

I knew I could not last much longer taking this kind of punishment, but I was determined to keep fighting for my life. With one good break I could shoot this guy. I also knew that if he picked up my stick he would probably kill me with it. I had to shoot him before he did that. After what seemed like much too long of a time, two other cops showed up and pounced on him. The guys were actually very quick to respond and help me. The entire fight took only a couple of minutes, but it felt like 15 rounds to me. Oh, how much I wanted to kill this guy.

Traffic had stopped dead to watch the show. I thought about that afterward. I felt a little resentment that no one got out of his or her car to help me. Then I realized that the entire incident happened so quickly that people might not have had time to react before the other cops showed up. At least I would like to think that was the case. The alternative, which is that that they would just stand by and watch the guy stomp and beat me to death, really sucked.

The other guys put the psycho in handcuffs and threw him into the back of one of the police cars. He began to scream and yell and kick the hell out of the inside of the car. The guys with me expected him to calm down when he realized he was caught, but instead the psycho kicked the driver's side rear window out of the police car. At that point they opened the door, wrangled his feet, and put a flex cuff on his feet to bind them together. Flex cuffs are two-foot long plastic cable ties that we keep inside the perimeter of our hats for just such a circumstance. Then one of the cops jumped into the back seat with the guy and sat on him to keep him from moving. The other cop asked me if I wanted an ambulance.

I said, "No. Just put me in the car and take me to the hospital, but I want a piece of this guy first."

Ok, now here was my dilemma. I believe in the biblical tradition of retribution. There should be an eye for an eye, and a tooth for a tooth. The people who established that standard of justice understood the human psyche and the human psyche hasn't changed since the inception of this standard of justice. They understood that the person who has been wronged is in the best position to know what will make him or her whole again. There may be room for mercy, depending on the situation. However, in this traditional view of justice, it is up to the wronged person to mete out mercy, not some judge or some legislative body with no personal stake in the matter. There is a reason why justice is represented as a scale. What this psycho did to me pushed my end of the scale very far down. He would have taken my *life* from me if he could. I knew what I needed to make my scale go back into balance. I was in the best position to say what will make me whole again. That is my morality.

The problem is that as members of our "civilized" society we are expected to forgo our morality if it conflicts with our ethics. The ethic called for me to simply place this man under arrest, with the minimum amount of force necessary, and to do so without exacting any retribution. Society's ethic for someone who did what he did is to simply put him back in a jail. There, he will be warm in the winter and cool in the summer. He will get three meals a day, access to a library, and cable TV. He also has access to a gym where he can work out so he can more easily beat the shit out of police officers when some asshole on the parole board lets let him back out again. The worst thing he has to suffer is that he is deprived of the company of normal people and he can't go on vacation. Boo-hoo.

Well, for all the times I rationalize my dilemmas in favor of my ethics, this time I rationalized in favor of my morality. I wanted justice for what he did to me and for how he tried to kill me. Simply putting him back in jail wasn't making it for me. Just jailing him again did not equal justice for me.

I sat in the front passenger seat and the three of us started driving toward the hospital. The psycho was lying down across the back seat. Every police officer should know that we live in a world where our words and actions can easily be recorded by audio or video equipment. If cops do not assume that their words and actions are being recorded, shame on them. I was very much aware of this. I told the cop who was driving to take me to a spot that I knew of on the way to the hospital where I was sure there would be no people or devices to observe or record us.

Even with three broken ribs I had enough adrenalin in my system to return what this guy had given me, with interest. I sent him to the hospital with a broken nose, a broken jaw, and I was in the process of emptying my can of mace into his mouth when the other two cops pulled me off him. He was eventually charged with resisting arrest, as well as felonious assault on me and the two officers who assisted me. They both suffered back injuries during the melee.

Later, during the bedside arraignment in the hospital, the guy kept insisting to his court appointed lawyer that I assaulted him while he was in custody. He also said that I purposely sprayed mace in his mouth, face, and eyes, and then just let him burn all the way to the hospital. Can you imagine that? This guy just tried to kick and beat me to *death*, and he didn't expect to get the shit beat out of him. This is the problem with ethics. Even the bad guys have societal expectations and they base their warped and evil decisions on them. He expected me to act ethically, even under these circumstances.

The two cops who saved my life answered these *false* accusations by testifying to how extremely violent and aggressive he was. They described what he was doing to me when they got there. They told of how he destroyed the inside of the police car and kicked out the window. They insisted that the physical force we used was necessary to subdue him. They verified that we did indeed stop the car on the way to the hospital, but it was to adjust his handcuffs which they said the defendant claimed were on too tight. The officers further testified that, while we were doing that, the defendant tried to escape and that is how the injuries occurred. I would have testified the same way for them.

I will never quite understand why parole boards are so easily fooled by these people. This is not the first guy to be released who went right out and committed another crime. Unfortunately, he won't be the last. I wonder if the members of the parole board would be so quick to release these people if they had to do time for their mistakes. After all, they turned this animal loose on society after we locked him up. The act contains all the elements of Reckless Endangerment. I'll bet there would be fewer people released if the people doing the releasing had some consequences to pay when the public gets hurt. Instead, the ordinary citizens have to live, and die, with their mistakes.

Anyway, this vicious psycho was sent back to finish the sentence for shooting the gas station guy before starting another seven years for what he did to us. Some charges regarding the attempted kidnapping and assault on his former girlfriend were still pending on him when I got assigned to clerical duty.

After my ribs finally healed and I was about to go back on patrol, Atwell intervened. He did not want to lose my organizational skills so he convinced the Commanding Officer to let me join the team, temporarily. My job was to continue doing the administrative work while I chauffeured the Sergeant. I would also assist on operations when needed.

That was our team. Our work schedule depended on what the precinct's needs were and the team's value was measured in convictions, not just arrests. Sometimes the Commanding Officer would attend a community meeting and then tell Atwell where the complaints of drug issues were coming from. We also got our information off the streets. Atwell would then tell us where to target our efforts. He trusted us as to how to target our efforts. Atwell survived

Vietnam by not telling his people how to do their jobs. Rather, he guided our efforts and supported us when necessary. Every single one of us would have taken a bullet for that guy.

The standard operating procedure (SOP) for NET 104 was buy and bust. A team member would cultivate a dealer and eventually conclude a deal under the watchful eyes of the other team members. The buys were audiotaped and videotaped whenever possible. Then, at a time of the team's choosing, other police officers would make the arrest. Sometimes the team itself would arrest the dealer. I am sure you can see the potential danger. The dealer might decide to rob the buyer. Sometimes the dealer thinks the buyer is trying to rob him. Sometimes the dealer learns the buyer is a cop.

In some cases the dealer who makes the deal does not carry the drugs. Once the deal is struck, the dealer signals or calls someone else (the mule) to bring him the appropriate amount of drugs from where they are hiding them. In cases where the dealer uses a mule he often uses an enforcer. The enforcer is a third member of his team who is armed. His job is to spot rip-offs and cops.

If everything goes down the way it is supposed to the team places a drug dealer under arrest and tries to flip him. That means they offer the arrested person a lesser sentence, or a complete pass if he will inform on a bigger fish in the organization. Another method of getting the "big fish" is to simply pay informants for information on criminal activity going down or about to go down. The department has a fund for this purpose. The narcotics officers request various amounts of cash to pay for information and support their informants on the street. It is a lot like fishing. When you go fishing you use bait and you often have to pay for the bait. In other cases the money is used to "chum." When you are fishing you often throw chum in the water to attract the fish. You hope the little you spend on these enticements gives you a big payoff in the quantity and size of the fish you catch.

Most days after we finished work we would all get together at the Do-Drop-Inn. The owner was a retired fireman who finally got tired of his place being a biker bar. He asked the police for help. One year we went to war with the Pagan motorcycle gang and we took over the bar. Now it is a cop's bar. No surprise. After all, we are the most powerful gang in the world. We just use our powers for good rather than evil. Anyway, the owner loved us because, among other things, we spent more money than the bikers did. We always attracted a crowd and they also spent more money than the bikers did.

When the 8 to 4 and 4 to 12 shifts ended the cops would often go to the Do-Drop to unwind. They would have a few drinks and most of the time more than a few. They would shoot some pool, or play some darts, or watch a game, but mostly they would shoot the breeze. The place was always filled with cop buffs. Cop buffs are just ordinary folks from various walks of life who appreciate what we do. They enjoy hanging out there with us and listening to the crazy things that happen on any given day. There were always good stories to be heard at the Do-Drop-Inn.

Thankfully for Caputo's sake, there was always a plentiful supply of cop groupies as well. These ladies of all ages and levels of attractiveness have a special place in their hearts for police officers. The Blue Magnet liked to call it a "target rich environment." As a typical evening progressed, and mostly after the four to midnight shifts, there would often be some music and dancing, and anyone who was interested in doing so could probably get laid.

On one particular day we had finished a day tour (8 to 4) and we were all waiting for Atwell to show up and have a little team meeting. Over a glass of beer he would tell us what we were going to be doing the next day and then go home to his kids. His usual parting words were, "carry on" and we would. On this day we waited so long for him that the whole team wound up having dinner at the Do-Drop. Kenny, the owner, had a decent grill. It was almost 8 PM when Atwell finally showed up fresh from a meeting with all the suits.

I was sitting at a table with Roger and Nancy discussing the finer points of Motown music culture when Atwell plopped himself down at the table and called out to the bartender.

"Kenny, please bring me a Bud."

The bartender/owner pointed in the Sergeant's direction to acknowledge his request and then began to bring him a beer.

Atwell turned to Roger and asked, "Where's Caputo and Murphy?"

Roger said, "Murph is over playing darts," and pointed across the room at Murphy who was playing darts with three other cops.

Nancy was quick to speak up and say, "Caputo is in the parking lot getting a hummer from some skank."

I jumped right on that and sarcastically I said, "Now Nancy, I am surprised at you. You don't know for a *fact* that he is getting a hummer, do you? I mean, that's all conjecture on your part isn't it? Oh, and how do you know for a *fact* that the girl is a skank? Maybe The Blue Magnet is just counseling that girl on the evils of hanging out in cop bars."

Nancy made a gimme-a-break face and the Sergeant said, "Bullshit."

Then he called across the room to Murphy and said, "Murph, go get Caputo and let's get this show on the road. I want to go home sometime today."

Murphy responded, "Sarge, can it wait a minute? I am about to win my game."

Roger, Nancy, and I all looked at each other when we heard Murphy's response. Then we looked at the Sergeant for his reaction. First, Atwell raised his eyebrows. Then he thought for about three seconds. Then he furrowed his brow.

Atwell called out, "Detective Murphy, have you got your cell phone with you?"

Murphy called back, "Yea Sarge why?"

Atwell said, "Well son, I ask out of concern for you. You see, I need you to stop what you are doing and bring yourself and Detective Caputo to me forthwith. I just wanted to be sure that when you were done you could call someone who cares whether or not you win your dart game. Do I make myself clear?"

Murphy said, "On my way Sarge."

He immediately made his apologies to the other players and went to get Caputo. The three of us just shook our heads and smiled at Atwell's predictability. You could tell the Sergeant anything, but you couldn't tell him much.

While we were waiting I asked Atwell what took him so long to get here. He said that one of the chiefs showed up at the meeting unexpectedly. Administrators who normally never say a word at these meetings suddenly had to take their turn to speak in order to impress the Chief.

Murphy walked over to the table, interrupted, and with a smile he said, "Caputo's coming. Ah, I mean he is on his way"

All the men chuckled and Nancy said, "That's disgusting Murph."

When she said that, we all laughed, including Nancy.

The Sergeant continued to regale us with the various ass-kissing techniques of his supervisors until Caputo came bopping over with a big smile on his face.

Nancy asked him, "Well, was she good?"

Caputo said to her, "Castillo, I don't kiss and tell, but I'll bet she was better than you are."

Nancy retorted, "First of all, you will *never* know, and I hope you catch a disease."

Caputo sarcastically said, "What is with you? I happen to be a loveable guy."

He then put a look of surprise on his face and said, "Oh, wait a minute. I get it now. You're jealous! You want me all for yourself, don't you? Yea, I can see it now. You've been *Magnetized*?"

We all started laughing and Nancy's beautiful eyes flared at him.

She said, "Fuck you Caputo. Any girl with any self-respect would have nothing to with you."

Caputo looked at the rest of us, spread his arms wide and said out loud, "But the world is filled with all kinds of women. They all need to be loved and the Blue Magnet is merely a humble servant of the public."

Then he and Murphy started singing a line from a country song that they had apparently rehearsed sometime in the past, probably at another bar.

"I ain't high class but I ain't white trash. I'm wild and a little crazy too. Some girls don't like boys like me … but some girls do."

With that, Murphy and Caputo grabbed Nancy and hugged her. She feigned disgust with a big smile and then pushed them away. I saw a smile come over Atwell's face also. He was looking at them with fondness. Roger and I looked at each other and started laughing with the Sergeant. Atwell told us what the plan was for tomorrow and then he finished his beer while we all discussed logistics.

About fifteen minutes later Atwell said, "Well, carry on."

Then he and Murphy left the bar together. They both went home to their families. Caputo left a short time after them with a girl in tow. My guess was that she was the one from the parking lot. Before long Roger's girlfriend Gail, who happened to be an attorney and always worked late, came into the bar to take him home. They had been together for about three years and Gail had his number.

I think Roger loved her so much because she could handle his brooding personality. He was a crusader who got very disappointed with life and people every now and then. We all appreciated him for who he was, but when he got too intense Gail would do whatever she did to mellow him out. I loved the way they were together. She hung out with us from time to time. We all knew her, appreciated her and liked her Roger, Gail, Nancy, and I, all left the bar together and went our separate ways.

CHAPTER 10
ROBIN HOOD AND HIS MERRY MEN

The dilemma for NET 104 began when the City ran into fiscal trouble. The government did not want to stop its supply-side enforcement efforts, but the politicians cut off the funds to the street narcotics enforcement teams all over the City. The teams could no longer obtain the cash to pay their informants or make their buys. It was a typical bone-headed maneuver designed by dilettantes. The police managers were responding to pressure from politicians to cut costs. God forbid they should have prepared a plan in advance for such a possibility.

One day, Roger and Nancy arrested a mid-level dealer, brought him in, and put him in the cage. They caught him with coke and about $1,000.00 in cash. I was in the office doing my thing and the Sergeant was out and about somewhere. It was my job to voucher evidence and property as well as other general clerical duties like ordering supplies and answering the phones for the unit. The cage, a 12 by 12 foot cell in which we keep prisoners prior to arrest processing, was located next door to the NET office in the stationhouse. I could hear the asshole whining about how he was a dead man for losing the drugs and the money. I also heard Nancy tell him to, "Shut the fuck up."

Roger said, "Good for you, you piece of shit. You deserve whatever you get for what you've been doing."

They walked into the office and dropped the evidence envelopes containing the drugs and the money on my desk. I started pulling out the blank arrest paperwork forms, the voucher, and the narcotics transmittal form. Out of the corner of my eye I noticed Nancy whisper something to Roger. They glanced my way and then they walked out into the hallway. When they re-entered the office they closed the door behind them. No one else was in the room with us.

They pulled chairs up close to my desk and Roger said, "Mike, we wanted to talk to you about an idea we had. Before we begin though, I just want to make sure we agree that this conversation is completely off the record. Are you cool with that?"

I said, "What's up?"

Nancy said, "You know how we don't have any more street cash. Well, (and she glanced at Roger) we have an idea. We want to take some of the money we recovered here and use it to go fishing. Not all of it, just some of it."

I said, "And you are telling me this why?"

Roger said, "Because we are not thieves. If we get caught the only way anyone would believe that we weren't taking money for ourselves is if we can prove it. We had this idea that since you voucher this stuff you can keep a record of what we used to go fishing just in case. That way there will be some evidence in our favor if the shit hits the fan."

I said, "You guys are nuts. Why in God's name would you want to do that? Management does not want to fund this operation anymore. That's it. Things will loosen up when the drug dealers get out of control again and bystanders start to get shot. I'm not keeping any records of anything you do. Records get people jammed up as much as no records, sometimes even more."

Roger said, "Mike, help us out here. You're a smart guy. You know what I'm trying to do. If you don't think records are a good idea, then give us another idea how to do it, you know, semi above board."

I responded with a chuckle, "Did you just say 'semi above board'? There is no such thing. Why do you feel the urge to do this? If you can't make arrests, you can't make arrests. Why do you want to risk your career on something when management does not give a shit? You are going to get caught, and the same idiots who cut off your funds are going to cut off your balls. In fact, they will probably be more pissed off that you did an end run around them, then at what you actually did. This whole idea is too stupid for words."

Nancy looked at me and said, "All right, then how about just this once. We will take 500 and see how far it goes."

I said, "I love you guys. I know what you are trying to do. It's noble, but it's really stupid." Then, with an exasperated tone I said, "Do what you have to do."

Nancy took $500.00 from the stack and handed it to Roger. He very deliberately and obviously put the cash into an envelope. Then, just as obviously, he put the envelope into his file draw. We all had file draws in these big four drawer file cabinets where we receive our department mail. That is also where keep our personal stuff when we don't want to walk all the way downstairs to our lockers. I started helping them with the paperwork and then I vouchered the remaining money as though that was all there was.

Very soon the air became heavy with unsaid things. Finally I said, "All right, just for a second let's think about this. One of you explain to me how you plan to do this without getting caught. How are you going to answer the Internal Affairs Division when the drug dealers start accusing you of stealing their money?"

Roger spoke first. He said, "I have had plenty of dealers over the years accuse me of stealing their cash. They actually have the nerve to call it their cash. IAD asks them for proof. Since they don't have any, IAD closes the case out as undetermined. It happens to Narcotics Enforcement Teams all over the city. IAD is used to it. If we are careful not to do it unless we are sure there is no record of the amount the guy has, we should be cool. Most of the time we don't even stop to count the cash at the scene of the arrest. You know the situation is usually just too out of control for that. We just bag it and tag it. As far as I know, you are the first person to count the cash when you open the envelope and voucher it"

Then Nancy said, "The way we'll keep from being tempted to use the money personally is to do it in front of each other. We both know how much we took and we both know how we will use it. It will be like checks and balances."

I laughed and shook my head when she said "checks and balances."

Then I said, "Guys, there is no way you are going to convince me that some of this money isn't going to be used for personal reasons. It's human nature. Maybe there were one or two pads that started that way – maybe. Maybe you are telling me the truth, but you are going to wind up the same way - on the take for personal gain. I won't be a part of that. I actually liked Frank Serpico.

Oh, and what about Murphy and Caputo? How do you plan to explain how you have street money and they don't? And what about Atwell? Atwell didn't just fall off a truck. He's been doing this shit for years. He is clean and at the very least you guys are going to get him jammed up with the Department when you get caught."

Roger looked at me and said, "You mean if we get caught."

I gave him an exasperated look and said, "Will you give me a break, please?"

Nancy said, "Well, maybe he will just look the other way. He doesn't have to be involved."

I said, "Nancy get real, people are going to ask him how his team is putting money out there when no one else is. He can't answer that question even if he 'just looks the other way'."

Roger, just looked frustrated and said, "Mike, we are trying to do the right thing here. It's not forever. It is just to get us over this money hump. We are not thieves."

My brain started working and I remembered a lesson I learned being the oldest of six children. Whoever gets to mom first is the one who gets believed. I had studied Atwell's personality for some time and it occurred to me that he really believed in what the team was doing. It also occurred to me that if he saw the trouble coming he might react more gently than if they did this without informing him upfront. The problem was how to work it out so I could talk to him without winding up getting everyone jammed up. I also did not want to be labeled a rat. It was a problem for me because I certainly could not live with being part of a crooked operation. I did not become a cop for that. I would rather go back on patrol.

After Nancy and Roger put away the $500.00 I told them about my plan to broach the subject with Atwell in private. I also explained my reasons why I felt it should be done. Both Roger and Nancy questioned the wisdom of my plan.

Nancy said, "I don't think that's a good idea Mike. I can't see him going along with it."

Roger nodded in agreement with her and said, 'She's right Mike. I would rather just go it alone."

I said, "Guys, are you being honest with me about wanting to use the money for good?"

They both nodded yes. Then I said, "If you are, then you have got to know in your hearts that Atwell needs to be part of it. If Atwell puts the kibosh on everything then it is probably in your interest anyway."

After much more conversation they both resigned themselves to what I was planning to do, but they didn't like it. I am sure they regretted ever talking to me about it.

A couple of days later Sergeant Atwell asked me to chauffer him around the precinct. The culture in the City PD called for supervisors to have chauffeurs. The chauffer served a dual purpose. First, the chauffer allowed the supervisor to concentrate on whatever he or she was doing. After all, they are supposed to be supervising. Secondly, if a situation arose where the supervisor had to get involved in some police action, his or her assistance was already present in the form of the chauffer.

That day, Atwell had a few personal errands to run and we needed to get some electronic equipment out to Murphy. Murphy was doing surveillance in an apartment across from where some coke dealers were operating. He was recording the operation on video, as much as he could. He was also trying to determine how many people were involved, how the operation flowed and what kind of weapons and security they had, etc. His long-range audio dish broke down and we were bringing him a replacement.

After squaring Murphy away, the Sergeant decided to just drive around a little and get a feel for what was happening in the Precinct that day. He wanted to put his finger back on the on pulse. As we drove around we talked about this and that, nothing significant. At one point we turned a corner and in front of us there was a car with a bumper sticker that read, "War is not the answer." The words were surrounded by the traditional peace symbol, you know, the circle with the upside down Y in it. There were also a dove and a daisy on the bumper sticker.

Atwell made an exasperated sound and then said, "Look at that shit, a peace symbol. Man do things come full circle or what?"

I said "Yea, most of the time."

He continued, "I haven't seen one of those since the 1970s. Pointing at it he said, "That is the footprint of the American chicken."

I just chuckled in agreement at his comment. He had no idea that I demonstrated with the SDS (Students for a Democratic Society) against the war in Vietnam. Once I learned what was really going on over there I wanted the war stopped.

I particularly resented that fact that if you were in college you could avoid the draft. Man that pissed me off. College deferments basically say that some American lives are worth more than others. College deferments also say that my investment in education is worth more than your investment in your own business, or in whatever other endeavor happens to be your own particular pursuit of happiness. There is just something ethically right about the people who decide to go to war also sending their own kids to fight it

Too many people had died just to prove to the Communists that we had the stomach to fight over some off-shore oil deposits. Yes, there was the "domino theory," but no matter what philosophical direction you approached Vietnam from originally, political interference wound up turning into a bunch of bullshit. Johnson, Nixon, and Ford, sent about 60,000 Americans to their deaths, and spent tons of money on the war, with nothing to show for it. Lord knows how many Vietnamese were killed.

John Fogerty's song *Fortunate Son* says is well: "...they send you off to war. And when you ask them how much should you give, the only answer is more, more, more." It had to be stopped. For me, chicken had nothing to do with my involvement in the anti-war movement. That is clearly evidenced by my choice of careers.

Then the Sergeant went into a soliloquy that was much closer to my heart (See Real Fact of Life # 3).

He said, "Yea, war is not the answer unless of course you count freeing our country, ending slavery, defeating genocidal fascists, and deposing brutal dictators."

He continued, "I'll bet if we were just a little friendlier to Hitler he would have stopped gassing Jewish people on his own. Oh, and the KKK, they would have stopped lynching us Black folks if we would have just shown them a little more love."

I could not help but laugh out loud at his monologue. Truly, there is no such thing as a former Marine. All of a sudden I got an idea on how to feel out the Sergeant about Roger and Nancy's plan.

I said, "Hey Sarge, you know how the Marine Corps teaches people to adapt and overcome?"

He nodded yes.

Then I asked, "You were a platoon leader, right?"

Again he nodded yes.

I continued, "What would you do if the managers of the Marine Corps made some decisions that left your platoon without the proper equipment and supplies they needed to do their jobs?"

He thought for a short 5 seconds and then said, "Well, you appropriate what you need to in order to accomplish the mission."

I quickly said, "I agree Sarge, but when you say appropriate you really mean steal right?"

He said, "Well, yea in a way, but you are not stealing from the locals or from the Corps for your own benefit. Anything you take is used to further the mission."

I said, "Sarge, I have a hypothetical I want to run by you. You know how the City has cut off the street money right?"

He nodded yes.

I said, "I want you to think about this in terms of the end justifying the means."

He turned toward me in his seat and focused on what I was saying.

"The money we recover from drug busts eventually gets destroyed right?"

He nodded.

I continued, "We have no mechanism in place to legally confiscate the money and use it for a productive purpose. I understand that this was put in place because recycling the money is corruption prone. However, from a purely philosophical point of view, do you see a problem with using the seized money for good purposes like buying police equipment or financing police operations?"

He diverted his eyes from me and looked straight out the windshield of the car, this time for a long 5 seconds. I knew he was thinking seriously about what I just said. I just kept driving.

Then he said thoughtfully, "Well, if you can eliminate the corruption issue, I actually don't see a problem with using the money for police purposes. There is no one who should rightfully get it, and the money would sure go a long way to helping us do our thing, particularly in times of financial stress. I think you've got a great idea here Mike. You should put it on an employee suggestion form. They pay you $75.00 if they adopt your suggestion, you know."

We both laughed at the thought of the department actually changing direction based on an employee's suggestion form. Then he continued musing.

"Man, if it could be done legally this is really a good idea. In fact, I wouldn't stop there. I say we should be able to seize any property that they use to further the commission of their crimes. We could get houses, and cars, and boats, and planes, and all sorts of other stuff. Then we could auction off what we don't need. We could really do God's work with that money."

I could see that he was getting into the idea and I said, "So you have no problem with the moral issue, the right or wrong of it?"

He said, "No, morally I am fine with it. However, the department will never go for it."

I knew he was talking ethics now and I just let him continue.

I said, "What do you mean?"

He said, "Well, we would need the people at the top to start thinking about using seized money as the right thing to do. Right now they don't. They just see it as too corruption prone. It's a shame in a way."

I said, "All right, let me ask you this then."

I slowed down the cadence of my words to get him to pay special attention to what I was saying.

"How would you react if a few dedicated police officers were willing to risk their careers by skimming some drug money seized in busts and using it for police purposes, you know, like paying informants and such. How would you personally react to that?"

All of a sudden the expression on his face changed to one of realization. He knew what I was getting at. Atwell took a long 10 seconds this time to respond.

He eventually said in a read between the lines fashion, "That is a very interesting *hypothetical* situation you propose. It definitely gives me something to think about. Rest assured I will certainly give the matter the attention it requires."

I just went silent and continued driving. I was waiting for the other shoe to drop. He let about a minute pass and then he paid me a very nice compliment.

He said, "You know Mike, you are a very smart guy. I like your style. I just hope the others appreciate you. Sometimes people's intentions are misconstrued"

It was obvious he was considering what consequences I would face for broaching the subject with him.

I said, "Thanks Sarge. I hope so too"

After about 20 seconds he said, "I don't understand why you have not made boss on this job. You certainly have the smarts for it"

I said, "Well, unless you just don't give a shit, it takes a certain kind of person to be responsible for the actions of so many other people."

I glanced to my right and we looked each other straight in the eyes with a full understanding of what we were really talking about. I knew I had just done something that Nancy and Roger were not comfortable with, but they knew I was going to do it. I also felt it was the right thing to do to keep everyone out of trouble. Atwell was a good man. He did not deserve to be blindsided and have his career ruined without knowing how and why it was being ruined.

Make no mistake; the higher ups would definitely hold him responsible for the actions of his team even if he did not know what was going on. Their attitude is that you are the supervisor. You are always supposed to know what is going on. The philosophy flies in the face of reality, but I can see its utility. Besides, the betrayal would have devastated this man. He was clean and he really cared for everyone. He just didn't deserve it. I believed that Atwell would handle Roger and Nancy without hurting them. He would keep them from making a big mistake. I kept thinking of that old saying, "The road to hell is paved with good intentions."

In the days that followed I picked up on the fact that Nancy and Roger had spoken with John and Dennis about their skimming plan. However, I got the sense that their plan was in fact, moving forward. I was hoping that the Sergeant would have spoken with all of them at some point, but no one else on the team spoke of this to me after my first conversation with Roger and Nancy.

I continued to properly voucher everything that was put in front of me. Still, each time they brought in cash to be vouchered I could not help but wonder if they had skimmed some off the top. The team's arrests continued at a good level in spite of the loss of street money from the Department Atwell went about his business and seemed to be on great terms with the crew. There was the usual joking and bonding experiences, and there was absolutely no sign of any issues between the Sergeant and his team.

About a month later I started getting some interesting calls in the office. The first call I took was from the Reverend Donald James. He was pastor of the Evangelical Church of Christ. He said he wanted to thank the team for their generous contribution to the Church's fund for a new furnace. He asked if it would be OK for him to mention us at service on Sunday. He said he was going to ask his congregation to pray for us My brain started to short circuit.

There was no way that NET 104 had passed the hat and taken up a collection for a new furnace. I would have been privy to and part of that. The money had to have come from drug busts. I did not want to insult the Reverend by saying no, but if I said "sure" I was afraid that a public mention of our "generous gift" might get everyone jammed up. This is the problem with not talking to each other.

I said, "Oh Reverend that is really not necessary. Please don't mention us at service. We were happy to do it."

The Reverend then said, "So you want it to be anonymous?"

I said, "Yes."

"I hope you don't mind me asking," He said, "but $3,000.00 is a lot of money. Did it come out of your own pockets, or did you fund raise for it at the precinct?"

Man I can think on my feet. I said, "Well Reverend, in a way it did come out of our own pockets. We buy lottery tickets as a group and we hit for a sizeable amount so we decided to tithe, but please keep it on the down low. OK? I don't know how the Department would react. They might actually consider the lottery to be gambling."

He said, "OK. I can do that. God bless you son, and please thank everyone again for us."

The next opportunity I had to talk with Roger and Nancy was the following day at the Do-Drop. The three of us were sitting there watching the news waiting for the rest of the crew.

I asked Nancy directly, "Have you guys been giving drug money to Reverend James' church?"

She looked at me and said sarcastically, "I thought you wanted plausible deniability? If I say, yea Mike we have, then you lose your precious plausible deniability right?"

I said, with exasperation in my voice, "It's already gone Nancy. Reverend James called yesterday."

Then I related the conversation to her. When I finished, I just closed my eyes for a moment and said to her, "You guys cannot get away with this. It is going to blow up in your faces."

Roger said, "Yea, well, we're doing the right thing Mike, and you know it too."

I asked, "Does Atwell know what you guys are up to?"

Roger repeated my question, "Does he know what we're up to? Well, let me put it this way. He is Robin Hood and we are his Merry Men. Did Robin Hood know what his men were up to?"

Roger waited for my reaction which I withheld while I absorbed what he just told me.

Before I could respond he said, "Come on Mike. Don't look so serious. It's really a good thing. The church needed the money."

I just shook my head in disbelief. The idea that Atwell would risk his career over this blew my mind. I could almost see Nancy doing it. I could definitely see Roger doing it because it would allow him to thumb his nose at "the man", but Atwell? Atwell has kids. Murphy has kids. Most of all, they all loved being cops. They were putting everything at risk and I was being drawn into the vortex.

With a sigh of resignation I looked at both of them and said, "Iacta est alea."

They looked at each other and then at me. Both of them were smiling with a "What the hell is he talking about now?" look on their faces that I have seen from time to time in the past.

I said, "That's Latin guys. Julius Caesar said it right after he ordered his troops to attack Rome. It means the die is cast. The way I see it, NET 104 is taking on Rome and this time Rome is going to kick our asses."

Shortly thereafter a local community youth group suddenly got an influx of funds for repairing the basketball courts and buying equipment for the kids. Ostensibly, Roger and Nancy had found them some generous anonymous contributor. Then the drug treatment center received a donation of several thousand dollars. They used it to take in people they never could have afforded to help. Things like this went on and on for months.

It was just before Thanksgiving that I really got involved beyond just looking the other way. I was the one who coordinated the purchase and delivery of turkeys to any families that came to our attention who could not afford their own. When Atwell gave me the job of coordinating the turkeys I looked for him to also supply me with an excuse.

He just smiled at me with a guilty grin, shrugged his shoulders and said, "I won a bundle at the track on a couple of long shots that came in. Get the money from Dennis."

I just shook my head, smiled back, and went with it. You should have seen Christmas time. The team actually went out shopping to buy stuff for the local free medical clinic. They also tried to make sure that no child in the precinct went without a toy or a tree. Dennis Murphy actually came back to the Precinct and delivered some toys on Christmas Eve after his own kids were sleeping. Santa Claus is definitely Irish.

The operation was in high gear and taking on a life of its own. Throughout it all I never forgot what Bob Marley said, "Each day the bucket goes to the well. Someday the bottom will drop out." NET 104 could have pulled over at any time, but they didn't.

One of the first things drug dealers do, after speaking with their lawyers, is accuse the arresting officers of stealing drugs and money. In their corrupt mental state, some of them actually think that the police department is going to trade them a dismissal for their silence. Their endeavor is extortion. Unfortunately, it is difficult to prove absolutely that they are lying. The arrested dealer might say he had $5,000.00 when he only had $500.00 or 10 kilos of coke when he only had a gram.

When the drug dealers first started doing it they actually did slow down law enforcement efforts. Internal Affairs did such thorough investigations and treated honest police officers so poorly, that many officers decided, "Screw this. I bust some drug dealer, he makes an empty accusation, and they treat me like the criminal. I don't need this hassle, I'll do the minimum."

In fact, some municipalities were so afraid of the bad press and lawsuits, that they eliminated all narcotics enforcement efforts that were not joint operations with the FBI, DEA, or Customs. As a result, the number of narcotics arrests plummeted by 80% during the days of intense IAD scrutiny. Drug dealing went wild and drug dealers became much more brazen. The movie *New Jack City* paints a pretty good picture of the problems the politicians and IAD caused by de-motivating the police.

Eventually, the public and the politicians trying to please the public, wanted to stop the violence and make more arrests. After a while, the lack of evidence to support the dealer's accusations and the sheer volume of complaints led the Internal Affairs Division to take a more pragmatic approach to the problem. IAD knew that they needed to start treating the officers better if they wanted the cops to make more arrests. Management came to an understanding with our union and that understanding put the arrest train back on track. Believe it or not, the Department took a statistical approach to the problem.

They developed a statistical norm for the number of complaints by drug dealers that they used to determine whether or not to investigate complaints that cops were stealing their drugs and cash. Simple accusations with no other evidence resulted in cursory investigations and a database entry. Unless there was some sort of credible evidence of theft, they waited for a statistical aberration before launching a full investigation. Guess what? Robin Hood and his Merry Men caused a statistical aberration.

People don't give police officers enough credit for creativity. Unlike many other professions, critical thinking skills are directly tested in the entrance examination. Not too many other professions do that. The result is a pool of people who are pretty good at problem solving. Although a knucklehead or two does slip into the system, most of the time if you are thinking, "that cop was stupid," you are probably wrong. He or she is most likely playing stupid to suit his or her own agenda.

There is a myriad of reasons. It could be that the cop just doesn't feel like working at that moment. It could also be that pretending not to see something, or letting something go, achieves the resolution that is in line with the officer's morality rather than his or her ethics. What is both interesting and telling is that the two jobs within the police department that require the most creativity are not obtained through civil service tests. They are appointed positions. One is Police Detective and the other is Internal Affairs Investigator.

There are some jaded police officers who would say that there are only two criteria you must meet in order to be appointed a Detective. First, you must be able to sharpen a pencil without stabbing yourself. Second, you must have a hook. A "hook" is police jargon for a person who has the power to influence the person or persons who make the appointments.

Currently, there is no mechanism in place for a police officer to become a detective based solely on measurable performance. The system has both plusses and minuses. A detective should have good people skills as well as a drive to make arrests. These attributes are subjective. However, the system tends to promote dilettantes to supervisory positions and these individuals wind up making the detective appointments. I am sure you can see the problem. Fortunately, within the Detective Division only the best get into the specialized units like Robbery, Homicide, or Special Victims. As far as Internal Investigator is concerned, the competition for the available positions is not that great, but the officers selected for Internal Affairs are usually very smart, honest, and dedicated.

Once the Internal Affairs people identified the statistical aberration, they devised a very cool trap for the people of NET 104. They interviewed one of the drug dealers that the team arrested who had made a complaint against the officers. They listened to his story, and then they offered him a deal that would give him probation on his drug offenses if he would help set up the cops who supposedly stole his drug money. They also insisted that he cooperate with the subsequent investigation and prosecution.

NET 104 made so many arrests that they sort of lost track of who was sentenced to what. It was easy for Internal Affairs to put this dealer named Henry back on the street a month after his arrest. He was wearing a recording device (a wire), and carrying an envelope filled with $3235.00 in marked bills. When Roger Thomas got the word from the street that Henry was back in business he was pissed. I remember him ranting about how he could possibly be out so soon. He called the prosecutor handling the case.

Roger asked, "Why is Henry back on the street? How did this bust go south?"

The prosecutor, who was working with Internal Affairs said, "Look Roger, I am sorry you don't like the way we do business, but that's life. Henry gave up some bigger fish, and making a deal with him is worth it for us."

Roger said, "Well you know what asshole? Henry is back on the street dealing drugs again as the result of your *deal*. I am going to bust his ass again, and if you make him another deal, I am going to start getting suspicious that maybe he paid you off. For your sake, this next bust better stick."

The sting went down exactly the way Internal Affairs planned it. Roger and Nancy made the bust and $800.00 was never vouchered. I found out later that Nancy and Murphy were going to use most of the money for a pet project. They were saving up to buy a van for the senior home and $600.00 of the $800.00 would have gone toward the "van fund". The other $200.00 was supposed to be used for fishing. IAD was able to show a chain of evidence that put the money from Henry's coat into Roger's coat. They had that on video. Somewhere between the scene of the arrest and the office, $800.00 disappeared from the envelope.

When I brought the voucher envelope with the balance of the money in it out to the desk to be put in the safe, they were waiting. They searched Roger's coat and found the missing cash. Roger said that he had been counting the cash before giving it to me to voucher. He said that he needed to go to the head really bad and just forgot to put the last $800.00 back into the envelope. He insisted that this interruption made him forget the other $800.00 in his coat.

It was a lame excuse. Internal Affairs wasn't buying any of it and suspended the lot of us, including Sergeant Atwell. For whatever their reasons were, Internal Affairs did not wait for a second or third offense to be committed. They did not wait to follow the money and see how it was used. They just shut down NET 104. By doing so, they limited the scope of the wrongdoing and gave all of us a much smaller legal problem to face. To this day I still wonder how that happened to work out for us.

During the investigation some interesting facts were revealed. Most important, no drugs were missing. Nobody took any drugs for any purpose whatsoever. Second most important, all personal purchases made by team members during the previous 24 months could be traced to money they had earned legally. The informants, who were paid using the money from the "skimming activity", as IAD called it, had no idea what was going on. They just knew that they were being paid for their information as usual. The team members explained the fact that they had money to pay informants by sticking to the stories of winning lottery tickets, anonymous donors, and good days at the track.

IAD heard the rumors that many worthy causes throughout the precinct had received donations that were traceable back to the Unit. They confirmed the rumors, but their official position was that NET 104's political friends in the community were trying to defend them and that those friends started the rumors.

CHAPTER 11
THE BLUE WALL OF SILENCE

For those of you who don't know, many cops despise the Internal Affairs Division and the officers who work in that division. Some cops are opposed to their existence philosophically. IAD is responsible for policing the police, and as we all know, no one likes to be policed. Other officers, including me, can appreciate IAD. Just like policing in general, someone has to do it. In fact, after completing investigations into the facts and circumstances, IAD sometimes clears officers of false accusations. However, some of us object to what the division sometimes evolves into. You see, when there are no large corruption issues to work on, IAD can become very picayune.

When there is nothing major going on, IAD will take on cases that would ordinarily be handled by supervisors at the Precinct level during busier times. They also begin to look for problems where there are none. Both of these behaviors piss off the cops who are out there doing the job honestly, and who now and then become the subject of unsubstantiated allegations. It is no fun to be hauled over to IAD based on what you know is a false accusation, or because your righteous enforcement efforts pissed off some politico. It is particularly irritating when you know full well that if some poor, powerless, person made the same complaint as the politico, IAD would let the precinct commander handle it.

I appreciate the concept of internal affairs. My knowledge of human nature and my experience as a police officer tell me that if IAD did not exist we would have a corruption nightmare on our hands. The good cops would be unable to do right by society for fear of the bad ones. Truly, IAD is necessary. It provides the police with a healthy fear of consequences that cannot be ignored. Unfortunately, we have to take the bad aspects of IAD with the good.

If the people of NET 104 were taking money from drug dealers for their own gain, I would have come down on the side of IAD. Since they were using the drug money to further police operations and benefit the community, I came down on the side of NET 104. I did not believe that the people assigned to NET 104 should lose their jobs, or be prosecuted for what they did. On the other hand, I believe that those who further the use of supply side enforcement are behaving unethically for reasons I have already described. Those people are the ones who should lose their jobs. Because of this philosophical position, I raised the blue wall of silence.

When I went for my interview at IAD, two Sergeants, Tiller and Danson questioned me. It was standard operating procedure for me to have a union rep and a lawyer present to make sure the interviewers did not violate my rights, the contract, or the rules and regulations. The subject of an IAD investigation is always given his or her Miranda rights. Whatever a cop says to Internal Affairs can be used in a criminal prosecution unless some type of immunity is specifically agreed to in writing by the District Attorney's office. Needless to say, I was very nervous.

Danson began. "You are the clerical man for the precinct's NET Unit correct?"

I said, "Yes."

He continued, "What involvement did you have in skimming money that was recovered during their drug arrests?"

I said, "I am unaware of any such activity."

He said, "Are you aware of any other team members who were taking some of the money they recovered during drug arrests?"

I said, "No. I told you I am unaware of any such activity."

Then they tried to flip me by offering me a deal if I would turn on the others. They said they already had enough evidence to indict all of us and the first one who flipped got a deal. I reasoned correctly that they did not have enough evidence to charge anyone besides Roger at that time. If they did, they would not have been offering me a deal.

The agreement within the NET 104 Unit was that we would cover for each other. Since no one took money for personal use, this was easy for me morally. Besides the criminal side of this, we committed major violations of the Department's Rules and Regulations. I hoped that the worst that would happen to us would be that we would all get charged with Tampering with Evidence and then get fired for that. I stuck to my guns and once again I applied what Ben Franklin said. "If we do not hang together, we will surely hang separately."

Then Tiller started to question me.

He asked, "Are you aware that the members of the NET Unit have been making financial contributions to community organizations throughout the precinct?"

I said, "Yes."

He asked, "Do you know the source of the money the team has been using to donate to those community organizations?"

I said, "I believe so."

You should have seen how the both of them leaned forward in their chairs. They were anticipating my next words.

"It is coming out of their own pockets," I said.

Tiller chuckled. Danson smiled and made a puffing sound with his mouth expressing his disbelief without the use of words. Then they sat back in their chairs again.

I went into a spiel designed to convince them of my innocence. I said, "Why is that so impossible? I realize you guys suspect they have been stealing drug money, but I don't think they have. One of the guys won a substantial amount in the lottery. Another guy hit a long shot at the track, which is completely legal. They used that money. I also know of at least one situation where two of our people got an anonymous donor to contribute some money. Don't even ask me because I do not know who the donor was. He or she was anonymous. There is nothing wrong with doing what they did."

Tiller said, "Do you know that for a fact?"

I said, "Well I was not at the track when they won, or in the Bodega where they bought the tickets."

Tiller said, "Then what you mean to say is that someone *told* you about winning the lottery. Someone *told* you about hitting a long shot and someone *told* you about some mysterious anonymous donors, right? You don't actually know where the money came from, do you?"

I said, "Well yea, that's essentially correct. I only know what I have been told."

Tiller asked, "So would you say that it is possible that the money could have come from drug arrests?"

I said, "I don't believe that for a moment."

Tiller asked, "Why?"

I said, "Because I do the vouchering. They place a sealed evidence envelope in front of me. I open it, count the money in front of the arresting officer, and voucher it."

Tiller asked, "Well how do you know they do not take the cash before they come into the office? It is possible right?"

I responded, "Look, I am only talking about what I think is true. I refuse to speculate on what is possible. It is the oldest, most irritating, lawyer's gimmick."

He be labored the 'possibility" point for a while longer. Then Tiller changed the subject slightly and asked, "So, who won the lottery? Who hit the long shot?"

I said, "I don't know. One day I was having a pleasant conversation with Sergeant Atwell about a call I took from Father Flaherty of St. Mary's Church. I commented about how much it must have cost the team to buy turkeys, and the Sergeant said that one of them won big at the track. I don't remember if he even said whose horse came in. I have to tell you that none of this seemed important to me at the time. What seemed important was that they were doing God's work."

Danson and Tiller both laughed at me in disbelief when I said they were doing "God's work," and then their questioning went on a while longer. The upshot was that they got nothing from me to use against the others.

Getting busted by IAD had to happen. I knew it from the start, yet I got swept away by the adventure of being one of Robin Hood's Merry Men. I have to admit that it was a thrill. It was an in-your-face defiance of the status quo based on a revolutionary concept that drug money should be seized and used for good purposes. During the IAD investigation I was kicking myself for not requesting a transfer out when the plan began to proceed. After it was over and the consequences known, I was actually glad I had been a part of it.

I had no problem with the morality of taking a drug dealer's ill-gotten cash and doing good deeds with it. I knew it was not ethical because the department's expectation was that the money would be properly vouchered. I rationalized my choice with the fact that the entire system of supply-side enforcement is unethical. It was pretty much a case of the pot calling the kettle black. I was very hard pressed to worry about *my* ethics in the unethical environment of supply-side enforcement. Since the system of supply side enforcement, stupid as it is, was not going to change anytime soon, an end run around the problem seemed appropriate.

We believed we were right. None of us wanted to allow them to punish us for what we did. None of us saw anything immoral in this. To destroy the cash without using it to help anyone seemed like a stupid ethic. The team may have been using the money for its own purposes, but they were good purposes. They were not using it for personal gain and that made all the difference to me. I firmly believed that the status quo was wrong and the blue wall of silence survived the storm.

One after another, the members of NET 104 and Sergeant Atwell made it through their interviews without getting locked up. I don't know if this made a difference, but there was a tremendous amount of political pressure from the community leaders brought to bear on our behalf. No one in the community would publically entertain the notion that the money came from any source other than the team's own pockets and fund raising ingenuity. That belief was supported by the fact that no one on the team, or the Sergeant, had anything unusual going on in his or her bank accounts. None of them had new cars, or new houses, or new jewelry. In that sense, everybody was pretty smart.

However, none of us got off Scott-free. We were all fined and took our slaps on the wrist. Roger lost his detective shield and was transferred to another command to do patrol. Eventually he got it back and began working as a regular detective in another command. They scattered the rest of NET 104, including Atwell, to the four winds. They were all transferred to other commands and assigned to ordinary detective duties to punish them for what happened.

That is everyone but me. I pleaded with IAD to do anything to me but put me back on patrol. I told them it would be torture for me. I was like Brer Rabbit from the *Tar Baby*. "Oh, please don't throw me in that briar patch." I received no fine, but for not cooperating with them, predictably, they threw me back on patrol. My life became uncomplicated and peaceful once again.

Here's the ethical kicker. Some years later, the New York State legislature passed a law that allows municipalities to seize money and property used to further, or obtained through, criminal enterprises. The municipalities may then use the money and property for a myriad of police purposes.

What was unethical, and in fact investigated as possibly criminal behavior, is now completely ethical and legal. Seizing and using money and property for police purposes is now the standard operating procedure. The process is handled through the Asset Recovery Bureau, a layer of bureaucracy that was created specifically for this purpose. Man, if I had only submitted that employee suggestion form I would be $75.00 richer today.

CHAPTER 12
HEARTS AND MINDS

When most people hear about the blue wall of silence they imagine a vast conspiracy of police officers who remain silent regardless of what crimes their brother or sister officers commit. This is Hollywood. If you take the time to read the details of police corruption cases in the media you will see examples, nationwide, of police officers who refuse to tolerate working next to criminal cops. Frank Serpico was just one of them. However, in police work we judge each other by whether the transgression is a sin of the heart, or a sin of the mind.

One example of a sin of the mind is a police officer losing control during an arrest. We are human beings like everyone else. We can only control ourselves and the events we become involved in to a certain degree. We too have natural self-defense mechanisms which once they are unleashed cannot be stopped on a dime. We too have the same natural desire as everyone else to even the score for a wrong done to us. So when a criminal runs from the police and that causes us to take our lives in our hands as we try to catch him or her, we understand each other's need to make that person can pay for that when we catch them.

We always yell "Halt" or "Stop- Police" or "Police- Don't Move." All these people have to do is comply. When we tell someone to stop, they should stop. If they do, 99% of them will not have any problem other than their legal one. Don't expect one officer to rat out another officer for getting physical with a criminal after that person caused the officers to risk injury in a chase.

On the other hand, if a police officer is so warped that he sadistically abuses prisoners, that officer commits a sin of the heart. If an officer goes out looking to shake down people, that officer commits a sin of the heart. Being on the take is a sin of the heart. There are actually few police officers who will tolerate sins of the heart from their peers.

Police Officer Adam Blaustein was a personal friend and a long time professional acquaintance. He came on the job three months after I did and for many years we worked together. We were both police instructors. During one of the department's purges of administrative personnel, we found ourselves back on the street patrolling sectors next to each other. We were happy to know the other one was around. Adam was a good honest cop and very professional. He had a good sense of humor and we worked well together.

Adam was part of the most phenomenal police training system ever devised. He was our precinct's Command Level In-service Trainer. The title is a mouthful, so the rank and file came up with a very unfortunate acronym for those in his position. Both the male and female Command Level In-service Trainers had their objections to the acronym. They preferred to be called Training Officers (TOs).

There was one officer in each of the six precincts. There was one for headquarters, one for the Detective Division, and one for Highway Patrol. Their work hours overlapped the day and the night shifts, which was a testament to their dedication and a burden to their families. Whenever there was a change in the law, or a court decision that affected police procedure, these nine people regularly trained a 2500 member police force, while the officers were in-service, in 90 days. It was an incredibly efficient use of time, personnel, and money. In addition, the U.S. Military has demonstrated time and again the positive effect training has on morale, enthusiasm, professionalism, and ethical behavior.

Then, one of our logistically impaired police commissioners decided that he wanted to impress the county executive by reducing the Department's patrol overtime bill. In a purge, he eliminated the Command Level In-service Training Program. He put the nine Command Level Trainers, including Adam, back on patrol.

Management's ethics, and the union contract, dictate that there must always be a minimum number of police officers on patrol to protect the public and each other. So now in order to train a police officer, that officer has to be taken off patrol and sent to the police academy for a day. His or her place on the street is filled by someone on overtime. I am sure that the commissioner would have thrown these ethics to the wind if he had been legally allowed to reduce the number of cops on patrol. Unfortunately, this is the kind of decision-making that occurs when political contributions are prerequisites for upper management promotions instead of previously demonstrated management skills and common sense.

One day I got called to assist Adam with an arrest. It started with a traffic violation for running a Stop Sign. The defendant, a male, white, 27 years old, was a local resident of the upper middle-class neighborhood we were patrolling. He was one of those people whose parents raised him to question authority. Accordingly, he immediately began giving Adam a hard time. Most police officers with time on the job have heard just about every line that motorists can think up. Over time, we develop a thick skin. We also use standard spiels to try to avoid confrontations, or long conversations about the drivers' many justifications for why they did why they did.

Our initial contact spiel goes kind of like this: "Good morning (sir or ma'am) you rolled passed the Stop sign at (whatever) road. I am going to have to examine your driver's license." After the driver complies, you say, "Sir/ma'am, please show me proof that the vehicle is insured." After the drivers complies you say, "Please remain where you are. I will be with you shortly."

Vehicle registrations stickers are affixed to windshields. At that point the officer goes back to the police car, checks out the documents and either writes a ticket, or makes the decision to give a warning instead. When the ticket is completed, the officer returns to the subject's car and says: "There's an instruction form here that explains how to handle everything. You can go now."

That is how it is goes when you stop well-adjusted mature people who admit, at least to themselves, that they rolled passed the Stop sign. That wasn't this guy.

This guy started with Adam by saying, "You've got to be kidding. I stopped at the sign."

When Adam told him his wheels never stopped turning he said, "This is all you have to do? With all the crime out there you have to persecute innocent citizens for *rolling* passed Stop Signs? I slowed down for it."

Then he refused to give Adam his license.

He said, "No, this isn't fair. I got a ticket just last week for the same thing and it is not fair that I should get another one. Go give it to someone else. There is nothing wrong with the way I drive. I am not giving you my driver's license so you can write me another ticket."

When Adam explained that the alternative to a ticket is an arrest, he claimed not to believe Adam.

He said, "Arrest me? You can't arrest me for running a Stop Sign."

Adam said, "Sir, tickets are issued in lieu of arrests so as not to clog up the courts. If I am unable to issue a ticket because I can't identify you, I am forced to arrest you."

The guy responded, "Then go ahead. I'll have your job for false arrest if you do."

That is when Adam got on his portable radio and called for assistance. It is not standard procedure to take someone's keys when you stop them for a traffic violation. It is common practice to take someone's keys if the person cannot, or will not, be identified. Doing so calls the issue out. Either the guy gives you the keys or you arrest him immediately.

Adam got caught flatfooted by this guy's refusal to surrender his license. It happens to the best of us now and then. He left the guy with his keys. Adam was standing right outside the guy's car, next to the driver's window, when the guy decided to just drive away. It must have occurred to the guy that since he refused to give Adam his license, and nothing immediately happened to him (like losing his keys or being dragged out of the car) maybe he could just drive away.

He put his car in gear, with Adam standing right there, and drove down the block. I turned the corner just as this was happening and I saw Adam running back to his police car so he would be able to chase the guy. It was obvious to me that the guy was trying to run from Adam, so I sped up, passed Adam's police car with my lights and siren on, passed the guy on the left, and cut him off. He had only two choices. He either had to pull over or he had to hit my police car. He chose to pull over.

Adam caught up to us with his police car and quickly told me what had happened. At this point, the guy was going to get tickets for running the Stop Sign and for Failing to Obey the Lawful Order of a Police Officer. The first charge carried three points, if he was convicted. The second charge would result in his driving privileges being suspended for six months. In the hope that this could be resolved in the street, Adam asked me if I would try and convince the guy to give up his documents rather than be arrested.

Doing so was a common practice. Sometimes the second officer who arrives can defuse the situation. It is a tactic that works well most of the time. I really did not want to spend the next four hours processing an arrest for something this stupid. The driver had gotten out of his car and was standing in the street in front of his vehicle.

I said to the guy, "Look, we need your driver's license to identify you. If you don't have your driver's license with you, then we can accept something other form of identification, but we have to Identify you."

The guy said, "Why, so you can give me a ticket?"

I said, "Well, you are probably going to get one or two tickets, but you may or may not be found guilty. On the other hand, if you force us to arrest you, you will wind up paying thousands of dollars in legal fees, win or lose. If you take the tickets, you will have your day in court. You will have the chance to tell the judge what the officer did."

The guy then said, "But that other guy has no right to give me a ticket. I didn't do anything wrong."

I said to him, "Think of it this way. If the officer is wrong, and he has no grounds to write you a ticket, the judge will dismiss the case against you. Then the judge will see to the discipline of the officer. But if the officer is not lying to you, if he is correct and you can be arrested for not giving him your license, it is going to cost you dearly. No matter how you slice it, the smart play is to give the officer your license or some other form of identification."

Although the guy looked right at me and heard everything I said, when I finished talking to him, he never responded to the issues I raised.

He took out his cell phone and confidently said, "I'm calling my father and he's calling my lawyer."

At that point, Adam, who had been listening to our conversation, walked up to him and said, "All right, I have had enough. You're under arrest! You will get your phone call just like everyone else after we have processed you. Put the phone away, turn around, and put your hands behind your back."

The guy just ignored Adam. Adam and I looked at each other to make sure we were on the same page. Then we grabbed the guy to put handcuffs on him. He started flailing his arms and hitting us with his cell phone as he did. We wrestled him onto the top of his own car and handcuffed him behind his back. Somehow, one of the three of us stepped on his cell phone after he dropped it on the street.

The guy began screaming at us, "You broke my phone! You have no right to do this! Let me go! Let me go now!"

Then he decided to play Gandhi on us. He dropped to the ground in an act of passive resistance. He became dead weight. That forced us to drag him to Adam's police car and put him into the back seat.

Once in the back seat he continued screaming, "You fucking bastards. You can't do this." Stuff like that.

When we closed the car door, he started kicking the car seat in front of him. He had worked himself into a frenzy of hatred and anger. At that point Adam and I began to think we were dealing with a mental case. We parked the guy's car on the street where we arrested him, locked it, and took his keys with us. I retrieved his phone from the roadway, but it was damaged beyond repair. I drove the police car and Adam sat in the back seat with the prisoner. For a while the guy kept insulting us and threatening us.

At one point I yelled at him, "Calm down, what is wrong with you man?" After that, he spit at me and he hit me in the neck with his spittle. Finally, Adam warned him that if he didn't shut up Adam would gag him. The guy refused to shut up so we stopped the car and got two rolls of medical gauze (Cling) out of the trunk. Adam stuffed one roll in the guy's mouth while he was ranting about how we would lose our jobs. Then Adam wrapped the guy's head with the other roll of gauze in order to hold the first one in. We left him nose holes so he could breathe. The guy cried the rest of the way to the stationhouse, but at least it was a little quieter in the car and he couldn't spit anymore.

Along the way, Adam and I discussed the guy's behavior. We concluded that he was not a mental case. He had responded lucidly when we were conversing prior to the arrest. He wasn't delusional. In fact, he seemed quite in touch with reality. He just concluded that we had no right to arrest him. We determined that he was just a spoiled little asshole. He probably threw temper tantrums all his life, even into adulthood. It was inevitable that his tantrums would get him in trouble outside his own family.

Sometimes the police wind up giving people like him their first reality check. I suspect it is because certain parents don't have the stomach to do it themselves. Other times, it is a case of the apple not falling far from the tree. Sometimes when you meet the parents you completely understand why the kid turned out that way. When we walked him into the stationhouse the cops working behind the Desk started laughing out loud.

One cop said, "Oh my God, they arrested the Mummy."

Another one said, "No man, that's Claude Rains, the Invisible Man."

We walked this guy into the arrest processing room, sat him on the bench, and chained him to the wall without removing his cuffs. After we secured our gun belts in lockers, we re-entered the arrest room to start processing the paperwork. As soon as we removed the cling from his head and mouth he immediately began spouting more venomous bullshit about us personally.

I never knew my mother did those things with my dog and I was pretty sure that I never had oral sex with Adam. After insulting us, he told us how we were both going to pay for what we were doing to him as soon as his father found out. I couldn't believe this guy was 27 years old. He was behaving like a spoiled child. We searched him and inventoried his property for safekeeping. During the search we, of course, came across his driver's license. Adam couldn't resist waving it in his face.

He said, "You see this, Dumbass? I get to look at it anyway. Only now you're chained up for behaving like an animal. How do you feel? Do you feel better, or do you feel worse than you did when I stopped you? It sure would have been smarter and cheaper to just show it to me when I asked for it right? …Dumbass!"

Any chance we had to get any cooperation from this guy that would have helped us process the arrest disappeared when Adam called him Dumbass. As we asked him for the standard pedigree information we needed to complete our paperwork, the guy kept demanding his phone call and telling us about his right to remain silent.

Eventually, we brought in the Desk Officer who explained to him that the courts had ruled that he would not get his phone call until after the arrest was processed. This included pictures and prints and that it would be a short or long process depending on his cooperation. We hoped that the Desk Officer, being a supervisor, could encourage him to cooperate with the process. After all, it was in the guy's interest to do so.

While the Desk Officer was talking to him, Dumbass began screaming at the top of his lungs, "I want my phone call! I want my phone call!" over and over and over again.

Finally, the Desk Officer gave up trying to talk to the guy. He said to us, "You guys need to get him to stop. This is a stationhouse not an insane asylum."

Then he left the room and returned to the main Desk which was way down at the other end of the building. After that, the guy began chanting, "I want my phone call" in this sing song way.

I calmly said to him, "Hey buddy, a couple of minutes ago you were bitching about your right to remain silent. Why don't you exercise it now and shut the hell up? You are really starting to get on my nerves"

He said, "Fuck you pig!"

Adam turned around and we looked at each other. Neither of us had heard that term for many years and we both started laughing. The guy just looked at us obviously wondering what we were laughing about."

I turned back toward the guy and I said, "You know something man? Someday I am going to retire and I won't be a pig anymore. You? You are going to be an asshole your entire life."

He just looked at me and said, "Oinker, porker, sowfucker, piglet."

Then he started making oink sounds with his nose and Adam and I started laughing again. He would not shut up and in a few minutes he started screaming once again for his phone call.

Adam decided to try a different tack to get Dumbass to shut up and cooperate. At least that's what I thought Adam was doing. He started out talking to Dumbass very calmly.

Adam said, "You know something? I think I know what the problem is."

To my pleasant surprise, the guy stopped screaming.

He looked at
Adam and began to listen.

Adam continued, "When you were a little kid your parents gave you coloring books right?"

Dumbass nodded and continued to listen.

Then Adam said, "You probably took the crayon and scribbled all over the page of the flower or whatever it was you were supposed to be coloring, didn't you?"

Once again the guy nodded and continued to listen.

"Now, what your parents should have told you was, 'No Dumbass, you are supposed to color inside the lines. That is the right way to color.'"

At that moment I realized that everything was about to go south. Dumbass began to glare at Adam with hatred in his eyes. I said to myself, "Oh shit, here we go"

Adam continued, "Instead, your mother probably looked at the scribbled on picture, showed it to your father, and said, 'Oh look honey, see what a beautiful picture Dumbass made.'"

When Adam said that, I burst out laughing. I could not control it. I had this picture in my head of the guy's mother saying, "Look honey, see what a beautiful picture Dumbass made" and I lost it.

Then Adam continued, "And so you grew to think that any stupid fucked up thing you did would be acceptable. Well, its not, and that is why you wound up here ... Dumbass!"

I could see the guy boiling inside. Adam may very well have been right, but saying so was not going to make a difference at this point in this guy's life. The guy spat at Adam and told us both to go fuck ourselves.

Then he said, "Leave my mother and father out of this. You don't know them you Nazi piece of shit."

I knew that when the guy called Adam a Nazi he pissed Adam off. Several of Adam's relatives were murdered in the Holocaust. He once told me that one of the reasons he became a cop was to do his part to make sure it never happened again (See Real Fact of Life # 2). We went on like that, trying to complete the paperwork prior to taking his picture and prints. After we went as far as we could on the paperwork, it was time for pictures and prints.

Adam stood up. Then he walked over to the guy and said, "Stand up." I'm going to take your cuffs off. We need to fingerprint you and take your picture."

I was surprised that the guy stopped chanting and stood up. He let Adam remove the handcuffs without a hassle. I was expecting a Gandhi thing again. As Adam was taking the guy's cuffs off, he whispered into the guy's ear.

I heard Adam say, "I am not going to deal with your shit anymore. You are being given everything the law requires in the same order as anyone else who gets arrested. Now if you don't shut the fuck up and cooperate with me on these pics and prints I am going to put you in the hospital."

At first I thought that there was a problem with Adam's timing. The guy was uncuffed when Adam was whispering in his ear. Later I realized that Adam planned it that way. Dumbass pulled his arm away from Adam and started heading for the door. I jumped up from the arrest processor and moved toward the door to block his way. However, my concern proved to be unnecessary because without missing a beat, Adam hit the guy with his slapper across the side of the head. The guy fell to the floor like a sack of potatoes. I didn't expect Adam to do that, although in hindsight I should have expected something like that. Adam was at his wits end and I was close to mine.

A slapper is a sizeable piece of lead that is sandwiched between two pieces of leather and sewn together. Its purpose is to give us a leg up in a hand-to-hand combat situation. However, the guy went down so hard that I thought Adam killed him. I stood there holding my breath and praying that this guy was still alive. Then he groaned and I breathed a sigh of relief. We immediately called for an ambulance and reported to the Desk Officer that Adam hit the guy when the guy tried to escape. Dumbass woke up in the hospital with a concussion. In addition to the charges of passing a Stop Sign and Failing to Obey the Lawful Order of a Police Officer, he was also charged with Resisting Arrest and Attempted Escape.

We had explained everything to this guy. We gave him plenty of opportunity to act like a civilized person. The guy was hell bent on pushing Adam passed his limits. He experienced the consequences of doing that. I'll bet Dumbass thinks twice about hassling the next cop who pulls him over for a traffic violation.

New York State courts still look at driving as a privilege rather than a right. Your privileges to drive may be suspended if you accumulate 11 points for moving violations, refuse to take a DUI test, or disobey the lawful order of a police officer. There is no doubt that Dumbass acted unethically regarding what was expected of him as a licensed driver in the State of New York. He was required by law to produce his driver's license upon demand of a police officer. He did not do that. Adam, on the other hand, behaved quite ethically through the entire incident.

Some people might argue that Adam used excessive force by knocking the guy out with his jack. Others would argue that the force Adam used on the defendant kept us from further injury. We were surely going to physically fight with this guy if Adam had not hit him. Obviously, our ethics call for us to terminate violations of law. People don't expect their police to stand by and watch the violations continue. In this case, prior to the defendant's attempted escape, the violations were disorderly conduct and resisting arrest. The issue is not that we used force to terminate his behavior. Law permits the use of force. The question is whether Adam actually used excessive force.

After the incident was over, I tried to think of how I would have achieved the end of modifying Dumbass' behavior if I were in Adam's place. First, we tried reasoning with the guy. That didn't work. I guess we could have gagged him again, but I know that some bleeding hearts would have considered that cruel treatment. Tazering him or macing him seemed excessive, so smacking him sounds pretty reasonable to me. I would have probably done the same thing that Adam did in this case.

In an emotionally charged situation physical strength is not completely under control. Adam may have smacked him hard, but he certainly didn't beat him unnecessarily. Adam committed a sin of the mind, not of the heart. I felt obliged to protect Adam from all the armchair quarterbacks and I did.

Another sin of the mind can occur when a police officer offers to pay for a meal and the proprietor refuses to take the money. Most officers will make a second attempt to pay and then, to save everyone embarrassment, the cop will usually stop trying. This is a sin of the mind. The cop knows he is supposed to pay, but he lets the proprietor treat him to whatever it is because the proprietor insists on doing that. An officer who goes out looking for something free is a different story. That is a sin of the heart. Police officers, who take payoffs from criminals or bribes from citizens, deserve to go to jail as far as I am concerned.

Rookies begin their careers in precincts by bouncing. This means every day you are assigned to a different sector. The practice serves two purposes. First of all, it familiarizes the rookie with the entire precinct. Secondly, it gives the supervisors an idea of how fast, or slow, you are developing as a police officer. When a rookie gets assigned to his or her first steady sector assignment it is a really big deal. You are the law in that sector. You are supposed to take care of the sector and its occupants like you are the sheep dog protecting them from the wolves. They depend on you.

In my first steady sector there was a bagel place. I began going in there in the mornings for my coffee and bagel and I tried to establish a rapport with the owner and the staff. I made small talk with questions like, "How's business going?" "Any problems I should know about?"

We just made conversation and there was some minor joking around. I would always offer to pay for what I bought and they would always take my money. Everything seemed fine on the surface, but I got the feeling that they were just tolerating me and that they had some sort of issue with the police.

Then one day, after we had established a rapport, the owner said to me, "Can I talk to you a second?"

I said, "Sure," and we went off to one side of the store where no one could overhear us.

He began by telling me that over the past few weeks he had gotten to know me and he believed I was a "straight shooter". He said he wanted to tell me something. He said that no matter what I decided to do, he hoped this conversation would not affect the relationship that had developed between us. He went on to say that he knew how the world worked. He was a businessman and years ago he was involved in one business that had to pay protection money to mobsters. He also said that no matter what business he owned, he always "took care" of the police. That meant he gave us stuff for free.

He said, "I never mind giving you guys a free bagel and a free cup of coffee, but I am really having a problem with one of the cops. He comes in here, goes over to the deli case, grabs milk and butter and cream cheese and whatever else he wants and brings it to the counter. My people ring him up and bag his stuff. Then he takes the bag and leaves without paying me a cent."

I asked, "Did this all develop out of a free coffee and bagel? I mean, why wouldn't one of your people say, "Excuse me, you forgot to pay for that?"

The bagel man smiled at me naiveté and said, "One day, one of my people, who didn't know any better, did ask him to pay and he paid. Then, within a couple of hours he was outside the store hassling my customers and giving them tickets. I cannot tell you how much money he cost me over that next week. The following week he was back in the store. Again, he put what he wanted on the counter. I bagged it and told him to have a nice day."

I must have had an incredulous look on my face because before I said anything the bagel guy said, "Yea, I have trouble believing it too."

I said to him, "Ok, you have got to tell me who this guy is."

He said, "It's Danny Donaldson. I've known him for years, and it's only been recently that he is behaving like this. I am not looking for any more trouble. Please don't do anything if it is going to make things worse, but I am asking your advice."

I said, "Danny Donaldson? This isn't even his sector, it's mine."

The bagel guy just looked at me quizzically. He had no way of knowing that it was a social no-no for one cop to eat in another cop's sector without telling the cop who is on duty in that sector. However, what Danny was doing went way beyond that.

I said, "All right, thank you for telling me. I have to think about exactly how I am going to handle this. Whatever I do, I will try not to cause you any more trouble than you already have. I will keep you out of it if I can. But like you said, you are a man of the world. You know how these things go. I am going to have to get back to you."

Up to that point my experiences with Danny Donaldson had been all good. Danny had 20 years on the job and was always ready to help me as I learned the ropes. He took care of his own sector (which was next to mine) and he was always prompt when backing me up on assignments. I just couldn't picture him doing this kind of thing, but I started to plan what to do about it as though it were true.

I felt I owed it to Danny to give him a chance to tell his side of the story. If the accusations were true, I wanted to give Danny a chance to pull over and stop what he was doing. If he did, this was going no further. I was not going to get Danny jammed up if I didn't need to. I felt I owed Danny the chance to do the right thing because of all he did for me.

On the other hand, if Danny's response was to continue the illegal behavior, no blue wall of silence was going to stop me from doing whatever would be necessary to shut him down. The alternative was not acceptable to me. I was between a rock and a hard place. I had to hope for the best and prepare for the worst.

The next morning I drove my car up to Danny's car and we went 10-69. 10-69 is when two police cars drive up next to each other from opposite directions so that the drivers' windows are right next to each other. After handing him his coffee, bagel, and paper (which I paid for by the way), I began making small talk.

Eventually I said, "Danny, I have to talk to you about something and try not to get upset immediately, OK?"

He looked at me and nodded in agreement, but I could see in his eyes that he was apprehensive.

I continued, "I have been told me that you have issues with the bagel place in my sector. The person I spoke with said that you are taking stuff without paying for it and that when they charged you, you hassled their patrons."

Danny was totally embarrassed. I could see his brain short-circuiting and then he said, "That's bullshit! The bagel guy complained about me, didn't he?"

I said, "Dan it doesn't matter. I just want to know that from this point forward this problem will disappear."

Danny sounded relieved once I told him the outcome I was looking for, but he was very defensive, understandably. He became indignant and said, "You know, I had that sector before you. I had a relationship with the owner of that place. I can't tell you how many times I stopped him, his wife, and their people. They were constantly running stop signs, or speeding. I always gave them the courtesy of a warning. Nobody got tickets. You know as well as I do that we are talking about hundreds of dollars in fines that they did not have to pay. Forget about how much money the points would have cost them in insurance increases.

I said to him, "Danny, I understand how these things develop. You give them a break. They thank you for saving them the fines and points by not charging you. I've been there. Look, I am not judging you. I am just telling you that it has to stop now. If I know about it, other people will also. It will become a much bigger problem if it continues."

Danny said, "Oh don't worry. There won't be any problem. Just wait until the next time I stop one of them."

I said, "Danny, please don't hunt them. Please just let it go. I mean, if you are sitting on a Stop Sign and one of them happens to be one of the five or ten tickets you write, fine, but if they are the only tickets you write, you are going to cut your own throat. Please just let it go."

This situation between the bagel guy and Danny might have started as a mistake of the mind. However, when Danny started hassling people in front of the store it became a mistake of the heart. For him to go after these people after I spoke with him would not only have been another mistake of the heart, but it would have been something my morality would have caused me to react to.

Thankfully, Danny let it go. He stayed away from the bagel place in my sector and my stock went way up with the bagel guy. As time went by I verified that Danny took no revenge on the bagel place. In fact, he never went in there after that. Danny and I continued to get along fine and I never mentioned the incident again to him or anyone else.

Hearts and minds are important. Months later, I got T-boned in my police car by some asshole. I was going on a "shots fired" call with my lights and siren blaring. The guy who hit my car claimed he could hear me coming, but he thought he could beat me across the intersection. He was in a hurry and couldn't afford to wait for whatever emergency vehicle was causing the traffic to stop. Yes, he actually said that in court. I guess it is all part of being an asshole.

It turned out that the bagel guy was in one of the cars that stopped to let my police car go by. He was the first one to call 911 when he saw me stagger out of the smashed car and collapse on the roadway. The seat belt that saved my life also compressed my chest. The accident knocked the wind out of me and it took me a minute or so to get my breathing back to normal. Other than that, I was OK. The bagel guy also helped me up off the pavement. So you see, hearts and minds are important. I wonder if the bagel guy would have helped Danny up off the pavement?

CHAPTER 13
STRESS CRACKS

Friedrich Nietzsche, the 19th Century German philosopher and poet proposed, "What doesn't kill us makes us stronger." He obviously had not experienced the detrimental effects of a Post-Traumatic Stress Injury. Ordinary stress does have a positive effect on our ability to cope with the world around us. In that sense, what doesn't kill us makes us stronger. However, traumatic stress does not make one stronger. Acquiring the symptoms of Attention Deficit Disorder (losing one's ability to concentrate and focus), and losing short-term memory, does not make for a stronger psyche.

Misdirected and inappropriate hostility does not make for better interpersonal relationships. Uninvited and sudden flashbacks of horrible events are very disquieting. In fact, psychological trauma caused by large doses of stress often negates the self-controlling influences of morality and ethics. We can all think of situations where people have disregarded their morality and their ethics because of their emotional stress. If the stress is great enough, it can even negate the fear of consequences. When that happens, people sometimes commit homicide or suicide.

The fact that one stressor, or stimulus, can cause different reactions in different people is a phenomenon we continue to study. For instance, I was a police officer who became a stockbroker who became a police officer again. Try to imagine human stress on a vertical scale from Zero to 10. Zero is peaceful REM sleep and 10 is something that you perceive to be immediately threatening your life. Put time on the horizontal scale.

During an average day, a police officer's stress can go from 3, where it might sit for several hours, suddenly up to 8 or 9 for a little while. Then it might go back down to 3 again. It might go up from 2 (particularly on a midnight shift) to 10 very quickly and then settle back down to 2. For police officers, stress makes large severe movements up and down along the scale, acutely, all day long.

A stockbroker's stress is very different. On an average day stockbrokers start about 3 once they are at work and go to

5 when the bell rings. The stress may fluctuate between 4 and 6 all day and drop back down to 3 after the closing bell. It is a rare thing for the stock market to be so volatile, or the day to be so troublesome, that a broker's stress goes above 6 or 7.

What gave me the most stress as a broker was the lack of job security. If you piss off a valuable client, or make a mistake on an account, the firm you work for can fire you. The contract you sign with the firm gives you no recourse. That situation does not sit well with people who are trying to pay mortgages, or provide daily for their families.

An employee must familiarize himself or herself with the concept of Kowtow and ass kissing is the order of the day. Of course, none of this applies if you bring in the big bucks. However, in brokerage you are only as good as your last deal. I think they invented the phrase, "What have you done for me lately?" Still, money always takes a back seat to having your life threatened and life-threatening issues are just not there for stockbrokers, except as skewed examples.

During my first stint as a police officer with the City I had no health problems whatsoever. After six months as a stockbroker I used to start my day swigging Maalox. Within one year I had an ulcer and a condition called spastic colon. When I became a police officer again, all my physical ailments disappeared within the first year.

In my case I think I know the reason for this. The human animal has a fight or flight response to life threatening stimuli. Your adrenal glands pump epinephrine into the blood stream when you go from 2 to 10 quickly on the scale. The epinephrine helps protect your system and aids you in your fight or flight response. Over time, that can make some cops crazy and they wind up resigning early in their careers. I happen to have no problem with this kind of stress.

On the other hand, my constitution is not suited for long-term steady stress, day in and day out, like the kind experienced by stockbrokers. My body stopped producing epinephrine because I had the same general gnawing stress every day.   I had nothing to protect my system and things started to break down.

Unfortunately, even people with my aptitude for handling up and down stress cannot adequately adjust to the devastating psychological effects of traumatic stress. No one can experience serious assaults to their senses year in and year out indefinitely. At some point in time cops burn out. When burnout happens, the culprit is most often PTSI.

The phrase "burned out" is very descriptive of what happens to some police officers over time. The officers have no more fuel left to burn. They have given as much as they can and they are emotionally spent. They have experienced so many traumatically stressful events that they just can't do it anymore. Each new traumatic event causes flashbacks to other events. This triggers PTSI symptoms and there are and layers and layers of traumatic events. It is like receiving a new injury before the first one has had time to heal, but even that does not really describe the situation accurately.

The problem is that the minimum amount of time a police officer needs to retire is 20 years. In fact, in some police departments the officers need 25 or 30 years service before they can retire. When they burn out before retirement age they are no longer much help to their peers or the public. The department finds some productive assignment for them where contact with the public is minimal. Our catch phrase for cops in this category is the "rubber gun squad." I went into the Property Bureau one day and saw one of the guys wearing a tee shirt that read, "Rubber Gun Squad – We're Here Because We're Not All There." He said it was part of his therapy. Before you can develop coping skills for PTSI you need to admit that you have it.

Police Departments tend to carry burnouts to retirement age in return for all they have done during their careers. After all, look at all that has been done to them to make them that way. They will suffer mental anguish for the rest of their lives because they ran at the things that most people ran from, and they did it for us.

Obviously, some officers encounter more stressful events than others do. All things being equal, you would think the officers with the most number of stressful events should burn out first. Unfortunately, all other things are not equal. Because all of our constitutions are different, there is no way to quantify the effects of traumatic events. You can't qualify them either, except in general terms. Each human being reacts differently to the same stimuli.

For example, shortly after I became a City police officer I was assigned to the precinct that geographically included the airport. The Port Authority Police handled the ordinary calls for service at the airport. My sector was adjacent to the airport just north of it. My partner on patrol was a guy named Stephen Delmont. Steve was a descendent of the original Delmonts who lost their estate when Robert Moses built the Southern State Parkway on Long Island. Moses compensated the Delmonts with money, which they had plenty of anyway, and by naming a racetrack, a state park, and some roads after them. Steve was a grandson, with a sizeable trust fund, who decided to become a police officer. I am sure his parents love that idea.

One day we were talking about the status of the recruitment effort. In the context of that conversation I asked him what motivated him to become a cop.

I said, "… it obviously isn't about money."

Steve smiled and said, "You are never going find out what you're made of by sitting behind a desk with a bunch of sycophants telling you how important you are. My father went directly from college into the family business. Right now he is on the board of directors of three companies and he makes about seven decisions a year. The decisions he makes are based on the recommendations of committees of employees who know what they are talking about. That way he doesn't have to. Don't get me wrong. He is a wonderful Dad and a great provider. In fact, I will probably wind up doing the same thing someday. He just doesn't need his life to mean anything more than that. I do"

Steve and I had been working together since the time I was assigned to the precinct. He had much more time on the job than I had, but we seemed to have the same philosophical view of policing. It made for a trusting and comfortable relationship. The southern end of our sector, just north of the airport, was a big swamp. Brookdale Boulevard is the road that goes through the swamp from north to south. It has one lane in each direction and terminates as the leg of a "T" intersection with Boundary Road, the road that runs along the perimeter of the airport. Brookdale Boulevard has one lane in each direction and no guardrails. It floods at extreme high tides. There were many times when we pulled cars out of the swamp because they tried to take that road too fast, or they just couldn't see the edge of the roadbed because it was under water.

One summer day we had just signed on at 3:30 pm and we were sitting in our police car on a side street just off the high and dry north end of Brookdale Boulevard. It was windy and raining and we were setting up our memo books for the night. At about 4:00 pm the roar of a landing jetliner coming in low over our heads interrupted our conversation. Seconds later there was a huge booming sound just south of us. It wasn't thunder. The plane went down.

The National Transportation Safety Board eventually said that the wind had forced the tail of the aircraft to dip. It hit one of the light towers that the plane was following in to the runway. The tail sheared off and the plane flipped upside down. As it was doing so, the wings hit the ground and broke apart. Fuel was spread everywhere and the plane burst into flames. Only 13 people survived. Some died instantly and others were burned to death strapped upside down in their seats. Many of the bodies were torn apart as the plane tumbled and plowed through the swamp. Luggage was strewn everywhere. Two flight attendants, whose seats were in the tail section that sheared off, survived with only scratches. They walked out of the swamp. All the other survivors had serious injuries.

Almost immediately, the ghouls who lived in the swamp homes along Brookdale Boulevard swarmed the plane. Dan Costello, one of the two cops in the first car on the scene, broke the rules and fired several warning shots toward the ghouls to shoo them away from the dead and the plane. He and his partner slogged through knee-deep water filled with rats, insects, and sink holes, to enter the burning wreckage and search for survivors. With the exceptions of the flight attendants who were in the tail section, these two police officers pulled any passengers who survived the crash from the burning plane. Months later they were given the Department's highest award for valor.

With Dan and his partner, whose name I can't remember, heading into the nightmare of the burning plane, it was understood that Steve and I should take control of the perimeter of the crash site. We needed to make sure that the ghouls left things alone and that the cavalry could get in and out. We call access to and from the scene of an incident ingress and egress. Our job became to insure ingress and egress and to try and maintain the integrity of the crime scene.

We considered it a crime scene because at that time we had no idea what brought the plane down. We left our car on Brookdale Boulevard facing south parked just behind Costello's car. Steve started jogging south toward Boundary Road and I started jogging north toward whatever. We were a lot closer to Boundary Road than we were to where I was headed. In any event, we needed to get control of Brookdale Boulevard.

I quickly lost sight of Steve because of the bends in the roadway. I was chasing ghouls as I went along, threatening to shoot anyone who crossed over the road behind me as I passed. It was no empty threat. I was so stressed I would have shot anyone of those sickos if they did so. Fortunately for everyone, to my knowledge, no one tested me.

At one point I caught this ghoul walking out of the swamp with an arm in his hands. He was holding the arm in his left hand while trying to pull a wedding band off the finger with his right hand. I threatened to shoot the ghoul if he did not give me the arm. He smiled at me in a sick way as he turned it over. The look on his face made me want to shoot him right there, but I had more important duties to attend to at that moment so I didn't. The whole scene was like something out of *Night of the Living Dead*. At that time rubber gloves were something that only the paramedics used, so I handled the arm with bare hands. It was bloody and still warm, but it belonged to someone. I was going to take care of it, gloves or no gloves.

I got to the point where Brookdale Boulevard met its first cross street north of the swamp and I got ready to deal with traffic. At that point, I was approximately one-quarter mile from the crash site. I put the arm on the side of the road for safekeeping and began passing emergency personnel and vehicles through. Before long a Lieutenant showed up. When he heard I was one of the first officers on the scene he wanted a quick briefing. He assigned another cop to relieve me on the traffic detail and told me to ride with him back to the crash site while I told him what was happening so far. You should have seen the look on his face and his chauffer's face when I ran back, got the arm, and began to get into the car. I had enough sense to put it on the floor in the back seat of the Lieutenant's police car because it was still quite bloody.

When we got to the crash site, cops, firefighters, and paramedics had erected a tent on the road that was going to serve as a temporary morgue. They chose Brookdale Boulevard rather than Boundary Road because there was less swamp to cross to get to the crash site. However, the tide was coming in and in my mind I questioned the wisdom of that decision. They obviously did not know Brookdale Boulevard very well or they would have chosen Boundary Road.

As I got out of the back seat of the Lieutenant's car he said, "Thanks for the briefing, and get that fucking arm out of my car."

He was freaked. I had every intention of doing so, but I understood his reaction. It was gross. I picked up the arm and headed over to the morgue site. Once I got to the morgue tent I got stuck there. A Sergeant, who had arrived at the scene from the south side, ordered me to take control of the morgue and start a record of what and who comes in and out.

I was working with two paramedics and another cop. When bodies were brought in we covered them with plastic morgue sheets to preserve some dignity and to keep them from being viewed by prying eyes and cameras. Most of them were burned severely. The stench of burned human flesh is unlike any other smell. Some of our police humor is quite dark. It is a way of coping. Accordingly, when two cops would carry in one of the burned dead they would say something like, "I've got another crispy critter here. Where do you want it?"

As the body parts came in we tried to match them up with torsos and heads as best we could. Unmatched parts were placed in a kind of "parts pool" from which we matched the parts with the rest of their bodies if we could do so. There were a lot of parts left unmatched.

At high tide the water covered the roadway about two inches deep and things started to float away. We scrambled to keep everything contained within the morgue tent and succeeded, I think. It was very dark by that time and what artificial light we had was not great. As all the extension cords from the light truck began to become inundated things got scary. Electricity and salt water don't go together very well. It would have been something out of a nightmare to be electrocuted in a morgue tent, in a swamp, surrounded by bodies and body parts. The topping on the cake was when the rats began to come out of the swamp looking for a meal. This was truly an assault to my senses from every direction and every level of bizarreness I could imagine at that time.

Eventually, I was relieved and started looking for Steve. He had been assigned to help carry the dead out of the swamp. He had to slog his way back and forth from the outside of the wreckage to the road, again and again, in knee high water. He was handing off the bodies and body parts to others who were bringing them into the morgue. That is why I did not see him before I got relieved. When I found him and told him we had been cut loose he was sitting on the fender of our radio car staring down at the ground. He looked up at me and I could tell he was traumatized. We both were traumatized and we were exhausted as well. It was three in the morning which can be a creepy time even when nothing is going on.

Back then there were no such things as PTSI debriefings. You were expected to suck it up and deal with it. That's what I tried to do, but my mind was having nothing of it. I had no schema to draw on. I began suffering all the typical symptoms with one addition. Almost 30 years later any time that I smell burning hair I have to fight the urge to vomit. Weird stuff right?

Steve Delmont did not fare as well. The PTSI he suffered as a result of dealing with the plane crash affected his mind in a really bad way. His personality completely changed. He became skittish and nervous about everything. He was hostile and became distant from both his family and me. I guess, out of an effort to cope, he began drinking a lot more than he did before the crash.

I gave up my seat in the radio car because I was trying to make a move into the precinct's Anti-Crime Unit. I would see Steve a lot around the stationhouse, but we no longer patrolled together. One day his sister called me. It was a few months after the crash and she was trying to determine what had happened to the brother she knew and loved. At that time I had limited knowledge of PTSI. I was not much help to her, but I did tell her that I knew it all started with what he went through at the crash site. Eventually, the assault to his senses that he suffered that day overwhelmed him. Steve had a bad career-ending event.

I guess the pressure had been building up inside him for days. PTSI does that to you. You become like a pressure cooker. If you don't find some harmless ways to vent the stress, you will eventually explode at someone. Some of us develop coping mechanisms. For instance, whenever my brain starts screaming inside my head because of a flashback I sing to myself. I used to sing to myself before the crash, but now it has a purpose. As I become emotionally involved with the song, I piss off the steam. It takes me away from the present for a while and lets me vent slowly. Sometimes the people I am with at the time that I start singing think I am crazy for just bursting into song. Singing works most of the time, but not all of the time. I use other coping mechanisms as well.

It is hard to put your finger on what stimuli will trigger a PTSI episode. There are so many. Steve lost it one day after catching up to a thief who had just led him on a car chase. When the other cops involved in the chase got there, Steve was trying to pull the guy out through the driver's side window of the car. Steve had him in a headlock and was actually choking the guy as he tried to pull him out. The choking was unintentional, but the beating was not.

When they eventually got the guy out of the car and they were trying to put him into handcuffs, he took a swing at Steve. The cops who were assisting him said that Steve was yelling, "You stupid fuck! You stupid fuck!" as he punched the driver over and over in the face. There were so many civilian witnesses that the investigation went badly for Steve. This incident was just one of many violent outbursts he initiated after the plane crash. Steve and the police department mutually agreed that Steve should resign because of his anger management issues. He told me he was going to take some time to "get his act together and maybe do something else with his life."

    This was a man who was dedicated to what he was doing and fearless in the face of danger. After being an active City cop for years, he certainly did not have to prove his bravery in any other way. However, he could not handle PTSI. It made him a loose cannon and even I was worried about what direction he might point at any moment in time. I lost track of what happened to Steve after that. The moral of the story is that we had pretty much the same stressors, but very different reactions.

    I had another serious bout with PTSI some years later when I was on field training with the County police. Field Training is six weeks long and it is the final stage of the Police Academy training before you go out on your own. You spend the time on patrol with a Field Training Officer (FTO) who lets you handle things and then evaluates your performance. Of course he or she jumps in if needed.

    My Field Training Officer was a guy with 15 years on the job. His name was Gary Theodore Jones. Everyone called him G.T. G.T. was in the army in Vietnam. He participated in and survived the battle that was depicted in the movie *Hamburger Hill*. He was a good guy with a lot of baggage, but he knew his job and he did it well.

    Some other cops warned me in advance that when I worked my week of midnights with G.T. he would talk all night about his experiences in Vietnam. He did. This was a coping mechanism he developed to deal with his own PTSI. The stories were quite interesting, sometimes frightening, and often heart wrenching. At some point each night he would emphasize how important sleep was to people. He would say again and again that sleep is a weapon. It is a weapon that you need in order to fight well and if you can deprive your enemy of that weapon, you will certainly have an advantage when you face that enemy the next day. I thought it was quite ironic that he kept me up all night talking about how valuable sleep was.

G.T. was very proud of his service to our country and he was very proud of what he was contributing now. After hearing his stories I internalized how much our military personnel give of themselves for us. It is one thing to know something on an intellectual level. It is another thing to know it on an emotional level. It is a wonder how so many of them remain sane.

The idea that this country should need a charitable organization like "The Wounded Warrior Project" to insure proper care for our vets is disgusting. So many bureaucrats are profiting from the Veterans' Administration. You would think that at the very least their morality and ethics would motivate them to keep the system functional for our vets. I say give the vets a medical ID card and let them go to whatever doctors they want to. All the government would have to do is pay the bills, which they are supposed to be doing anyway. Well, G.T. and I bonded over the midnights and wound up becoming career-long buds.

One day we signed on duty for a 4 to Midnight tour. Everything seemed normal. We got coffee, took care of our police housekeeping duties and went on patrol. Then things started to get bizarre.

Before long G.T. said, "Listen Mike, I need to go see the Babalawo. I have a bottle for him."

I asked, "The Babalawo? Who is that?"

G.T. said he was an Indian holy man who lived on a street off Plainfield Avenue.

I questioned, "An Indian holy man? Who lives in Plainfield?"

G.T. said, "Yea, do you think only white people live in Plainfield?"

I said, "Well yea, but give me a break, an Indian holy man? Wait a minute, are we talking dot Indian or feather Indian?"

G.T. said, "He's feather you fucking racist and he happens to be half-Black too. Do you have a problem with that?"

G.T. was Black.

I said, "You know G.T., you have a big chip on your shoulder. For your information some of my best friends are half-black, feather Indian, holy men. I just don't know any who live in Plainfield."

We both laughed and he directed me to the Babalawo's house turn by turn.

The house was a small ranch style home on an isolated piece of property near one of the major parkways. It was a pretty place with a white picket fence and flowers everywhere. We parked the police car on the street in front of the house and walked up to the front door. There was no doorbell, but there was a doorknocker that depicted some fantasy creature. I half expected it to come alive and bite me. Like I said, things were getting bizarre.

G.T. gave the door a couple of hard knocks and then he called out loudly, "Hey, witch doctor. Open up, it's the police. We're here to deport you."

When the door opened, there stood a dark-skinned man about five feet seven. He was heavy set and balding. He wore loose fitting, lightweight, brightly colored clothing. It looked like traditional sub-continental Indian garb to me. The Babalawo embraced G.T. and then turned his attention to me.

In the spirit with which G.T. called him a witch doctor I scowled at G.T. and said, "Who are you kidding man? This guy's dot, not feather."

Without missing a beat, G.T said, "I'm telling you he's feather. He's a West Indian Holy Man, a Santeria priest. Now apologize to him. Go ahead, apologize to him before he puts a spell on you and fucks you up."

I looked at G.T. with a disbelieving smile and said, "Oh, a *West* Indian Holy Man. You didn't say he was *West* Indian."

Then I looked at the Babalawo and said, "I'm sorry sir. I did not mean to insult you. I misread your clothing and my mentor here is not the best communicator sometimes."

The Babalawo glared at me and said to G.T., "Why did you bring this white man to my house. He is obnoxious."

Both G.T. and the Babalawo started to smile. I guessed they wanted me to know they were only playing. When I realized this, I continued in the moment.

I said, "What do you mean white? I happen to be an all-American mutt. I am one part Swiss and three parts Italian. And don't start telling me what my people did to your people. My people didn't get here until the 1920s and they got pissed on too. Don't forget, a whole bunch of white people paid with their lives to free the slaves. You got an issue? Don't take it out on government that freed you. Besides, I've got soul in my soul.

I looked at them with a face that communicated righteous indignation and then I started to smile to make sure they knew I was playing also. In spite of my rant they looked at each other and in stereo they said, "White man." Then we all laughed.

The Babalawo was a Santeria priest, but he was also much more than that. He had the gift of prophecy. G.T. said that the Babalawo prophesized that Castro was going to win the civil war in Cuba and he got himself and his family out before it happened. He has been living on Long Island ever since. The Babalawo nodded his head proudly. I just rolled my eyes and said that I wasn't all that impressed, that I could have predicted Castro would win also (See Real fact of Life # 2).

I asked, "You got anything better than that?"

The Babalawo said, "Yea, how about this. I predict you are going to get your ass off my porch before I turn you into a zombie you disrespectful pup." Again we all laughed.

G.T. took out the bottle of Captain Morgan he had stashed in the bag he was carrying.

He said to the Babalawo, "Thank you, Babalawo. The troublesome person is gone."

The Babalawo took the bottle, smiled, and said, "I knew he would be."

When G.T. realized that I had no idea what they were talking about, he half turned toward me and told me the story while the Babalawo stood there and listened. Some time ago, G.T. started having problems with a newly appointed Sergeant who came to the precinct. The Sergeant began to hassle G.T. because G.T. refused to pick up the Sergeant's laundry at the dry cleaners. That is the kind of thing that selfish supervisors ask rookies to do. G.T. was no rookie. The Sergeant had no right to even ask someone with G.T.'s time on the job to do menial tasks like that.

Besides, G.T. had issues with authority anyway. Add to the insult the fact that the Sergeant was white and trouble was inevitable. The Sergeant began giving G.T. a hard time about everything. G.T.'s police car suddenly started to fail the monthly inspection. G.T. also started getting all of the shitty details that rookies were usually assigned to.

G.T.'s response was to stand his ground on contractual and procedural issues and grin and bear the rest. He also went to see the Babalawo. He told the Babalawo about the problem and the Babalawo put a curse on the Sergeant. G.T. and the Babalawo did not describe the particulars of the curse. I don't know if he used a voodoo doll or some other type of curse. First, the Sergeant developed a rash on his neck that caused him to go sick for about two weeks. This gave G.T. some immediate relief. Then the Sergeant managed to wrap his car around a telephone pole on an icy road one night. That was the end of the problem. It was solved within three months after the Babalawo put the spell on the Sergeant.

According to G.T., the custom in the Santeria religion was to give an offering to the Babalawo to thank him for his help. Captain Morgan served that purpose. Before we left, G.T. asked the Babalawo to predict what my career would be like in the police department. The priest reached out his right hand and placed it on my forehead. He closed his eyes and drifted off for a moment. Then he took his hand away abruptly as though something shocked him. I could not help but wonder what he saw. I also speculated that he did not see anything and that he just did it for effect.

He looked me in the eyes and said, "You are like my friend here (meaning G.T.). Your path will not be easy. Still, in the end your soul will belong to you and to the Lord of course."

Then he turned to G.T. and said, "The devil will not be able to take this man."

I just nodded my head, looked the Babalawo in the eye, and with a smile I nodded and said, "Very cool."

He smiled back. Then we said our goodbyes.

We left the Babalawo's house on a spiritual high and began to do our patrolling with G.T. driving.

I asked him if he really believed in this voodoo stuff and G.T. said, "I don't know."

Then he turned toward me and said, "It sure worked for me."

We both laughed and shook our heads in disbelief of the wonders in the world around us. Neither one of us had any stress at that moment.

Within minutes, Communications Bureau (CB) sent us an assignment over the radio for a motor vehicle accident – two aided, at a busy intersection in our sector. "Aided" is police jargon for people injured or sick and in need of help.

G.T. said, "OK. Rookie, its time to do some serious police shit. This one's all yours. Let's go make the Babalawo proud."

Apparently, some guy and his date were on their way home from a day at the beach. They were in his convertible Chrysler two-seater and they were following an 18-wheeler. Witnesses said that as they were approaching a large intersection the truck signaled a right turn. The road they were on had a parking lane. The guy in the convertible tried to pass the truck on the right side. It wasn't happening. The truck sheared across the car decapitating the guy and dropping his head into the girl's lap. The car was so crushed that she was pinned inside. When we got there she was screaming and going out of her mind with this head in her lap.

While G.T. was taking care of everything else, I ran to the girl and tried to calm her down. I saw her staring down at the head and screaming. I looked down at the head and it looked back up at me. I would have sworn I saw the mouth move a little bit like he was trying to say something. It was probably, "I'm sorry my stupidity is going to mess up the rest of your lives. What can I say? I lost my head."

I took a deep breath and I told the girl to focus on me.

"Just look into my eyes," I said.

I assured her that everything was going to be OK while I asked her about her injuries. She said she thought she was unhurt except for being pinned in the car. Then I could see her mind turn to the head in her lap. She started screaming again, quite out of her mind and right in my ear. The car was crushed pretty badly. I was unable to determine if she had injuries because when the guy's head was coming off his heart kept pumping blood for a while. It was all over the girl and the car. I wondered if it was her adrenaline that may have been keeping her from feeling her own injuries. I started wondering all sorts of things like how long these two had known each other, whether they were in love, whether she had even enjoyed the date. There is little accounting for what your mind will do when it is being assaulted by such an event.

Even though I was holding her face with both hands and trying to maintain her attention she kept trying to glance down at the head. Then she would start screaming again. Out of sight being out of mind, I finally took off my jacket and draped it over her chest and lap covering the head. That helped her calm down to a steady cry. After what seemed like much too long a time, the volunteer firefighters and the EMTs arrived. There were other cops at the scene also. They were controlling traffic and such. I continued holding the girl while they used the Hurst tool to pry the car open and free her.

I felt that it was my responsibility to deal with the head. I reasoned that I was already damaged goods from previous traumatic incidents. Why let one of these volunteers suffer more PTSI if they don't have to? The headless body was going to be bad enough for them to handle. When it was appropriate to do so, I brought the head to the morgue wagon wrapped in my jacket. I assisted with the body as well. Once the girl was on her way to the hospital one of the volunteer firefighters brought me my jacket. It was covered with blood and I would never wear it again, but I needed to retrieve my shield and nametag from it.

I thanked him and after a pause he said, "I never saw anything like that before."

I said, "Yea, now the adventure begins."

He asked, "Adventure?"

I said, "Shit yea, depending on your makeup you may be thinking about this for a long time. I have developed some effective ways of dealing with it. If you ever start having issues with sleeping, or aggression, or nervousness call me. I might be able to help you work through it. I'm serious. If people start telling you that you have changed, or if you notice a change in yourself, call me."

Then we introduced ourselves and I gave him my police business card. That was when I decided to become a PTSI counselor even if I had to develop a program myself. There were no PTSI debriefings available for G.T or me. Later, when we sitting in the police car having coffee, we talked about what had happened. He was worried about how I would deal with the incident emotionally. Besides being my Field Training Officer he was also a caring human being. This guy, who had every reason in the world to be more messed up than most, was worrying about me.

He asked me, "Are you OK?"

I said, "Yea, I'm fine."

He said, "Good, because that shit can make some people beaucoup dinky-dao."

I questioned, "Beaucoup dinky-dao?"

He said, "Yea, very crazy in the head."

I smiled and asked, "Why couldn't you just say very crazy in the head?"

G.T. said, "Where's the fun in that? It was cooler to say beaucoup dinky-dao, don't you think? Besides, now you know some Vietnamese."

I chuckled and shook my head. I turned toward G.T. and smiled.

I said, "You know, someday I am going to meet some Vietnamese people and the only thing I am going to be able to say in Vietnamese is that they are crazy in the head. Haven't we messed with those people enough? They're going to think *I* am beaucoup dinky-dao."

With an exasperated tone I continued, "Do you know any useful Vietnamese?"

Then we both started laughing. We were both very stressed out and the laughter helped a lot. My Vietnamese lesson went pretty well. Afterward I assured G.T. that I expected it was going to be more nightmares and flashbacks, but that all in all, I would be OK.

I consider myself a lifetime learner. After doing PTSI counseling for several years, I have gathered a lot of data and I have learned a lot about the subject. The traumatic incidents that have the most detrimental effect on human beings are those that involve children or animals. Yes, animals. I have handled a couple of horrific crimes involving children and animals and I have counseled others who have had similar experiences. What makes these the worst is the complete trusting innocence of the tortured and murdered victims.

    In our effort to gain control of the world around us we want to remember certain negative things. That way we can head them off and keep them from happening again. However, the uninvited thoughts, pictures, and flashbacks to these same events, are a consequence of our effort to gain the very control we seek. Truly, it is a double-edged sword.

    Burnout was certainly possible for me, but it did not happen. In fact, by most accounts, I am doing pretty well. I am not completely "dinky-dao," and I still do my job effectively. However, whenever I meet cops who appear to be burned out, I give them the benefit of the doubt. God only knows what experiences brought them to that point.

CHAPTER 14
SPECIAL ED

It is true that you never get a second chance to make a first impression, but first impressions can be problematic. What you see during a first encounter is a cross-sectional view of the person. You don't get to see all the facts and circumstances that, over the years, resulted in what you are looking at. You don't even get to see the events in that person's life over the past few hours that may have influenced a person's behavior and attitude at the time you meet them.

The most important thing you can glean from a first impression is how well a person behaves in spite of such things. When two police officers who never met before get assigned to something together, what matters is how well you and that other cop perform your duties at that time. Everybody has bad days, but if a cop fails to do his or her duty over a long period of time there are usually only two reasons. One is that the cop is burned out. The other is that the cop is just plain lazy. The latter is usually evidenced by a career of being a lazy.

Police officers are evaluated monthly on the totality of their activity. They are compared with other officers who patrol the same area. One officer may not have written a lot of tickets, but he or she may have answered many more calls for service than the officer who did write a lot of tickets. One officer may not have investigated many criminal cases, but he or she may have handled a large number of motor vehicle accidents or aided cases. However, every now and then someone falls through the cracks and management fails to catch that person who is doing very little of anything. Such was the case with Ed Doughty. For some reason he thought he should be treated special. Everyone who worked with him called him Special Ed.

Responding to burglar alarm calls is statistically one of the most useless things we do. The latest statistic I know of is that only 1 out of every 180 alarm calls can be verified as a legitimate burglary. That is way less than one percent. Obviously we need to respond to burglar alarms, but the people who install, maintain, and use the alarm systems need to improve their track record. Seriously, if we can put a man on the moon why can't we make our alarm systems more reliable?

If the public wants the police to take their house alarm seriously, the alarm should be real most of the time. Otherwise, don't expect us to go lights and siren taking our lives in our hands to answer your ringing alarm. My life is worth more than that and you owe me legitimate calls for service. As it stands, the situation causes all sorts of problems like the one I had with Special Ed.

Complacency is the police officer's greatest enemy. It occurs as the result of responding over and over to assignments or events that turn out to be non-threatening. Then, when the real one comes along somebody winds up getting hurt. Whenever I am assigned to do field training with a recruit I stress this issue. When it comes to car stops, or responding to alarm calls, I say, "If you discipline yourself to do it the right way every time, you will be doing it the right way the day your life depends on it."

One day, this twenty-year veteran named Brian got an alarm call in a middle class neighborhood in his precinct. Law enforcement history teaches us that sending one cop to investigate a burglary can be very dangerous for the cop. Prior to the proliferation of automated burglar alarms most of these calls were for real. Some human being would hear or see a prowler and call it in. If the call for the burglary is real, there might just as easily be more than one burglar. The burglars are usually armed with at least the tools they used to break in. Also, it is easy to get the drop on the officer who is searching a home when you are already in the building and you know the layout. Besides, you need two cops to transport an arrest safely anyway. Therefore, responding to burglar alarms is a two-person assignment. They send two cops.

On this day Brian responded to an alarm call with a rookie. Some people don't like responding with rookies because they miss a lot of cues that experienced cops see. On the other hand, every rookie is completely paranoid. Rookies look for snipers on rooftops and in their mind every car they stop is filled with armed terrorists or drugs dealers.

Their skills are excellent. In addition, they just got out the academy and they will never be in better physical shape.

The Police Academy trains everyone the same way. If there is a change in training, police officers who are in-service already are re-trained in the new procedure. We are all trained to stop cars the same way. We are all trained to search buildings the same way. You need to be able to anticipate what your partner is going to do. Good or bad, when the chips are down, we all do what we have trained ourselves to do. Rookies are not complacent.

When Brian got to the private house in which the burglar alarm was ringing the rookie was only seconds behind him. They exchanged pleasantries quickly and Brian took the lead walking around the house. The rookie followed a short distance behind double-checking Brian as he passed windows and doors looking for signs of a break in. All the time the rookie kept his eye on Brian who he knew would be the first to encounter a problem.

At one point Brian came to an open double hung window in which the lower glass and screen were up. What Brian should have done was to flatten himself against the wall and approach the window slowly. Then, very quickly, peek his head inside the window to see what he could see and pull it back out just as quickly. We call this a peek-a-boo. It is effective and safe because our action is faster than the reaction of the burglar who might be waiting inside the house.

Instead, Brian complacently walked past the window. He reasoned that since the glass was not broken the owners probably just left the window up. He thought that might have been what set off the alarm in the first place. The screen being up should have been a warning to him. Before he had taken three steps past the window, the burglar who was hiding behind the wall next to the window stepped into the window and fired two shots at Brian.

The gun he used was a .22 caliber pistol with a plastic bottle on the barrel. The plastic bottle served as a cheap but effective silencer. It was pretty creative thinking on the burglar's part for keeping the sound down. It was real dumb if you expected to make an accurate shot. Thank God that most bad guys are not both evil and smart. One shot missed Brian completely, but the other went right through his hat grazing his scalp and knocking the hat from Brian's head.

The rookie, being on top of his game and right on the edge, didn't miss a beat. He heard the dull thuds of the silenced shots and saw Brian's hat go flying. While Brian was reaching his hand up to his head and bending over to pick up his hat, the rookie stepped into a position to get a better angle on the burglar. He could still see the burglar in the window preparing to take another shot. The rookie drew his weapon and began shooting bullets into the window and the wall of the house where the burglar was standing.

You have got to love the Sig 26. It carries 15, 9mm rounds. The bullets we use are hypersonic jacketed hollow points which serve two purposes. When the bullets hit flesh they use the physics of hydraulics to spread out to almost twice their diameter. They deliver a powerful blow and expend their energy within the body. That way the bullet does not pass through the bad guy and hit a good guy. When those rounds hit things like walls or other objects they close up on themselves. This makes them capable of penetrating most of the things we would shoot at. In this case the bullets had to penetrate vinyl siding, three-quarter inch wood sheathing, some insulation, and one-half inch sheetrock.

Some police departments train their cops to fire two rounds and then re-asses the threat. This is a really dumb training policy. Statistics show that while you are assessing whether or not your bullets hit the target, the bad guy is shooting back at you and trying to kill you. I am confident some politician put that policy in place because he or she was afraid that the municipality would be criticized for the number of bullets a cop might fire. How's that for ethics? To hell with the cop's safety, worry about the bad guy being shot with too many bullets.

Our department trains us to keep firing until the threat is gone. The question should not be whether you are justified firing 2 or 10 or 20 shots. The question is whether you are justified in firing the first one. If you are justified in firing one bullet, then you can shoot until the threat is gone.

The rookie did exactly what he was trained to do. He splattered the window and wall with seven bullets before he heard the burglar cry in pain and watched him drop below the windowsill. Only then did the rookie stop to "reassess the threat." It turned out the burglar lived to serve time for attempted murder of a police officer. Stories like this are not common. Most burglar alarm calls are false alarms, but things can get very real, very quickly. That is why alarm calls are two person assignments.

When I first got assigned to the sector next to Special Ed I met up with a cop from a neighboring sector who we called Carl. Carlos Garcia is an interesting character. He is an Iraqi War veteran who joined the Department shortly after he got out of the service. Carlos was a squad leader in Iraq in charge of one of the teams that searched for Saddam Hussein. Carlos' team did not catch Saddam Hussein and he was imprudent enough to mention that when he was in the Police Academy. They never let him forget it. One of his instructors, who is a Gulf War veteran and also of Latino decent, told him that he disgraced the name his family gave him by not finding Saddam. He started to call him Carl instead of Carlos. The nickname stuck. It was no big deal. The instructors gave me the nickname Snake when I was going through the academy, but that is another story.

Carlos did two tours of duty in Iraq. He is fluent in English, Arabic and Spanish. He is also a good cop. He backs up well and he engages the people in his sector. He is very smart, a natural leader, and I knew he would be a good boss one day. I was one of his instructors when he was going through the academy. He tells people that I was his best instructor. He told me that he loved the way I always treated the recruits as little brothers and sisters, teaching them how to be good cops and teaching them how to stay alive. Carl had a special place in his heart for me.

However, Carl also had a very bad habit of cursing all the time. You cannot have a conversation with him without hearing the word "fuck" over and over and over. I was sure he did not talk like that around his family and friends. I can't imagine his family and others putting up with his cursing all the time. It was definitely selective because he did not speak that way to complainants or supervisors.

At that point Carl had about four years on the job. My first day on patrol with him, he came to visit in the morning bearing coffee and bagels. We smiled at each other as he pulled his police car up 10-69 to mine. We had not seen each other for some time so I had to break his balls a little.

I said, "Carl, are we going to be able to get through a conversation without you cursing? I would really like to be able to do that."

He said, "Fuck no! Cursing makes a point. A lot of famous and important people curse all the time. It's just the way I express myself."

As he spoke he handed me my coffee and bagel.

Then he said, "Besides the word fuck is a really cool word. There's no other word like it in the English language. Did you know that?"

I said, "No Carl, enlighten me."

"It can be used so many ways that you don't have to know very many other words and the person you are talking to knows *exactly* what you are trying to say."

I said, "So, let me make sure I understand what you are telling me. Instead of increasing your vocabulary by using new and more expressive words, you seek to limit your vocabulary by constantly using one word."

He said, "Exactly. It is an economy of scale."

I chuckled when he said that. He knew full well what economy of scale means, but I played along.

I said, "Carl, using the word fuck has nothing to do with an economy of scale. Economy of scale has nothing to do with cursing."

Carl was smiling and he had a twinkle in his eye. I could see he had given this some thought and I was about to receive the benefit of his deliberations on the matter.

He said, "Think about it. It can be a noun. 'What a stupid fuck.' It can be a verb. 'Fuck you.' It can be an adverb, 'That girl is very fuckable.'"

I interrupted at that point and said, "Carl, that's not an adverb."

He smiled a satisfied smile and said, "See, but you knew what I meant right?"

I smiled, shook my head and then he continued.

"It can be an adjective. 'He's a fucking idiot.' There is past tense, 'He got fucked.' There's future tense, 'He's gonna get fucked.' There's just is no other word in the English language like it. I got more. You want to hear more?"

I very dramatically put my hand up to my forehead, covered my eyes and shook my head. In teacherly fashion, I slowly dragged my hand down to my chin. Then I shook my head again as teachers do when they are dealing with a difficult student.

Finally, in an exasperated tone I said to him, "Carl, I have seen you with complainants. You don't curse when you are with them. Just try to think of me as a complainant and let's have a conversation in which you don't curse, OK? Can you try that?"

He said, "Sure, what the fuck?"

When he said that, we both started laughing out loud.

Then I said, "You know what Carl? I've got an adverb for you. You're fuckingly hopeless,"

We both laughed again.

Carl welcomed me back to the street and started giving me the run down on what was going on in that part of the precinct. He described the people we would be working with as well as who and what the problems were around us.

When I mentioned what squad I was in he said, "Oh, lucky you. You're going to be working 5 out of 5 with Special Ed."

I chuckled and said, "Special Ed? What makes 'Special Ed' special?"

Carl said that Ed Doughty was the laziest cop he ever met. He suspected that Special Ed had to have a hook because the Academy instructors wash plenty of people out who they think might become drones for the next 20 years. Somehow Ed made it through and I was now assigned to the sector next to his. This meant that when I got an alarm call Ed would probably be assigned to go with me and visa-versa.

In spite of what Carl had said, I decided to give Ed the benefit of the doubt. I knew what PTSI could do to a person and it was completely possible that Carl's information was inaccurate. People say things based on bad information all the time. I also thought that if Carl's info was correct, maybe it was PTSI that made Special Ed what he is today. If that were the case, then Special Ed deserves some understanding and consideration. Ed was also a little older than I was so I started out our relationship by granting him respect and trust. However, regardless of what his experiences might have been, PTSI or no PTSI, I expected him to do his job. After all, I was doing mine in spite of my experiences.

Well, it turned out that Special Ed was not a casualty of PTSI. As time went by I researched his career. He really was just lazy as shit. Before long I began to notice that he never got to the alarm calls even when they were in his sector. After the third time he let me go on an alarm call without backing me up I decided it was time for a talk. I found him sitting in his police car in the park, which was in my sector by the way, and reading the newspaper.

I drove my car 10-69 to his and said, "Man, where were you on that alarm call?"

He said, "Well, I figured you would call me if you found something."

I said, "Do me a favor. In the future please don't do that. You went over the air and acknowledged the assignment. I'm thinking you are coming to back me up."

He never looked at me and continued to pretend to read the paper. Maybe he was actually reading the paper, but either way it pissed me off.

I said, "Ed, are you listening to me? This is important."

Then a smile crossed his face and without even turning to look at me he said, "You handle your calls your way and I'll handle my calls my way."

My brain started to short circuit. After a short 5 seconds I said, "Ed, when I am involved you need to ride on the call. If you don't want to ride on the call, then don't tell radio you are en-route. Tell radio that you are otherwise engaged and let someone else go with me"

I knew why he was playing this game. The supervisors listen to the radio as they are driving around on patrol. Ed knew that if he did not acknowledge an assignment his supervisor would want to know why. His solution was to act like he was working, but then not respond unless he actually had to. He was playing the odds. The odds were that the burglar alarm would be false, the house would be fine, and he would be wasting his time. He would rather sit there reading the paper then come and back me up. That spoke volumes to me.

In bureaucracies there are three kinds of discipline. There is downward discipline. There is upward discipline, and there is lateral discipline. Downward discipline the traditional type. An employee does not fulfill the terms of his or her employment and the supervisor initiates some sort of disciplinary procedure to modify the employee's behavior.

Upward discipline takes two forms. The first form is direct sabotage. It will usually occur when you have a boss who is a true asshole. He or she might be completely incompetent, or maybe the boss has an attitude that he or she is superior to you by virtue of this supervisory position. Sometimes, the uppity attitude is the supervisor's way to cover the fact that he or she is incompetent. The employee secretly does things, or fails to do things, and the result is that the supervisor does not achieve his or her objective. If it is done well, the supervisor will never know it was intentional.

The second type is called a "rule book slowdown." This usually occurs when management in general behaves unethically toward the employees. Willful contract violations are a good example. Grievance procedures are notoriously slow even when the violations are blatant. They favor management. In this case, the employee does exactly what he or she is told to do, no more and no less. The supervisor, being human, will eventually forget to tell you to do something, or will not see the negative consequences of telling you to do something and you simply don't say or do anything to help him or her. Eventually, circumstances occur that cause the supervisor to fail to reach some sort of management goal.

In the military, where a pompous supervisor or unethical management can actually get people killed, the upward discipline might take the form of a stray bullet or hand grenade. Problem solved for the military, but we can't get away with that in the police department.

With Special Ed, I had to consider lateral discipline. Once again I faced a dilemma. My morality told me that this guy needed an attitude adjustment. My ethics called for me to report him to his supervisor, a decision that would not sit well with all of the other officers or the supervisors. I would be called a rat, or a baby. Police culture called for me to solve the problem at my level, on my own.

I began getting angrier and angrier as I tried to convince Ed to do the right thing and respond to his calls, particularly when those calls are with me.

Finally, to get his attention, I said, "Look man, I have put up with this for some time now. I am not putting up with it anymore. If you get assigned to another alarm call with me and you don't show up, you and I are going to war. All I am asking you to do is show up when you are supposed to, or let someone else take the assignment."

Ed turned, looked at me, and said sarcastically, "What are you going to do tell the teacher on me? I told you. You handle things your way and I'll handle things my way."

I didn't say any more. I backed my car away from his and started driving around. I started thinking about the fact that if he treats a brother officer this way, how he must treat the public? Sometimes when the call was in his sector I used to hear him tell people, "Well ma'am there's nothing we can do." Up to that point I had always backed his play. It was his sector, his assignment, and ultimately his responsibility. If it were my assignment I may have handled it differently, but I was just there to back him up.

Then I realized that this piece of shit has gotten to the point where he is useless to the people he swore to protect and he is useless to the people he works with. I was working myself up to conduct some lateral discipline, but for the rest of that shift I just thought about it. Fortunately, I had no more assignments with Ed that day that would have forced my hand before I was ready.

Lateral discipline in the police department is not the same as lateral discipline in a business setting. In an office the most that might happen is that the employees might get into a fistfight. Maybe one or both would get fired. *Maybe* they might make cross complaints against each other for Assault. Police officers carry guns and all sorts of other weapons both lethal and non-lethal. Police officers are also used to using violence to solve problems. Let's face it, violence, or the threat thereof, is the main tool we use to modify behavior. Lateral discipline in a police setting can wind up as a clash of the titans.

There is an old saying out of Vietnam that my field-training officer taught me. It goes something like, "If you are not prepared to go all the way, don't get off the boat." Forget about the moral or ethical issues here for a moment. Going to war with this asshole could get one of us killed. I had to think long and hard about whether to do something about Ed, or just stand by while he cheats both the public and his fellow officers out of the contribution he should be making. I had to weigh the possible effects on my career and my family and whether it was all worth it. I decided I couldn't just suck on it. The thought of it revolted me. If it happened again we were going to war.

The next day when I came to work I was building to an emotional crescendo. One part of me prayed that on the next assignment we had together he would just show up and this cup would pass me by. The other part of me had prepared a plan. I played chess with myself the previous evening as to what his move would be if I did this and what my move would be if he did that.

It was about 0930 hours on a beautiful day in the bedroom community in which Ed and I worked that Mr. Dolan left for work and did not close his front door properly. Within minutes of his leaving, his alarm went off and Ed and I were assigned. I acknowledged receiving the assignment and put a code into the computer that told the dispatcher that I was on my way. Ed did the same. When I got to the house I put in another code that told the dispatcher that I had arrived at the assignment. Ed did the same. The only problem was that Special Ed was nowhere in sight. The son-of-a-bitch was doing it to me again. My blood started to boil as I walked around the house looking for signs of a break. Fortunately, there was no burglary.

I knew exactly where to look for Ed. He was in his favorite spot in the park sitting in the police car reading the paper. It was fairly hot that morning and I was sure he was sitting there with the car's air conditioner running. As I approached his location he looked up. He saw it was me and didn't even bother to roll down the window. As I brought my car up next to his 10-69, I lowered my window, reached out with my left hand and began to discharge mace into his front grill and air intakes. I emptied the whole can into that car in a matter of seconds. Ed didn't even look up from his paper to see what I was doing.

Then I put my car into reverse and started to back away. At that point he looked up from his paper and I gave him the finger. He smiled and I guessed he was thinking, "Is that all he's going to do after threatening me yesterday, give me the finger?" I was about 30 feet away from him when the mace began to take effect. All of a sudden he threw the paper down and threw the driver's door open rubbing his eyes, coughing, and struggling to see as his eyes teared up from the spray.

I yelled at him, "Next time it will be something worse. If you want me, I'll be at the firehouse … asshole."

The firehouse is where we often go to the bathroom and hang out when we need to decompress. Cops will go there to have their meals, watch some TV, or unwind from a traumatic experience. During the weekdays the firehouse is virtually empty. The fire district has a small budget and there is only one firefighter on duty 24/7. Whenever there is a fire, volunteers come from all over town to fight it. I got to the firehouse, parked my police car, and went out of service on a personal. I said hello to the guy on duty and then I proceeded upstairs to the meeting room where we usually hang out.

I considered that when Ed got there he might do something to my police car, but I wasn't too worried. If he did any vandalism to my police car it would not really hurt me. I would just report the vandalism by some "unknown person or persons," and Ed would have more work to do for the rest of the day as I dealt with the issue. No, it was more likely that he would do something to my personal car. Since he knew where my relieving point was, I parked my car somewhere else that morning.

If Ed retaliated, then I would have to retaliate in kind and this thing would continue to escalate until something drastic happened. However, I was completely prepared to fight a war of attrition. I learned something early on by being a skinny little kid. Although you might not win the fight, if you give the other guy a bloody nose, or hurt him bad enough, he will think twice about messing with you again. He will always ask himself, "Is it worth the fight to mess with this guy?" Sometimes that answer would be yes, but more often the answer was no.

Ed showed up at the firehouse in about fifteen minutes. He stormed in and I could hear him ask John (the fireman) where I was. Then he stormed up the stairs and burst into the room. I was standing there with my nightstick in my hand ready to break some of his bones if he charged at me. When he saw me at the ready he stopped dead in his tracks.

I knew what he was thinking. He was evaluating the consequences of his choices and he had few. Charging at me was not a good idea given the fact that I had my stick and I obviously anticipated that possibility. He had to decide whether to use his mace on me tit for tat, or draw his gun.

Before he made his choice I said, "If you go for your spray I'll split you skull, and if you go for your gun don't miss, because I will kill you where you stand."

His face went completely blank when I said that. Then the revelation hit me. This asshole wasn't going to do anything. He never dreamed that anyone would stand up to him in this fashion. He was completely unprepared to deal with someone like me. He was scared. I could see it in his eyes. He was posturing well enough, but he was too much of a lazy piece of shit and too close to retirement to blow his gig now. He just stood there and ranted at me.

"If you ever do anything like that to me again I'll have your job," he said.

He was full of shit. If this thing came to the attention of our supervisors he would have to answer for its origins. Most of our colleagues who knew the kind of cop he was would be on my side. The supervisors might have to take action, but they also knew him for what he was and there was no way he wanted to deal with the uncertainty of getting supervisors involved.

I responded, "There is a very simple way to stop this Ed, answer your goddamn calls. If you don't want to do that anymore then get the hell off the street."

He just repeated his threat that if I messed with him again he would have my job. Gee, I only heard that about a thousand times and it usually came from someone I caught doing something wrong – duh!

As he turned to leave the room I said, "Ed, we are probably going to get more alarm calls today. Do the right thing and this ends. Do the wrong thing and it escalates"

It was only about ten minutes later that I heard him go out of service and respond to the stationhouse. A few minutes after that I got a phone call from the stationhouse officer (the cop who acts as receptionist, security, and answers the phones at the stationhouse). Apparently, Ed had gone on sick leave. He told the Desk Officer that his mace had leaked and that it contaminated both him and his car. I had to cover his sector for the rest of the day, but at least I got a backup when I was sent on an assignment.

Morally, I had no problem with my actions. What Ed was doing was wrong and needed to be stopped. I rationalized my ethical lapse by blaming the system. If the system were set up to solve the problem without negative consequences to me I would have used it. Once again, it was not our morality or our ethics that dominated either Ed's or my behavior. Morality and ethics informed our decisions, but it was the fear of consequences, or lack thereof, that drove our choices.

Ed got himself transferred to the Arrest Processing and Detention Bureau. There, he would be warm in the winter, cool in the summer, never got rained on, and had his meals delivered to him every day. He eventually retired and moved to Arizona. Carl took his place and we had a ball. Eventually I went on to become part of the Community Police Unit. I still occasionally ponder whether there would have been a better way to handle my clash with Special Ed. I guess all is well that ends well.

CHAPTER 15
A LOVE-HATE RELATIONSHIP

The public and the police have a textbook example of a love-hate relationship. People love us when we are catching a rapist, pulling someone from a burning car, or stopping a terrorist attack before it happens. But they hate us when they perceive we have intruded into their lives, or have in some way abused our authority. For our part, we love the public enough to risk our lives for you and we don't even know you. However, we hate it when some people blame us for catching them doing something illegal, or when some people falsely accuse us of abusing our authority because of their own vindictiveness or ignorance.

The simple fact is that society has given the police a mandate. Police managers like to call it a "mission statement." To some officers it is a mantra, the focus of their energy and attention. I happen to be a Star Trek fan so I like to call it the "Prime Directive." Our prime directive is to "Protect Life and Property."

Society has told us that this is our most important function. Above all the other things we do as police officers, this is the most important. Why? Because it embodies your two most important rights, you're right to live, and your right to keep what is yours. You worked hard, you earned money and you bought something. It is yours. No one gave it to you and no one has the right to take it from you.

If you have any doubt that these are your two most important rights all you have to do is think of them in terms of your other rights. If someone takes your life, your First Amendment rights to free speech, and freedom of religion, and the freedom to assemble, or petition the government, don't amount to very much, do they? How about this? You are stopped at a red light in your brand new car and someone walks up to your window, sticks a gun in your ear, and says, "Get out of the car, I'm taking it." I guarantee you that your Fourth Amendment right to protection against unreasonable search and seizure and your Sixth Amendment right to an attorney will not be helping you at that moment.

Make no mistake, these are your two most important rights and protecting them is my most important function. Just look around the world at the places where we don't do it. In those places people have to fight to protect their own lives and property every day. This is the love part of the relationship. People love us when we are doing this. However, built into the Prime Directive is also the reason for the hate part of the relationship and I think I have come up with a good way of explaining it.

Robbery is forcible stealing from a person. If someone comes up to you, sticks a knife to your throat and says, "Give me your money," that's Robbery. If I wait until after someone has robbed you to do something about it, obviously I have not protected you. If I wait until someone is in the process of robbing you, I still have not protected you. The word "protect" means to *keep* from harm. So, the only way I can accomplish this, my most important function, is to do something about it *before* it happens. That is the rub.

I have no magical way of knowing who is about to commit a crime, or who is involved in criminal activity. I have only three tools. I have my natural suspicion, which we all have. I have my experience as a police officer, which theoretically gets better over time and I have one power that society has given me. It is called "The Common Law Right of Inquiry." It is the authority to stop you, to temporarily seize your person, that means hold you there by force if necessary, and to question you. Who are you? Where do you live? What are you doing here? Where are you coming from? Where are you going? Those are the only tools I have to accomplish what all reasonable people know is my most important function.

Now let us consider Mr. and Mrs. Nicepeople. They are out for a stroll after dinner. They happen to fit the description of a male/female burglary team that has been breaking into houses in the area. I exercise the common law right of inquiry on these two folks. Since they are just walking along minding their own business in their own neighborhood do you think they might consider that an unnecessary intrusion into their lives? Depending on how we do it, some people have even considered it to be an abuse of authority. Like we have nothing better to do than to hassle them for no reason. Are there no bagels? Are there no donuts?

But think about it for a moment. This is a huge power society has given the police. There is no doubt that it is commensurate with the task society has asked us to do, but it is still huge. No one else in society has this power. Even judges, who are probably the closest thing to God that some people are ever going to see, have their powers limited to the court room. They don't stop you on the street, hold you there by force, and go through your pockets looking for weapons. Only the police have the power to do that.

So what has history taught us about power? Power tends to corrupt. Think in terms of the elements of self-control. Humans rationalize violating their moral and ethical codes every day. If you give police officers that kind of power and they don't have a healthy fear of consequences, you are going to have a major problem on your hands.

Fortunately for all of us, the people who organized our government were very much aware of this. They had just come off a war with England during which the agents of the government were acting without any fear of consequences. They were not about to let that happen again. It was our very first Supreme Court that took up the problem of controlling police behavior. Obviously, there were no formal police departments back then. The founding fathers were focused on any agents of the government who would eventually be authorized to enforce the laws. The Chief Justice of that court was a man named John Jay, as in John Jay College of Criminal Justice

John Jay was a staunch supporter of individual rights. He did not trust the government, or the agents of the government to control themselves. He was one of those people who believed in the notion that it is better to let thirteen guilty people go free than to convict one innocent person. By today's standards, John Jay would be considered an extremely liberal judge. But even *he* knew that we needed some members of our citizenry to do the job of protecting life and property. Accordingly, he came up with a way of controlling the agents of the government, like the police, that no one has been able to improve upon in over 200 years. We still use it today, and he called it "The Reasonable Man Rule."

According to the reasonable Man Rule, whenever a police officer takes an action, society has the right to ask this question: "Would a reasonable person, looking at what you just did officer, consider it necessary to protect life and property?" If the answer is yes, then the officer has done exactly what society wants him or her to do. In that case, we aught to thank the officer for risking his or her life to protect our lives and our property. If the answer is no, then not only can the officer lose his or her job, but if what that officer did cost someone financially, that officer can be sued personally. Also, if what the officer did was fundamentally a crime, he or she can be put on trial just like anyone else. As you can see, for abusing the power and trust society gives us, police officers face life-ruining consequences.

In a minute or two a question will come to your mind so I will ask it and answer it for you. Who decides? Who decides what is reasonable and necessary? It can't be the police because they will rationalize their behavior and everything they do will be reasonable and necessary to protect life and property. It can't be the suspects, because then nothing the police did would be reasonable. It is the courts that decide. We have over 200 years of court decisions that tell both the police *and the public* what is reasonable and necessary in most situations. That way, the police make very few mistakes. Often, what the public perceives as an abuse of authority has already been determined to be reasonable and necessary.

For example, the courts ruled a long time ago that if you are driving a vehicle on the streets of New York and I pull you over, it doesn't matter why I pulled you over. You have to produce a driver's license and proof that the vehicle is registered, insured, and inspected. If you don't, you are subject to arrest. I don't have to worry about that being reasonable because the courts have already ruled that it is.

Why? Because you are driving a three thousand pound machine on the streets of New York and unlicensed drivers and poorly maintained vehicles kill more Americans each year than murderers do. Society considers this a significant threat to life and property. So much so, that the courts have told us that we can pull people over at random to check such things. We call them safety checks. However, if we are pulling over every 10th car and you happen to be the 10th car driving along minding your own business, or worse than that, late for something, you might not like the intrusion right?

Another instance involves the Common Law Right of Inquiry. The courts ruled that if I exercise the Common Law Right of Inquiry on you, you do not have to answer my questions. To compel you to do so would be a violation of your Fifth Amendment right against self-incrimination. However, in a similar case the courts ruled that just because you don't answer my questions does not mean you are free to go.

You could still be the rapist, or robber, or drug dealer that I am looking for and I am charged with protecting life and property. So if you do not answer my questions, the courts said I could hold you at that location for a "reasonable amount of time" while I try to discover, through some other means, if you are the criminal I am looking for. This is why most people talk to us. If you answer our questions you are usually out of there pretty quickly. If you don't, we can wind up holding you there for up to 20 minutes, unless further facts and circumstances emerge to justify holding a person longer.

Still another example involves the Vehicle and Traffic Law (VTL). Police officers are exempt from the VTL. The courts ruled long ago that to force the police to adhere to the VTL would severely hamper their efforts to protect life and property. Think about it this way. A guy robs a bank. He jumps into his getaway car and speeds off at 60 MPH. The speed limit is 30 MPH. If the police were forced to obey the VTL how would they catch him?

How about this one? All police officers are Emergency Medical Technicians (EMTs) when they graduate the Police Academy. They are trained to save lives. Someone in your house has a heart attack. Do you really want the officer waiting for the light to turn green? Do you really want that officer to poke along at 30 MPH to get to your house? However, the courts have also ruled that the Reasonable Man Rule *always* applies. If that officer causes an accident while he or she is breaching the VTL, the officer better be able to prove that he or she was not on the way to buy coffee and donuts.

Another case in point is what happens when a police officer tells you to do something. The courts have ruled that if a police officer tells you to do something you must give the officer the benefit of the doubt. You must assume that there is a good reason for the order and comply with it. If you don't, you are subject to arrest. The lowest charge would be under the VTL, "Failing to obey the lawful order of a police officer." However, the charges could be even higher. You could be charged with Disorderly Conduct, or Obstructing Governmental Administration. You might even be charged with Reckless Endangerment if, by failing to comply with the officer's order, you put the officer or someone else in danger of a serious physical injury.

However, in similar cases the courts ruled that after the exigency (urgency) of the situation has passed, you are entitled to know why the officer gave that order. After you have complied with the officer's order, if it really matters to you, you are welcome to contact the police department and ask why that officer did what he did. You will usually find it was in compliance with some law, or court ruling that you are unaware of. Other times the officer may be acting legally to protect the privacy rights of someone involved in a police related matter. The courts have ruled that in those situations a person's privacy rights outweigh your need to know why the officer directed you to do or not do something.

I am sure you can see how some of the things the police have to do to protect life and property can be misconstrued as an abuse of authority. Abuses certainly take place, but considering the millions of contacts with the public that the police have each year, abuses are few and far between. I hope that what I have told you here will encourage you to take another look, a more informed look, at the actions of the police and understand why they occur.

We teach police officers that *how* they say something is as important as what they say. Unfortunately, some officers are better than others at communicating. As instructors, we tried to come up with a strategy that we could employ to get everyone to be more sensitive to the way police officers are perceived by the public. As we considered different approaches we were guided by the KISS Principle. The KISS Principle is a tried and true method to get the lowest common denominator in any bureaucracy to understand something. KISS stands for "Keep It Simple for Stupid."

We went with the Golden Rule. "Do unto others as you would have them do unto you." We teach police officers that when they approach a citizen, and the situation is not life threatening, they should apply the Golden Rule. They should treat that citizen the way they would want their mother, father, sister, brother, wife, husband, son, daughter, or friend, to be treated in a similar situation.

Interviews with officers who receive civilian complaints show that the overwhelming majority of those who receive complaints did not employ the Golden Rule in their contact with the citizen making the complaint. The officers who do employ it seldom receive complaints. When they do, the complainants are usually irrational people, or the complaints are just unfounded.

In the end, the police and the public are all human beings trying to make our human community a better place. I see no end to our love-hate relationship. The police have ethics regarding how they should treat the public. In turn, each citizen has ethics with regard to how they should treat the police. We know ours. It is important for the public to know theirs and not challenge authority just for the hell of it. We just all need to behave as ethically correct as we can.

CHAPTER 16
FUNCTIONAL FICTION

As a student of psychology and sociology I was very lucky to become a police officer. I have been able to witness some human behavior first-hand that most of my colleagues only hear about in therapy sessions or read about in professional literature. I have paid for the privilege with a case of post-traumatic stress, but I have no regrets. I would not trade my first-hand experience for the mental and emotional safety zone provided by an office, or some professional journal.

One thing that has always fascinated me is the way we humans react to things we do not want to believe. During my 30 years as a police officer I have run into several situations where people were either doing things, or not doing things, because of invalid information. I still ponder why we humans often cling to our traditional beliefs and behaviors in the face of sometimes overwhelming evidence that our belief should be abandoned.

Sometimes the issues are insignificant and it really doesn't matter if someone continues to believe something that has been proven inaccurate. Other times the issue may be significant. It may result in public officials perpetuating a behavior which new information has rendered useless, or even unethical, according to current social norms and mores. We do not expect our public officials to behave like that. It is unethical for public officials to behave like that.

For example, in 1490 when Columbus was preparing for his first voyage to the New World there were some sailors who did not want to go with him. They still believed that the world was flat. They did not want to sail off the edge. It really didn't matter what those people believed. There were enough enlightened sailors to go with Columbus. However, if the person responsible for financing his voyage believed that the world was flat it would have made a great deal of difference. Columbus never would have gotten the financing he needed to mount the expedition.

When you become a police officer you accept society's mandate to "protect life and property." There is no doubt that society expects that the police will put a larger portion of their effort toward those police functions that go the farthest to achieving the goal of protecting life and property. Society expects, that as experts in this field, we will figure out how to give the public the most bang for its buck. That is the ethical thing for us to do.

Every police officer I have met agrees that responding quickly and safely to the clear and present danger of a 911 call for help tops the list in our efforts to protect life and property. After that, opinions vary. Some people say that constant and irregular patrol, commonly referred to as "routine patrol," is number two on the list. They claim it serves as a deterrent to criminals and would be criminals. Roving patrol does raise the public's awareness of a police presence. It gives people a sense of security and it lets them see how their money is being spent. However, there is little evidence that it serves as a deterrent.

First of all, the ratio of police officers to citizens is so small that the odds of a police officer actually catching someone in the commission of a crime while on routine patrol are microscopic. The ratio of arrests to man-hours spent on the task bears this out. To prove it, I searched our arrest records to see how often we arrest someone based *solely* on routine patrol. Keep in mind that in our precinct we put 24 officers on patrol 24/7. There were plenty of arrests based on 911 calls for service. There were many arrests based on detective investigations after the crime has been committed and many resulting from car stops based on VTL violations. However, I had to look at 72 days' worth of records before I found one arrest based *solely* on routine patrol.

The bad guys know that the odds on getting caught in the act are extremely small. Interviews with apprehended criminals reveal that our roving patrols did little to deter them from committing their crimes. Those who felt any deterrence at all were deterred by the fact that they might eventually get apprehended after the fact, not during the act. The police are really good at catching the people who commit crimes, just not during the act. Here is an example.

At one point during my stint as Crime Analyst for my precinct we began to experience a rash of pedestrian robberies. The perpetrator was a male, Hispanic, in his 20s, 5-8, thin build, wearing green hospital scrubs and black and white running shoes. He was armed with a "Rambo Knife," that he carried in a shoulder scabbard and drew out from under his scrub shirt to threaten his victims. His victims were all women and he would steal their purses. The robberies were taking place on the streets in the vicinity of one of our hospitals.

I worked up a profile on the guy based on the patterns of his behavior and told the officers who patrol that sector everything I knew. Their routine patrols amounted to nothing and for weeks the guy continued to strike. Then management arranged to place the sector car on "intensive patrol." That meant that the car would not be called away from its sector to back up on assignments. The car would only be assigned to calls for service in its own sector. This resulted in even more time being spent patrolling the vicinity of the hospital looking for the bad guy.

While the intensive patrol was in effect the guy struck two more times without being caught. At that point I recommended, and was granted permission, to put an unmarked car on "targeted patrol" in the area where the crimes were being committed. Police officers on targeted patrol will not interrupt their patrol duty unless there is an officer in trouble, or some other major incident. The operational problem was that we had no officers available to do the targeted patrol assignment.

There were no other major crime issues in the precinct at that time so I felt I would actually be helping myself if I volunteered. Besides, no one knew this guy's patterns as well as I did. Even with me patrolling the area five out of every eight days the guy struck again. I had altered my days off so that I would be working when he was most likely to strike, but he hit on a day when I wasn't there. However, the sector car was still doing intensive patrol 24/7. Believe me when I tell you, it was not for lack of trying to catch him. He was embarrassing all of us.

It seemed obvious to me that this guy was smart enough to look around for the police before he committed his crimes, but he was also hedging his bets. I studied the calls for service just prior to the crimes being committed and I discovered something. There consistently seemed to be an unfounded call for service in just prior to one of his attacks. It did not happen in the first case, but it happened in the subsequent six cases.

The type of call varied. Three times he called in a motor vehicle accident with injuries. That took two cars out of service each time. Two times he called in a heart attack. That took two cars out of service each time. The last time the son-of-a-bitch called in a robbery in which he described himself. All the locations of the calls for service were several blocks from the hospital. He wanted to draw us away so he would have the time to rob people. I was determined to be ready the next time he played his game.

As part of our effort to catch the guy, we made sure that the hospital personnel were aware of what was going on. One day a nurse walking to work after parking her car spotted the guy behind some bushes. He never would have been visible to passing patrols. He was putting his scrubs on over his street clothes. She called 911 and I was right on it. In the time it took for the nurse to call 911, for the call to get dispatched, and for me to respond from three blocks away, the guy had found another victim.

When I rolled up in the unmarked car he was running down the street with the knife in his right hand and the purse in his left. I called for back up and chased him as far as I could with the car. I wanted to get close to him before letting him know he was caught, but he made me. He made a left turn and ran across the lawn toward one of the hospital delivery doors which, of course, was propped open. I jumped the curb with the unmarked car and chased him with the car across the lawn toward the door. There was no way I could head him off, so I stopped the car, took the keys and jumped out to chase him on foot just as he entered the building. I was right behind him and I let radio know that I was chasing him into the hospital.

The ground floor of the hospital is a labyrinth of hallways and doors. As I entered I was yelling, "Stop – Police!" and all the other appropriate self- identifying and commanding things that I had in my repertoire. I wanted him to stop running from me. Since I was in plain clothes, I also wanted everyone listening to know I was a cop. I didn't need some armed guard or off duty cop shooting me by accident. One of the workers pointed down the hall to left and I could see the guy just as he made a right turn and disappeared from my sight. When I got to the turn in the corridor I stopped, drew my gun, and did a peek-a-boo just in case he was waiting for me right around the bend. He wasn't. He continued running down the hall and I gave chase.

My radio was useless once I entered the building. This was a long- standing problem we had with the hospital which the politicians and the hospital have taken years *not* to resolve. The technology existed to remedy the problem. It was all about who would pay for it. Isn't it wonderful how much our safety means to them?

The guy kept making lefts and rights following the exit signs. I kept him in sight most of the time. Then he made a mistake. He zigged when he should have zagged and ran down to the end of a hallway from which there was no escape. He tried the doors on both sides of the hall and then he realized he was trapped. I stopped chasing the guy when I saw he was trapped. I stood about 30 feet down the hall between him and freedom.

Then, some of my father's words came back to me. He said, "Son, unless they see you as food, most animals will try to run rather than fight, but there is nothing more dangerous than a trapped animal." I also remembered an incident in which a City Sergeant tried to *negotiate* the surrender of a man armed with a machete. As the guy charged the Sergeant, two other cops hit him with five of the bullets from their revolvers. He still managed close the distance. He nearly severed the Sergeant's left arm just below the shoulder before he dropped to the floor and died. If his swing was three inches higher, the machete would have severed the Sergeant's head.

The guy turned toward me, dropped the purse to the floor and took up a fighting posture with the knife in his right hand. I finally got a good look at it. The blade was about 10 inches long. I raised my gun to shoulder height and took aim at him.

With my shield and ID hanging from a chain around my neck I called out, "Police! – Don't Move! Put the knife on the floor and put your hands above your head."

He just stood there at the end of the hallway looking at me.

In broken English he said, "If you want this knife you are going to have to fight me for it."

Then the guy started doing tricks with the knife, flipping it from hand to hand and twirling it in a threatening fashion. Just then I realized that this is what they mean by life imitating art. I chuckled a little at his antics. I was watching a guy, who was armed with a knife from the movie *Rambo* and he was brandishing it menacingly like the sword wielding Egyptian from the movie *Raiders of the Lost Ark*. He might have seen *Rambo*, but I don't think he saw *Raiders of the Lost Ark*. Things did not end well for the sword wielding Egyptian in that movie.

I smiled and with a touch of incredulousness in my voice I responded, "Fight you? I am not going to fight you. You take one step toward me and I am going to shoot you."

Then in a serious voice I said, "I have 15 bullets that are going to keep you from plunging that knife into me. So if you want to commit suicide, just take one step my way. If you want to live, put the knife down and put your hands above you head."

With a look as sincere as a heart attack I continued, "Now shit or get off the pot."

I had already made the decision that this was not going to become a barricade/standoff situation. I was not calling for a negotiator to resolve this. Besides, no one resolved the radio issue did they? I might have called for a negotiator if *only* my radio was working. Too bad. With my rationalization in place I focused on the center of his torso. If he so much as twitched in my direction I was going to unload into him. He had no body armor so it would be a good test for those hypersonic hollow points the Department issued to me. (See Real Fact of Life # 4)

While all this was happening, I was aware that several people, hospital employees, had been following me during the foot pursuit. I could feel them standing some distance behind me and watching all this go down. I had to wait until this guy came at me in order to be justified in shooting him.

He thought about it for a very long five seconds during which I held my breath. Then he bent over and put the knife on the floor. When he stood back up, I told him to turn around and put his hands behind his back. I cuffed him to the sound of cheers.

The point of telling you about this incident is that hours and hours of routine patrol did not catch this guy. Neither did intensive patrol, even though we were dealing with a known problem in a limited geographical area. Targeted patrol did affect his arrest, but not without the help of a 911 call for service.

Patrol is just not an effective function for protecting life and property. However, there is a much more effective use of our time than routine patrol. It is a police function that goes a very long way to accomplishing the goal of protecting life and property and it may surprise you.

Insurance industry statistics show that traffic accidents cause more deaths, injure more people, and cause more property damage than all criminal acts combined. (Terrorist acts not withstanding). In today's world, motor vehicle accidents are the single largest threat to life and property faced by Americans.

Most police departments have a list of accident-prone locations and most police departments keep extensive statistics on their attempts to mitigate the dangers. If they have the resources, they send out Traffic Safety Officers to evaluate the problems. In some cases, improving things like signage, visibility, pavement markings, and traffic control devices can make a difference. However, the single most powerful way to reduce the number of motor vehicle accidents is to write moving violation tickets.

Nationwide, police statistics show that traffic accidents are significantly reduced in those places where VTL enforcement is increased. In other words, writing moving violation tickets goes a very long way to reducing the largest threat to life and property, after the immediacy of a clear and present danger, of course. In fact, driving records show that people who are given moving violation tickets have 27% fewer accidents in the next 18 months than the same number of drivers who are given warnings instead of tickets. This nationwide statistic was easy to verify.

At the time I was doing this statistical analysis I was stopping between 100 and 200 vehicles a month. For two months, quite a large sample, I kept the info on the persons I issued warnings to. I had copies of the tickets that I gave out. At 18 months, I compared the drivers' records for accidents. The evidence was there that approximated the nationwide statistics. This means that the deterrent effect of ticket writing stays with drivers way beyond the day they get the ticket. To anyone who is familiar with statistical significance, this is huge.

Here's the clincher for those of you who are still not convinced. Forget about the idea of protecting life and property and the fact that the public actually wants more VTL enforcement for a moment. Instead consider this. Even though so many more hours of police time are spent on routine patrol than are spent on traffic stops, traffic stops generate 65.5 times the number of arrests that routine patrol generates. They include arrests for warrants, drugs, DUI, weapons, stolen property, and so much more.

When we arrest a criminal we resolve the current crime. However, we are also protecting life and property because this person, who has already evinced the willingness to commit crimes, will not be doing so in the future. At least not for the time he or she is incarcerated. We can only estimate how much crime is prevented because a criminal gets arrested.

Remember, we are supposed to be concentrating the majority of our time on those tasks that do the most to protect life and property. That is our ethic! The upshot of all of this is that there is no logical reason to continue believing that cops should do more patrolling than ticket writing. It just doesn't make sense.

So why should this be a problem for law enforcement? Well, it is a problem because this flies in the face of 200 years of tradition. Traditionally, if you are not answering a call for service, you should be out there on routine patrol looking for bad guys. Traditionally, that is what good cops are supposed to do.

So the first problem is traditional police culture and the inertia that goes along with it. People don't like to change and you will not achieve much success by just telling people to do so. The next generation of police officers has to be properly educated to the point where they understand that writing moving violation tickets is, in fact, good police work, that it actually does more to protect lives and property than routine patrol.

Another problem is that management wants police officers to write tickets. Police managers constantly get requests from politicians, community organizations and individual citizens to increase VTL enforcement. The people, who the police are sworn to protect, consider VTL violations and motor vehicle accidents to be a significant threat to their lives and property. It follows that the police should give them what they want. That is the ethical thing for the police to do. We have no right to determine that a community concern is insignificant, or somehow incorrect. After all, they do actually pay our salaries.

Unfortunately, whenever rank and file police officers perceive they are being abused by management, or unappreciated by the general public, one of the ways they hit back is with a rule book slow down. It is a form of upward discipline. I described upward discipline earlier in this book, but in essence, the cops only do exactly what they are told to do. No more and no less. They follow the rules to the letter of the law. No more and no less. The practice is very effective because people who cannot accept the Real facts of Life have created so many unrealistic laws and rules. Those people get to see firsthand how disadvantageous life is when the police actually play by their rules.

Historically, a rulebook slowdown results in slower response times. That means more bad guys get away without being caught and people do not get help as fast as before. Ticket writing is another casualty of this lack of self-initiated activity. There is always a tremendous drop in ticket writing. Officers begin to "not see" VTL violations. This increases the number of traffic accidents. It reduces revenue for the municipality as well.

Eventually the loggerhead is broken through negotiations, as it should be, and the differences get resolved. However, police officers will continue to use this unethical weapon whenever police managers and the public act unethically toward them. (See Real Fact of Life # 3)

It is important to remember that the police managers are put in place by the promotional system. The politicians put the promotional system in place and the public puts the politicians in place. The ultimate responsibility for how the people who protect the public are treated lies with the public. We, your police, know this!

The inertia of tradition and the utility of upward discipline are difficult problems to overcome. However, they are not insurmountable. With education, as well as ethical management and employment practices, the next generation of police officers will adapt to the new information and this new way of doing business. We always have throughout history (See Real Fact of Life # 5). Routine patrol lost a tremendous amount of significance when traffic accidents became such a large threat to life and property. To believe otherwise results in functional fiction. It is unethical. In today's world, no matter how you slice it, writing moving violation tickets does much more to protect life and property than routine patrol.

CHAPTER 17
MOON TIDE MAYHEM

"There are more things in Heaven and Earth, Horatio, than are dreamt of in your philosophy." William Shakespeare, along with so many other writers, sometimes used ghosts to capture readers' imaginations. Writers also use them as tools to simply further their story lines. I have always kept my mind open to the supernatural. So much so, that for a while I used to go on patrol with a vial of holy water on my belt. It was blended holy water, half Lourdes and half Fatima. Anyone who knows holy water can tell you how powerful that stuff was. I carried it in case I ran into any vampires. Also, the bullets in my revolver were silver tips. The department issued us ammunition, but I went out and bought the silver tip cartridges just in case I ran into any werewolves. I did not necessarily believe in this stuff, but I always believe it is better to be safe than sorry.

Years ago there was a group of "vampires" who had occupied some of the catacomb-like spaces under the City of New York. New York is filled with lots of weird people and the police basically leave them alone. It is a free country after all. They came to our attention when bodies started appearing on subway trains and on subway train platforms, drained of blood. When I heard about the investigation, I volunteered to be part of the search team. I had already worked with another task force that investigated grave robbers. The grave robbers were digging up coffins and breaking into Mausoleums. They were robbing the graves of anything valuable. Then they would use the skulls and other body parts in some ghoulish rituals. Having had some experience with these kinds of whackos and armed with my holy water on my belt, I was ready to face the vampires.

It turned out that the "vampires" were not supernatural at all. One of them died just fine when he was shot and no wooden stakes were necessary to keep him dead. The others we arrested seem to be doing fine upstate in the bright sunshine of the prison workout yard. I still have not run into any werewolves, but when we transitioned from revolvers to semi-automatics, I bought the appropriate silver tip bullets. They will be devastating to any werewolves I happen to shoot.

Ghosts, goblins, and other supernatural things that go bump in the night are bound to cross-purposes with the police. Before my ghost experience I occasionally thought about how I would report it if I actually encountered a real one. Ethically, I should report the event as I experienced it. That way the information could become part of a database to guide enforcement efforts in the future with regard to the supernatural. However, everyone would probably think I was joking, gullible, or just losing my mind. All of those eventualities are not positive, so I believed that my fear of consequences would probably motivate me to come up with a more plausible explanation, even if the experience was real.

It was a hot August evening when I got a call to respond to a house in the sector next to the one I was patrolling. Marie Terenzi was the cop patrolling that sector and I was responding to assist her. Marie had only three months more on the County job than I did, so we knew each other as far back as the Academy. Having served as a paramedic in our Ambulance Bureau for five years before becoming a cop, she was flexible enough to handle anything and she had a great sense of humor. Marie was also very academic. I knew she would rise through the ranks as time went by and she had all the right qualities to make a great supervisor.

The house was on waterfront property. It was a center hall colonial on about an acre of land. It had two stories and the backyard led down a gentle slope through some trees to the open bay. The call came over as "Panic Alarm – Unknown Problem." Most house alarms are equipped with panic alarm buttons. Some panic buttons are on the keypads; others are on key fobs that the homeowner can carry around. Panic alarms don't go off because of wind or open doors. You have to press the button to activate a panic alarm.

We arrived at the house at almost the same time and we walked up to the front door together. Marie was on the left and I was on the right when we rang the doorbell. The door handle was on her side and when the door opened a woman about 30 years old stood there in tears and in a panic. She was obviously glad to see us and began to speak a mile a minute in Spanish. I do not understand a word of Spanish. I communicated this fact to Marie with the expression on my face. Her skills in Spanish were limited to two years of high school Spanish classes, so she put a call over the radio asking for someone who spoke fluent Spanish respond and help us with this problem. Then she tried to make some language headway with the woman.

As Marie was doing this, my eyes darted about looking for any immediate threats. From my position, I could see a coat closet to the left of the front door. An archway led into a formal dining room next to the closet. On the right side of the foyer, just behind the open front door, there was an archway leading into a formal living room. The arches created a symmetrical effect on the left and right sides of the foyer. The foyer itself had a cathedral ceiling all the way up to the second floor. About eight feet behind the woman, against the left wall, a staircase began its climb up to the second floor landing. The staircase was open on its right side with a banister that made a right turn at the top of the stairs. The banister formed a railing to protect people from falling into the foyer. The second floor hallway led left and right out of our sight. There was a closed door at the top of the stairs.

Back on the first floor, on the right side of the foyer, a long hallway led back toward the rear of the house. Down this hallway, some 20 feet back from the front door, there was an open door to the kitchen. It was one of those commercial type kitchens with a long island and there were many pots hanging from hooks above it. Beyond the island I could see a back door that lead from the house to the back yard. Through the glass in the door I saw that there was approximately 70 feet of yard to a thin row of woods. Behind that was the bay.

After I concluded that there was no immediate threat, I began to refocus on the woman and Marie. She had determined that the woman was the maid. The maid pushed the panic button and called us on purpose. The maid said that she was tired of putting up with the ghost.

I heard Marie say, "Ghost? You say there's a ghost in the house?"

The woman said, "*Si, fantasma.*"

Marie looked at me to make sure I had heard what the maid had said and then she asked the maid to tell us more about this ghost. At that point Marie and I were still trying to evaluate what the problem really was. Is the woman a whack job? Is she just trying to get us to leave? If so, for what reason? She was surly frightened by something.

Suddenly, there was a loud crashing sound upstairs. It sounded like a piece of wooden furniture fell to the ground and it sounded like it came from the room behind the door at the top of the stairs. The maid screamed.

I blurted out, "Ghost my ass," and then Marie bolted up the stairs with me right behind her.

I suspected, at that point, that the maid was being pressured to blow us off by whoever was in that room. The noise continued and it sounded like someone was destroying the inside of the room. We both drew our guns. We were in position on either side of the door and we could still hear things being thrown about Inside. I opened the door quickly and when we looked inside the room everything went still. It was as though we surprised someone, but we saw no one.

The first thing that hit us was the smell of decaying vegetation mixed with the smell of the sea. The room was an office and it was in shambles. A wooden bookcase, formerly on the right wall, had either fallen or was pushed over. Books and papers were all over the floor. A floor lamp lay on its side next to a wooden desk in the center of the room. The desk faced the door and behind it was a large window looking out over the back yard. The desk chair was on its side behind the desk. The desk itself was turned over as though someone stood up from behind the desk and just pushed it over toward the door.

Marie viewed the room from her position in the hallway and said, "Clear."

This indicated that she saw no threats to us. I viewed the opposite side of the room from my position and said the same. We both entered the room expecting someone to jump up from behind the desk, but no one was in the room. We verified with each other that we heard the noise coming from this particular room. Then I heard Marie gasp and I did the same. Books and papers were being stepped on by something invisible as it walked toward us. A cold breeze that seemed to move right through our bodies suddenly hit us both. The breeze did not move around our bodies, it went right through us and I got the distinct feeling that someone had just walked passed me. However, the window was closed. In fact, it turned out to be locked tight. Later, I could find no sign of any draft coming into the room through that window, or from any other source for that matter.

We both turned around and walked out on to the landing. We looked over the banister and down the stairs and saw no one except the maid still standing in the foyer. She was looking up at us. It was visible from her facial expression that she was still frightened and she was wondering what was going on upstairs. The smell of decaying vegetation and the sea was strong.

Then, right before our eyes, the foyer closet door at the foot of the stairs opened, seemingly by itself. When that happened, the maid screamed and pressed herself into the furthest corner of the foyer away from the closet and nearest the front door. I was half expecting her to go running from the house. I guess she was paralyzed with fear. The closet door remained open for about as long as it would take for someone to take out a coat. Then it closed again, by itself, right in front of our eyes.

I ran down the stairs right behind Marie. I was running out of reflex to protect the maid. As I passed the closet at the bottom of the stairs, I just gave the closed door a look, made a left turn, and put myself in front of the maid, my back to her. I was trying to protect her from I don't know what. Marie stopped and examined the closet and was looking around for any threats. Then everything went quiet for a moment. Before we could evaluate what we had just seen our attention was drawn to the kitchen.

Apparently, whatever this thing was, it seemed to be walking through the kitchen toward the rear door. Along the way it was hitting the pots hanging above the kitchen island. One by one starting from the point nearest to us the pots began to clang into each other. One fell to the ground creating quite a racket. Marie, the maid, and I just stood there with our mouths open. We were all stunned by what we were watching. When whatever it was reached the kitchen door at the rear of the house, this invisible thing opened the door and then closed it again. I assumed it went outside.

I reacted to that while Marie remained with the maid. I ran down the hall and through the kitchen glancing at the swinging pots as I went by. I was looking for some sign of a hoax. I saw no one in the kitchen and I saw nothing that might have been controlling the pots and pans. I threw open the rear door and looked outside for whatever it was. I scanned left and right and then I just paused a moment and looked. In the twilight I could see all the way back to the tree line. There was a path running through the trees that led to the bay. In just about the amount of time you would think it would take to walk from the house to the trees, I would swear I saw bushes being pushed aside as something seemingly invisible moved through the trees toward the bay.

I made the decision not to follow whatever I thought I saw. First of all, it seemed too much like it wanted me to follow it. That scared me a little. Secondly, I really believed, at that time, that I was the victim of a hoax and the source of that hoax was alive and well and inside the house. When I turned back into the kitchen I immediately began to examine the hanging pots for gimmicks. I found none. They were swinging exactly as you would expect them to if someone had just done what I watched happen. When I walked back into the foyer, Marie was more thoroughly examining the closet and its door for gimmicks. She found none.

While all of this was happening, the alarm company was notifying the emergency contact people on their list and telling them that there was a panic alarm set off at the house. I went back upstairs and I was examining the interior of the office when the homeowner arrived. She was a woman in her sixties and the alarm company called her cell phone while she was at dinner with some friends. She was accompanied by her husband who entered the house with her. The homeowner spoke fluent Spanish. After begging our pardons for just a moment the woman began conferring with the maid. At that point, Marie put over a call to cancel the Spanish interpreter that we had requested to respond. I slowly descended the stairs and joined everyone in the foyer.

Shortly thereafter, the homeowner turned to us and said, "Officers, I don't know any good way to explain this except to just explain it. We have a ghost in the house and Veronica (the maid) never should have called you. This type of thing happens sometimes when we have a moon tide. We told her to expect this when she came to work for us."

Marie said, "I don't believe in ghosts. What I do believe in is magicians and trickery. That is what is going on here and someone is going to get arrested for it." Marie was not pleased.

The woman said, "I am not a magician. I am a retired teacher."

She looked at her husband and said, "My husband is not a magician. He is an accountant. This is not a joke. It is not a trick and you never should have been called."

The woman looked deadly serious. As I stood there listening to the exchange between her and Marie, I was also watching the husband's face. He was either the greatest actor in the world, or he was completely mortified by what was going on. I believe he was very frightened by what we, the police, might do next. I could tell that Marie was getting frustrated and she appeared to be close to putting the homeowner in handcuffs for falsely reporting an incident. I decided to de-escalate things a little by asking about the ghost.

It turned out that Marie was as curious about this as I was. She just stopped talking and started listening. The woman invited us into the living room. She asked us to sit down and she offered us something to drink. We both sat down, but declined a beverage. I told radio that the situation was under control and no further assistance was needed. Then the woman began her tale.

She said, "What you witnessed was the spirit of my brother Paul. He has not moved on to the next life. Either he is stuck here, or else he does not want to leave here. I am not sure which it is. In 1953 my brother Paul came home from college for the summer and began having an affair with a married woman who lived two houses down from us, also on the water."

"She would tell her husband she was going for a walk by the bay. Paul would do the same to our parents. They would meet on the beach and make love in the woods. I know this because I was 13 years old at the time and I used to spy on them. I told Paul that I knew about them and he made me swear to keep his secret."

"Her husband began to get suspicious having seen how friendly they were. He told her that he would divorce her if she did not stop 'flirting' with the young man down the block. Paul came back up to the house after one of their meetings visibly upset. I asked him what was wrong. He did not tell me what had happened except to say that she told him she would no longer see him. He was devastated."

"My parents were not home, so Paul went up to our father's office and raided our father's liquor cabinet. He sat at the desk drinking and when he was good and drunk he went into a rage. He destroyed the inside of the office. I remember hearing the phone ring and Paul answered it. It must have been a wrong number because Paul hung up the phone quickly. Shortly after that he ran down the stairs and took his jacket out of the closet. He exited through the kitchen purposely trying to knock the pots from their hooks as he walked by. Paul went down to the bay. Why? I will never know."

"Apparently, while Paul was walking along the concrete seawall he tripped and hit his head on the wall. He fell unconscious on what should have been the beach. It was a moon tide. The tide came in twice as high as normal. The coroner said that the fall knocked him unconscious, but it did not kill him. Paul drowned and he would probably have lived had it not been for the moon tide. Now his spirit seems trapped. He doesn't behave like this at every moon tide, but it happens at most of them. His spirit seems to repeat the things he did just before he died. I used to think he was trying to tell us something by remaining here. As though he wanted us to see something, or know something, or find something. I gave up trying to figure it out long ago"

All of a sudden Marie went from being a total skeptic to being intrigued by the woman's story.

Marie asked, "And you just put up with all of this?"

The woman said, "Yes! This is my home! It was my parents' home! It was Paul's home! So I just clean things up and hope he behaves at the next moon tide. It doesn't happen every time"

Then Marie said, "I am going to promise you something. I am going to research the story of your brother's death. If I find you have been lying to us, I am going to personally arrest you. I am giving you one more chance to tell me the truth. After we leave here, there is no 'Oh, it was just a joke,' you are going to go to jail"

The woman told Marie, "Please do whatever research you want to. The story is true. I am so sorry that the police department had to become involved in this. I will try to make sure that you are never called again for this reason. Please just look the other way this time."

Then the woman gave us all the information we needed to facilitate Marie's research of her story. It turned out that the story of Paul's death was true. Way back in the 1950s the coroner had ruled the death an accident. The ghost story? I don't know.

Here was my dilemma. Although it was not a serious one, it was an interesting one. Let's not call it a ghost. Let's just say that Marie and I had just witnessed an invisible entity that was interfacing with our world. We both smelled what we smelled, felt what we felt, and we saw what we saw. We both knew that what we experienced was real. Under the circumstances and with the players involved, it could not have been a hoax. So how do we report it?

I wanted to call it the way I saw it. I figured that no one would believe us. That way, the detectives would work on it as some sort of a magic trick that was used to falsely report an incident. Marie and I would then either have further confirmation of the event, or it would be debunked.

Marie did not want to go that route. She felt that either we would be looked at as easily fooled, or we would be looked at as crazy for believing we encountered an invisible entity. She was afraid that either result would impair our reputations and that would not be good for our careers. I pointed out that making rank on our job was really not dependent upon reputation. She responded by reminding me that if someone had a "questionable mental state" the department could prevent their promotion. She believed that if we reported that we saw a ghost it might cause us a problem down the line. As a courtesy to Marie, and maybe myself too, I agreed we should report the incident as "alarm set in error."

Years later, after Marie had achieved the rank of Deputy Inspector, we were both attending a Department award ceremony and I had the occasion to converse with her. We talked about all the old times and people we knew when we were both on patrol.

When I reminded her of our ghostly encounter she said, "Ghost? What ghost? Only crazy people believe in ghosts."

We both raised our eyebrows at the same time and smiled. After that, she moved in close to me so that only I could hear what she was about to say.

She began, "Do you remember when I did the research on the incident with that guy Paul?"

I said, "Yea, you verified the story."

She said, "Well, not exactly Mike. I discovered that both the police investigation and the coroner's investigation were very shoddy. The incident happened all right, but I think I know why the ghost is still hanging around."

Marie completely captivated my attention. This incident had stayed with me ever since it happened. I nodded in an effort to encourage her to continue.

She said, "Do you remember how the sister said there was a phone call just before Paul went flying out of the house?"

I said, "Yea, she was 13 at the time."

Marie said, "Well, I suspect that the person on the phone was the husband. I'll bet he invited Paul to meet him by the bay to 'discuss' things. Then he killed Paul out of jealousy, or maybe out of fear that Paul might become loose cannon and spill the beans on the affair. That would certainly explain why the sister got the feeling Paul was trying to tell her something. Now wouldn't it?"

I was incredulous.

I said accusingly, "You suspected that this incident was a homicide and you never said anything?"

She said, "Like what was I supposed to do about it Mike? It happened over 30 years before you and I became involved. The husband died of cancer in the 70s. There was no way to prove anything. It was just a hunch I had."

I resignedly nodded and said, "Yea, I see what you mean."

Then Marie said, "I'll tell you what I did do though."

I was totally intrigued and asked, "What did you do?"

She said, "I told the sister everything that I suspected. She called me about a year later. She said that she contacted the wife, who was then living in Florida, and told her about what I suspected. She also told the wife that Paul was haunting the place."

I nodded.

Marie continued, "Here's the creepy part. After I told the sister my suspicions, the sister tried all sorts of spiritual mumbo-jumbo to get Paul to go wherever he was supposed to go after death. Nothing worked. About a month after the sister told the wife the story, the wife killed herself in Florida. All of a sudden Paul stopped haunting the place."

We both nodded to each other and thought for a moment.

Then Marie said, "I guess my hunch was right. It was a homicide."

I smiled at Marie and said, "That was a very cool thing to do Marie. I can't believe you never told me about this."

Then a thought made me chuckle.

Marie asked, "What are you laughing at?"

I said, "Well, there's obviously an afterlife right?"

She cautiously said, "Yea, but I will never admit I saw a ghost."

I rolled my eyes at her and said, "Paul stopped haunting the place after the wife died right?"

Marie nodded.

I asked, "You know how they say living well is the best revenge?"

She said, "Sure."

"Well, to pay the guy back for murdering him, wouldn't it be cool if Paul is making love to the guy's wife for the rest of eternity now?"

Marie said, "That would be some strange justice."

I said, "It sure would."

We smiled and high-fived each other.

CHAPTER 18
PACIPHONIES

When I was doing my graduate work in Psychology I was required to take a course in Child Psych. I was fortunate to have a brilliant professor, Dr. Helen Gerhardt. One day she gave us an in-class assignment to watch some video footage of the playroom at a day care center. We were to comment on any behaviors the children exhibited that were note-worthy. The video was about 20 minutes long. She obtained the video from a security camera that was trained on the playroom. Dr. Gerhardt had carefully edited the footage for us and it wasn't long before we saw what she wanted us to see.

At one point, male toddler # 1 was sitting on the carpeted floor playing with a toy. I think it was a Star Wars action figure. Male toddler # 2 decided that he wanted the toy. Toddler # 2 walked over and sat on the floor facing toddler # 1 within arms-length of him. Toddler # 1 ignored toddler # 2 and continued to play with the toy. 25 seconds after he sat down, toddler # 2 reached out with his right hand and grabbed the toy. In response, toddler # 1 put both hands on the toy in an effort to retain it and a short-lived tug-of-war ensued.

The tug-of-war was short lived because toddler # 2 switched hands and then smacked toddler # 1 across the face. Toddler # 1, stunned by the smack, released his grip on the toy and toddler # 2 took it from him. He then turned his back toward toddler # 1 and began to play with the toy himself. It took about 5 seconds for toddler # 1 to start crying. Since a reaction to pain would have come much quicker, I concluded that it took that long for him to process what just happened to him. It probably never happened to him before.

About 10 seconds passed before a female caregiver came into the picture. As she approached the crying toddler, he pointed at toddler # 2 in an effort to communicate to the caregiver what had just happened. He continued to point at toddler # 2 as the caregiver picked toddler # 1 up into her arms and began to administer all of the appropriate comfort and nurturing that one would expect. However, it became apparent that the caregiver did not see the slap.

She said, "Oh, now it's OK. If he doesn't want to share his toy with you we will just find you one of your own. Come; let's find you something nice to play with."

Scenarios like this one play out every day in day care centers, in homes, playgrounds, and on streets all over the world. This is how early in our lives we learn, either by experience or observation, that violence can be used successfully to solve problems. As people get older some of them embrace the utility of violence and use it regularly to achieve their ends.

Other people grow to abhor violence. They shy away from people who use it and they try to avoid becoming involved in violence, sometimes at all costs. Some people find violence so revolting that they deny it has any utility at all. This state of denial in the face of overwhelming evidence can cause some people to not recognize dangers. Still others, like me, find violence to be very distasteful. We always try to think of viable alternatives. However, we use it when we believe it is appropriate and necessary to do so. We acknowledge the utility of violence.

Merriam-Webster's dictionary defines pacifism as: "(1) Opposition to war or violence as a means of settling disputes. (2) A refusal to bear arms on moral or religious grounds. (3) An attitude or policy of non-resistance."

I once went on a tour of Amish country in Pennsylvania and the tour guide mentioned that the Amish do not serve in the military. He said that they are pacifists. I remember thinking, that's not very fair. They reap the benefits that are gained by others risking their lives to defend our country and they put nothing of their own at risk. I was further surprised when the tour guide said that they do not pay taxes either. So they don't even pay, in dollars, to support the people who *do* risk their lives to preserve our and the Amish way of life. I had always opposed the idea that religious organizations do not have to pay taxes so this opened an old wound for me. If Mike ruled the world everyone would pay taxes. Then, being a cop, another question occurred to me. What do they do when someone commits a crime in their community?

My tour guide explained, in so many words, that if the crime is containable within the community, the community "shuns" the offender. He explained that the offending person is ostracized and physically separated from the community until some acceptable combination of restitution and remorse is achieved. At that point, the community takes the offender back to its bosom. So I asked the tour guide what happens when the crime is not containable within the Amish community. For instance, what if the offender is from outside the community and the crime is something like rape, or assault, or grand theft of property? The tour guide said that in such cases the Amish report the crimes to the local police who investigate and arrest the offender if they can. He went on to say that the Amish let the "English" punish their own people according to their own (English) laws.

All of a sudden I came to a realization. These people are not pacifists. They just want someone else to do their dirty work for them. They are not opposed to using violence against their fellow human beings as long as they are not actually the ones doing it. Don't misunderstand me. It is the function of the police to handle these things for them, but they shouldn't call themselves pacifists. If they do, they are phonies – paciphonies.

I came away from my Amish country experience wondering how many other people out there go around saying that they are pacifists when they really aren't. I also came away wondering how the Amish, and other religious organizations, rationalize the fact that they selfishly take advantage of the "English" in this fashion.

The most fundamental ethic of any human community is for its members to contribute to the continued survival of the community. In a community based on a capitalist system, the ethic calls for people to contribute "their fair share." In a community based on a socialist/communist system, the ethic calls for them to contribute "according to their ability." In both cases the ethic still calls for the members of the community contribute *something* to its survival. From what I saw, the Amish contribute milk and tobacco and I won't even address tobacco.

On one occasion when I was teaching at the FBI Academy, I had a student who was a deputy sheriff from Ohio and the son of a dairy farmer in Ohio. The farmer contributed milk to society. He also had a daughter in the air force and a son who was a deputy sheriff. The Ohio farmer was a volunteer firefighter and his wife was a public school teacher. Guess what? All of them paid taxes. I am sure there is some religious dogma that helps "tax exempt" people like what they see in the mirror, but I can't imagine what that might be. Not paying taxes is unethical and just plain selfish.

During the tail end of the Vietnam War there were a lot of self-professed pacifists running around out there. I encountered plenty of them during the normal course of conversation at social events. I encountered even more of them when I attended anti-war rallies. I would listen to them deny that violence has some utility in solving human problems and then wonder how they can deny the overwhelming amount of evidence to the contrary.

One year I went to a New Year's Eve party that was attended by one of these self-professed pacifists. He was a very arrogant and pompous philosophy professor. This night he was spouting all sorts of this non-violent trash. Many of the guests were listening to him as though he were speaking for God himself. Unfortunately for him, at the time he was pontificating I was two sheets to the wind. I was also in the process of running the third sail up the mast. I am sure you have experienced how alcohol lowers your inhibitions and tempts you to do and say things that you would not ordinarily do or say. It works the same way for me.

At one point, the professor was talking about how it was not necessary for the police to physically remove the protestors who had occupied several buildings on his school's campus. The protestors had brought education to a standstill. The school administration tried to negotiate their departure for over two weeks to no avail. Apparently the protestors expected the school administrators to use their magical powers to convince the U.S. government to stop supporting the Contras in Nicaragua. That was the condition that had to be met before the striking students would end their occupation of the college buildings. Finally, when other students (and their parents) threatened to stop paying and start suing for an education that they were not receiving, the school administration called in the police to remove the protestors. (See Real Fact of Life # 3)

The professor went on to talk about an anarchist philosophy which espouses that police are unnecessary in society. He insisted that given enough time and patience people would sort out their own differences. Then he began to spout that people who demand things from society should be given what they demand. According to the professor, they would not be asking for those things if they did not need them. He cited the communist doctrine of "from each according to their ability, to each according to their need." I don't think I had ever heard so much philosophical bullshit come out of one person in my entire life. This guy just loved listening to himself talk and he loved having others hang on his words.

Almost everyone at the party knew I was a police officer, including the professor. Because he knew I was a police officer I could not help but take what he was saying personally. I felt he had to be looking for a reaction from me or he would not be engaging in this discourse with me present. Guests began turning and looking at me to see if I was listening. Many people in attendance also knew I was an educated man, and that besides experience, I would also probably have good academic support for my opinion on such matters. It became increasingly clear that everyone was waiting for my response to what the professor was saying. After all the alcohol I had consumed, I was happy to grant their wish.

In a social setting, the professor would introduce himself as Dr. Phil. Not merely Phil, Dr. Phil.

Finally I said, "Excuse me Dr. Phil, but you must admit that there are some people out there who just cannot be reasoned with."

The professor responded, "I will admit no such thing! Everyone can be reasoned with given enough time and the proper approach."

I looked at him for about 5 seconds while I tried to think of a way to make my point. I decided to take a basic human response and express it with some SAT words so it sounded cool.

I responded, "Really? Well I happen to believe that the philosophies you have been promoting tonight are extremely detrimental to our society. In fact, I am seriously questioning the value of your continued existence on this planet. The course of action I am considering is to reach across this table and knock your teeth down your throat. I think that might be a good way to both terminate your trash talk and disprove your theory in front of all these people. The notion is very attractive to me, so by all means, please try to *reason* me out of doing do."

He was struck dumb by the picture I placed in his mind and the immediacy of the threat I was making. It was the first time he had shut up all night. He looked to our host for help, but our host was intrigued by the exchange and did nothing to help him. Neither did anyone else. I think they were all waiting for the show to continue. To his credit, his brain stopped short-circuiting and he began to speak again. I stood there listening while he suggested three reasons why I should not hit him.

After each suggestion I shook my head and said, "No, that's doesn't work for me, hitting you is still too satisfying. Got anything else?"

I could see the fear in his eyes and the frustration building up inside him. It was like he knew his doom was imminent. He seemed trapped, so I let him off the hook and pointed him in the correct direction.

I said, "Let me ask you something right now in front of all these witnesses? I am about to punch you in the face. Can I do that without worrying about you calling the police on me?"

He jumped on that with both feet.

He said, "Well of course I am going to call the police. If you can't handle a simple difference in philosophy without turning to violence then you are obviously a dangerous person in need of control."

I said, "Ah, there you go professor. That convinced me not to hit you. However, please realize that it is only the fear of the police keeps me from putting your lights out. I guess you did *reason* me out of hitting you after all, with the help of the police of course."

When I finished speaking I smiled at him like the Cheshire Cat. The professor was incensed. I guess he thought he was still in the middle of the herd, but he had inadvertently drifted toward the edge. (See Real Fact of Life # 1) He announced that he was not going to condone this kind of behavior (mine) by remaining at the party. Then he began to make his good byes.

I cut him off and said, "No professor. You stay. I am the one who pooped the party. I should be the one to leave."

That suited him fine and I left after thanking my host for an interesting evening. Believe it or not, I got invited back the following year. I guess I must be an entertaining fellow.

The fact that there are so many paciphonies, like this professor, prompted me to develop a "pacifist test." After all, there might actually be a real pacifist out there. I would hate to confuse the real thing with the pretenders. These days, this is what I like to ask professed pacifists:

"Suppose you are living alone in a house you own outright. During the night while you are sleeping, two men break in. They beat you senseless, steal your valuables and then leave (which is not an uncommon occurrence in some quarters). Are you going to tell the police what happened to you?"

The response has been invariably, "Yes," and every one of them fails the test. Most of the time I just say, "Thank you," and walk away feeling no need to prove my point to anyone.

Whenever I am pressed, I explain that a real pacifist would just take the beating, forget about the valuables and never tell the police about the incident. Just like the Amish, when you report an incident to the police you press the start button on a vast machine that uses violence, or the threat thereof, to coerce people into modifying their behavior.

Violence, or the implied threat of violence, is certainly used to take them into custody. In fact, there are very few summary arrests in which some sort of physical force is not required. In some cases, the threat of death has to be expressed or implied in order to achieve the criminal's surrender. Once again, if someone reports something to the police that person is not a pacifist. He or she is just letting us do the violence for them and that is the way it should be (See Real Fact of Life # 3).

People cannot relieve their moral and ethical responsibility for the violence that ensues after you make a police report. The courts ruled on a philosophically similar situation a long time ago. When a mob boss orders an underling to "take care of the problem," he is responsible for what his henchman does to "take care of the problem." The boss is responsible because the boss knows what method the henchman is going to use to "take care of the problem."

In the same way, any ordinary citizen with only half a brain knows what method the police are going to use to "take care of the problem." It is violence, or the threat thereof. Real Fact of Life # 3 is not an illusion. Since I have never met a true pacifist, I sometimes wonder if maybe pacifism is an illusion.

CHAPTER 19
BENNY THE BULLY

I find it very frustrating to watch people make things more complicated than they really are. When the people who engage in this behavior are responsible for solving it, I get very suspicious. I can't help but feel that they are trying to get out from under their responsibility with "a complicated problem" as their excuse.

One example of this involves bullying and other school violence. Like with most societal issues, the solution really lies in the political will to do something about it. Investigators get to use 20-20 hindsight to try to determine why events like Columbine occur. With the advantage of 20-20 hindsight, they usually get a clear picture of the origins of the problem.

All too often, the kids who come to school with weapons to kill or maim their fellow students have had a history of being bullied, either physically or psychologically. Bullying among females frequently takes the form of psychological torture, and both sexes are victimized by what has come to be known as "cyber bullying."

The bullying experience often drives these individuals into the category of social outcasts. In other cases, emotional disturbance or mental illness is what causes students to be social outcasts. It is not usually the football captain or the home coming queen who commits acts of horrific violence against their fellow students or their schools. That is because they are not social outcasts. They are invested in the school and its social structure. On the other hand, football captains and prom queens have been known to engage in all sorts of bullying behaviors.

Sociologists and psychologists (the experts) made the connection between bullying, mental illness, and retributive school violence a long time ago. Of course they informed the politicians, law enforcement, and the educational community of their findings. In a nutshell, if we want to head off Columbines in the future, we need to stop the bullying in schools and identify and treat those students with mental issues. Across the country there have been thousands of school conferences, training programs, and professional development presentations to try to implement one plan or another designed to reduce bullying and other school violence.

The most popular response from the non-professional community is that it is impossible to stop bullying. The infamous "they" say that bullying has been around as long as there have been schools and children. Obviously, we can never stop 100% of school violence. We can never stop 100% of anything. However, most of the bullying and other school violence can be stopped if people are willing to do what is necessary to stop it. The fact is that they choose not to do so. Here's an example.

This incident occurred while I was assigned to the Community Police Unit (CPU) in my precinct. The CPU handles the kinds of assignments that the average officer patrolling a sector does not have time for. For instance, we can devote hours of time to citizens' complaints of VTL violations where the patrol officer cannot. The sector car has calls for service to answer. We execute warrants, which if done by the patrol officer would take him or her out of service for several hours processing arrests.

The CPU does traffic surveys to try to find ways to reduce motor vehicle accidents. We do security surveys for people who have been victims of burglary and robbery. A security survey teaches people how to "harden the target." It helps keep these victims from becoming victims a second time. CPU cops also act as school liaisons. We do school presentations on a variety of subjects to schoolchildren of all ages and we attend meetings with school officials on a regular basis. The CPU is a resource for the school administrators. I was the liaison with this particular high school, and because of that, this incident came to my attention.

The situation involves a young boy in his freshman year. One day, he made a huge mistake when he innocently sat at the football table during his lunch period. Being a freshman, he was still learning the school culture and did not know that only varsity and junior varsity football players could sit at that table. When the football players came to the table he was already engaged in eating his lunch. One of them, call him Benny the Bully, poured the boy's milk over the rest of the food on his tray without explaining anything to the boy and without giving him a chance to move.

Then Benny, along with another football player, physically lifted the boy from his chair, held him upside down by his legs, and carried him to another table. There, they deposited him on the table headfirst into some other childrens' lunch trays. The boy, whose name was Jonathan, was unhurt physically, but he felt humiliated and emasculated to have this occur in front of both male and female students who were in the cafeteria at that time. The fact that other children had their lunches ruined did not endear the boy to them either.

Jonathan's father had taught him not to fight in school. His father told him that if he had a dispute of any kind he should report the problem to school officials and let them take care of it. Students have a homeroom period at the beginning and end of school. It is not a full class period, but it serves to take care of school housekeeping chores. The homeroom teacher also serves a dual role as guidance counselor for the students assigned to him or her. Based on his father's direction and the school bureaucracy, that afternoon Jonathan told his homeroom teacher what had happened to him earlier in the day.

The homeroom teacher told the student that unfortunately the football table was a school tradition and that he would have to find somewhere else to eat in the future.

In response to the physical maltreatment and emotional upset that the boy experienced the homeroom teacher said, "Ah, nothing got hurt except your pride. I'm sure it won't happen again."

Well it did. The next day at lunch Jonathan sat three tables away from the football table. Benny the Bully sought him out. He came over to Jonathan and again he poured the boy's milk all over the rest of the boy's food. Then Benny told him that he did not want Jonathan to sit anyplace where he (Benny) could see him. Witnesses said that Benny told Jonathan, "If I ever see you again I'm gonna kick your ass."

Jonathan looked around the cafeteria. He realized that Benny would be able to see him no matter where he sat. He then went down to the principal's office to request that his lunch period be switched with a class period so he could avoid the problem in the future. The boy was genuinely frightened that the football player, who was twice his size, would hurt him physically.

When the school secretary in the main office asked the boy if she could help him, Jonathan related his request and the reason for his request. The school secretary verbally explained an extensive bureaucratic process that Jonathan was to follow in order to switch lunch periods. She gave this high school freshman no written direction or other assistance with his problem. Jonathan left the main office frustrated. He knew that he could not possibly accomplish the task by himself and he was still frightened.

During that day's afternoon homeroom Jonathan related the day's events to his homeroom teacher. The homeroom teacher's response was to say he would schedule a meeting with the football coach to get the coach to talk to the players and stop the harassment. The harassment occurred again the next day and the day after that. Each time, Jonathan ran from the lunchroom with Benny the Bully chasing him and many of the other children laughing at the whole situation. Each time it occurred Jonathan told his homeroom teacher what happened and pressed the homeroom teacher for the football coach's response. The homeroom teacher said he was "working on it." The boy finally gave up on the school system that did not help him. That night he told his father what had been going on.

The father took the day off from work and came up to the school the next morning. He was concerned and angry and he demanded a meeting with the school principal. He refused to leave when he was told he needed an appointment, even after the school secretary threatened to call the police. Eventually, rather than have their malfeasance exposed by calling the police on the father, an Assistant Principal (AP) was called and took a meeting with the father. When the father finished, the AP assured the father that he would look into the problem.

The father commented, "Please don't 'look into the problem.' I want assurances that my son will no longer be harassed. He needs to be able to eat his lunch in peace.

Don't you have teachers on duty in the lunchroom to handle things like this? What are they doing while this is going on? Station one of them near my son so they can and catch this bully in the act."

Instead of addressing the issues the father just raised, the AP blew smoke on the issue. He said, "Do not tell me how to do my job. I will not be threatened by your aggressive posture."

Since the AP did not give the father assurances about his son's safety, the father told the assistant principal that he would instruct his son to fight back if his son were harassed again. The assistant principal warned the father that if Jonathan fought back, he would be suspended.

The father commented, "That's great. You won't protect my son, but you will suspend my son for defending himself. What is wrong with you?"

The AP said, "There is nothing wrong with me. I said I would look into it."

The line in the sand had been drawn and the father left the school frustrated.

The next day, as soon as Benny the Bully entered the cafeteria and saw Jonathan, he started running toward the boy. Jonathan, fearing the football player's promise of a beating, left his lunch, jumped up from the table he was sitting at, and ran out of the cafeteria. Benny just laughed along with his fellow players at the boy running away once again. Other students who witnessed the event were laughing also and none of them stepped up to help the boy. Once again, no teachers got involved.

Jonathan stood in the stairwell and struggled with what to do next. After using whatever reasoning 14 year olds are capable of, the boy took a fire extinguisher off the wall and headed back into the cafeteria. Without giving any warning, he swung the fire extinguisher and struck Benny the Bully on the back of the neck and head. He then hit him again and again and again venting all his rage and frustration from the fear, intimidation and humiliation he had been subjected to.

Eventually other students pulled him off, but by then Benny was a bloody mess. He had lacerations on his neck and head. He was bleeding profusely from his scalp and he suffered a concussion. The principal called 911 for an ambulance and then he called me. When I got there, Benny was on the way to the hospital and Jonathan was in the Principal's office. The teachers on duty in the cafeteria did not see Benny harass Jonathan nor did they see Jonathan hit Benny with the fire extinguisher. At least that is what they claimed.

    Since Jonathan was the primary aggressor in the incident, protocol demanded that I custodialize the boy. When you are under 16 you are considered a Juvenile. You don't get arrested, you get "custodialized." There is no difference in the way we treat someone in the field. They still get handcuffed because juveniles have certainly done the police harm in the past and they have also tried to escape. However, when they get to the stationhouse they are not put in the arrest room for arrest processing. Persons under 16 are placed in a special youth room, rather than be placed in a cage, or chained to a wall with adult arrestees. If Jonathan had been over 16, he would have been charged with Assault.

    It is not considered interrogation to ask someone, "What happened?" so I listened to Jonathan's side of the story all the way to the stationhouse. He continued to tell me what happened while we were waiting for the Juvenile Detective and the boy's father to show up.

    Jonathan's story was disturbing. It was almost unbelievable and I needed to verify the facts with the school. It took some time, but I did so. Believe it or not, the school officials I spoke with were very forthright and there were many student witnesses. I came to the conclusion that the boy acted in self-defense. My belief that he acted in self-defense dissolved my reasonable cause to believe that Jonathan committed any crime at all. The defense of Justification negates the charge of assault. I refused to charge the boy.

    Instead, I wanted to release Jonathan and arrest the assistant principal, the homeroom teacher, and whatever teachers were on duty in the lunchroom at the time. I planned to charge them with Endangering the Welfare of a Child. They had adequate means and opportunity to alleviate Jonathan's hostile environment. They were responsible, by law, with ensuring the child's safety and they did not do so.

The Desk Officer (supervisor) on duty in my stationhouse understood my reasoning regarding the boy, but he did not agree with me that Jonathan was justified in doing what he did. The Desk Officer did not think that Jonathan acted in self-defense. He also refused to allow me to arrest the school officials. The Desk Officer acknowledged that the elements of the crime of Endangering the Welfare of a Child were present, but school officials had never been arrested before in such a situation. He did not want to be the person who authorized the setting of such a precedent. (He had micro balls as far as I was concerned).

Turnabouts being fair play, the Desk Officer ordered me to leave the responsibility of charging anyone in the case up to the district attorney's office. It was a lawful order since the problem would eventually be addressed. Temporarily, Jonathan was released to his father pending an appearance in Family Court and no school officials would be arrested at that time.

So whose fault was this incident? Was it the 14 year old who felt he had no recourse and just couldn't take it anymore? Was it the fault of the football player who the school allowed to bully the boy without fear of consequences? Was it the school district employees who did nothing to help Jonathan with the problem? I'll bet you are tempted to use those infamous words, "There's enough blame to go around" aren't you? Not me.

When school officials place the blame for the high amount of bullying and school violence on anyone but themselves they are using offense as a defense. If school officials do not want to get the police involved from the start, then they need to take on the role of the police in the schools.

Think about what happens in grownup world. If one of these school officials were to be harassed and intimidated while eating at a restaurant, the way the boy was harassed in the lunchroom, what would they do? They would call the police or ask the management to do so. That's what they would do. The police handle these situations in grownup world. In situations where there are no police available to stop the violence, some grownups choose to run just like Jonathan did originally. Other grownups choose to fight just like Jonathan did eventually.

Jonathan did not have the option of calling 911 for help. In fact, he was not even allowed to carry his cell phone in school. Parents expect that the school employees, teachers, and administrators, will provide their children with a safe educational environment. The New York State Penal Law Section 260.10, Sub. 2 codified this ethic. The school officials in this case behaved immorally, unethically, and illegally.

They knew right from wrong (morality). Yet they found something more important to do than protect a child from harm. They knew what was expected of them as custodians of his safety (ethics). That didn't motivate them to take action either and they had no fear of consequences. All the school assemblies and non-violent conflict resolution programs have done nothing over the past 30 years to alleviate this problem. Some people would even argue that school violence is worse than ever. Bullying and cyber bullying in particular will continue to plague schools until people start applying Real Fact of Life # 5 to the problem.

There was a time in recent history when a student could come to school bearing evidence of child abuse, neglect, or maltreatment and those cases would go mostly unreported. The reason the cases went unreported is completely logical. First of all, no one was required to report cases of child abuse, neglect, or maltreatment. The problem had inertia working in its side. Secondly, there were no negative consequences if a school official "failed to see" the evidence. Third, school officials who chose to become involved and make a report were subject to lawsuit should the report be erroneous. The idea that the school district could be sued caused school districts to discourage their employees from making a report, unless the official was really sure that the abuse, neglect, or maltreatment actually occurred.

In this situation there were negative consequences for trying to do the right thing and there were positive consequences for doing the wrong thing. It is the perfect behavioral model for perpetuating a problem, whatever that problem might be.

The New York State legislature successfully addressed the issue by adding a section to the Family Court Act. The first thing the new section of law did was to specifically designate which school officials were required to report. Then the legislature made it consequential if a school official "failed to see" evidence of child abuse, neglect, or maltreatment. From that point forward, if a reasonable person should have seen the evidence and the school official did not report it, that official could lose their professional license. Finally, the legislature indemnified both the reporting person and the school district from lawsuits if the report turned out to be erroneous.

This approach to the problem of child abuse, neglect, and maltreatment proved to be very successful in bringing cases of abuse to the courts where they are dealt with appropriately. It is surprising how much evidence of abuse the school officials began to see when their careers depended on them seeing it and they no longer had to worry about being sued for making a mistake about it.

The same issues that de-motivated school officials from reporting suspected cases of child abuse, neglect, or maltreatment are at work in the bullying/mental health problem. Instead of re-trying approaches to the problem that have been unsuccessful, why not apply a solution that has already proven to be successful? The school officials' behavioral issues are the same in both situations. Therefore, there is every reason to believe that a similar solution would significantly reduce the incidence of bullying and school violence.

Bullying is a petty offense called Harassment. It is punishable by up to 15 days in jail. When bullying results in a physical injury, it becomes a crime called Assault. If the bullying puts the victim in fear of a serious physical injury, it becomes a crime called Menacing. Both of these crimes are Class "A" Misdemeanors. Class "A" Misdemeanors are punishable by up to one year in jail.

"Cyber bullying" is a crime right off the bat. It is a form of Aggravated Harassment, a Class "A" Misdemeanor. Persons over 16 who commit Assault, Menacing, or Aggravated Harassment (cyber bullying) can be arrested and prosecuted. Those under 16 who commit those acts can be custodialized and then dealt with by the Family Court.

      My point is that we already have the appropriate tools to deal effectively with bullying and school violence. There is no need to reinvent the wheel. Bullies know right from wrong. Morality does not stop them. Bullies know what is expected of them as students. Ethics does not stop them. Watch how getting locked up (the fear of consequences) will stop bullying behavior in its tracks. It is not as complicated an issue as some would have you believe. It just requires political will.

CHAPTER 20
THE REAL McCOYS

During the late 19th and early 20th centuries the robber barons and other captains of industry built summer homes just outside of New York City. Some wanted to enjoy lavish parties, polo matches, and other high society pursuits. Others sought a more secluded and quiet summer lifestyle. Until the rise of the Hamptons many years later, the location of choice for those seeking a quiet summer was a secluded and heavily wooded Hamlet on the bay.

Each of these two and three story sprawling mansions is situated on about 2 square acres of property. The mansions in the Hamlet certainly rival the ones in Newport, Rhode Island, and they have the added advantage of being occupied and well cared for to the present day. Today, if you are the right sort, you might be able to purchase one for about 16 million dollars. That is, if anyone was selling.

The police officers in our precinct have nicknamed the Hamlet the "retirement community." This is because very little ever goes on there. The cops assigned to patrol that sector are selected for their special temperament. They must be morally and ethically flexible to accommodate the eccentricities and idiosyncrasies that are sometimes more overtly expressed by people of wealth, privilege and power.

The people who live in the Hamlet are old money and they are very well connected. For instance, if a resident comes to believe that a police officer patrolling the Hamlet is not a good fit, it usually only takes one phone call to a judge, or powerful politician, to have a more suitable officer assigned to that sector. It would be extremely rare for someone who lived in the Hamlet to be arrested in the Hamlet. An accommodation is usually made to spare the family any embarrassment or legal entanglement.

There was a time, later in my career with the County, when I was assigned to patrol the sector that adjoined the Hamlet. One time, I responded to a call there from a resident who had a squirrel in her basement. She called 911 and actually told them that she had a squirrel, not an intruder, in her basement. Instead of telling her that she needed to call an exterminator, the Department dispatched a police officer to respond. You see, she lived in the Hamlet.

I was assigned to the call since the officer on duty in the Hamlet that day was on his meal period at the time. When I arrived at the house, I verified the nature of the call. Then I told the homeowner that she had three choices. I could try to club the squirrel to death with my baton, but I might miss and break something. I could spray it with my mace, but then she would have to evacuate the house until the spray wore off, or I could shoot at it until I hit it. If none of those choices were satisfactory she would have to call an exterminator. I know what you are thinking and you are correct. I was not a good fit for the Hamlet.

Before the start of each tour of duty I would get together with the officer who was patrolling the Hamlet on that tour of duty for a cup of coffee. We would shoot the breeze and exchange information about what was going on in the precinct before starting to patrol our respective sectors. One morning I had coffee with Artie Malone who was assigned to the Hamlet. Artie had over 20 years as a police officer under his belt and he was just the sort of officer that the residents appreciated. He was like a concierge. I used to tease him and ask him how many of their dogs he walked this week. I would also remind him that the law required that he pick up after the dogs. Artie had a good sense of humor and he knew he also had a good gig. Artie and I had a cordial and supportive relationship.

Right after coffee that day he told me he needed to drive to the stationhouse to get the mechanic to look at the air conditioning unit in his police car. He said it should take no more than an hour because either the mechanic would fix it quickly, or he would have to schedule the car for repair. In the second event, Artie would take out a spare car to use for patrolling the Hamlet. We both knew that radio would assign me to cover his sector if there were any calls.

It was 8:15 AM when Artie left for the stationhouse. At about 8:45 a call came over for an "Aided Case – Possible Dead One, at 14 Beachwood Crossing" in the Hamlet. Radio assigned me, another officer who would be coming from some distance away and an ambulance to respond to the call. The ambulance was necessary because there are many times when the person calling 911 thinks someone is dead and they are actually still alive. Therefore, radio assigns an ambulance to respond. It is better to be safe than sorry. I was the primary car on this call and I was expected to give the ambulance a disregard if it turned out the person was really dead.

 I had never been to that home before but I found it within 5 minutes. When I got there I saw a gardener's truck that was parked in the street in front of the home. I told radio that I had arrived and asked who the complainant was. Radio said he identified himself as the gardener. His name was Jose Avilla. I asked for him and one of the men working in the front of the house pointed me toward a small thin man giving orders to another man. Mr. Avilla saw me walking toward him and moved toward me also.

 I reached out to shake his hand and while doing so asked, "Are you Mr. Avilla?"

 He shook my hand and said, Yes, I am the one who called."

 I asked him where the dead person was and he told me to follow him toward the rear of the house. The place was huge; three stories and spread out.

 As we were walking, Mr. Avilla said, "You got to see this officer, it looks like the guy died playing cards with himself."

 As we turned the corner at the rear of the house I saw a large solarium protruding off the back of the building on the ground level. It was an octagon shaped room. It would have been about 20 feet in diameter if it were a circle. The room was all glass from floor to ceiling and the roof was made of glass also. The glass panels were all casement windows. They were the old fashion type from the mid 20th century. Because of the way the glass sections were separated by the black metal frames, from a distance the solarium looked like a leaded glass lampshade. There were three doors. One was in the rear leading out to the back yard. The other two doors were one the sides and the whole structure was surrounded with beautiful landscaping and old fashion cobblestone walks.

As we were walking I asked Mr. Avilla how long ago it was that he spotted the guy. He said it was about 10 minutes ago just before he called 911. I did the math and concluded that time was of the essence if this guy wasn't dead yet. I asked him if he rang the doorbell or knocked to see if anyone was home. He said he did both of those things and there was no answer. He thought the dead guy might have been the only one home.

Mr. Avilla led me right up to the solarium and pointed at one of the casement windows for me to look inside. The solarium was void of furniture. In fact, it was completely empty except for a man sitting at an old fashion wooden card table. His was the only chair at the table. Beyond him, over his shoulder, I could see a large old oak door that lead from the solarium into the house.

The man appeared to be in his 70s. He was holding a deck of cards in his left hand and a single card in his right hand. Cards were spread out in front of him on the table. The configuration of the cards made it clear that he was playing solitaire. His head was tilted downward as though he was looking at the cards, but it was tilted a little too far forward. He looked like he had fallen asleep in the middle of a game or that he died that way.

I couldn't resist the urge to tap on the window and call out, "Hey, are you ok?"

Before I even finished speaking Mr. Avilla said that he had tried that already. I commented that maybe the guy was narcoleptic. Maybe he really did just fall asleep. By that time two of Mr. Avilla's men had wandered over to us to see what we were doing. I heard the radio crackle. Then the Advanced Medical Technician (AMT), who was driving the ambulance, told the dispatcher that he had arrived at the scene. The cop they sent to assist me, Dave Drayer, did the same.

As the primary car assigned, I would be calling the shots and taking the responsibility for the call. I went over the air and told both of them that I had a man slumped over a table, possibly dead, possibly asleep, in the solarium at the rear of the house. I told the ambulance driver to bring a trundle (rolling stretcher) to the rear of the building. I asked

Dave to see if anyone was home and to try to see if he could find a way into the house without having to break in.

If the old guy actually was in distress, there was no time to find someone with a key. We would need to act quickly and the solarium doors were locked. Whenever the police have to break into a place we try to do it with as little damage as possible. We will break a window before we kick in a door and we will force a lock before we break a window, etc. That is why we never go anywhere without a knife, preferably a Swiss army knife, which I just happen to have. I saw a place on a window frame that I thought I could jimmy. Dave told me he could find no access either.

By that time Eric, the AMT, had come to the rear of the house and was waiting with the trundle and his medical bag to do his thing. I managed to jimmy the window lock and after about 30 seconds, I was inside. I immediately opened the side door to the solarium nearest the AMT. He rushed in with his bag while Dave and I brought in the trundle.

In about 10 seconds Eric announced, "False alarm guys. This is a mannequin."

Dave and I looked at each other and I questioned, "A mannequin? Are you sure?"

Eric said in an exasperated tone, "Yea Mike, I'm sure. I think I've done this just a couple of times already in my career. This thing is made of plastic or plasticized wax or something, but it is not alive."

I had to see for myself. I had seen some bizarre things in my day but this was way up there on the list. I walked over next to the table and squatted down to get a close look at this thing. I have to tell you it looked incredibly real. The features were distinct. It had hair exactly where it was supposed to be and from my squatting position I could see that the eyes were open. I guess he was supposed to be looking at the cards. It was also covered with a fine layer of dust that I could not see until I got close to it.

I had to touch it to see what it felt like. I poked the cheek with my finger and it was hard. It felt like plaster to me, but I guessed that is what a wax figure feels like. Dave joined me at the table and was also looking closely at this thing. He touched its hair and felt it like I did. We were all dumbfounded by what we were looking at. None of us said anything for a good 30 seconds.

Then Eric announced that he was taking the ambulance back on patrol.

He said, "If you guys don't mind I would like to get to a central location in the precinct in case a *real* human being needs my help.

Dave and I looked at Eric and we both smiled at his sarcasm. Then I waved Eric on.

Dave said he was going back on patrol also and I said, "OK Dave. Just let Mr. Avilla know what's going on as you leave. I'll start taking care of the paperwork."

I was still squatting down looking at this thing. Just as I began to stand up I noticed something that blew my mind. I thought I saw ridges, loops, and swirls on the fingertips and lines all over the palms of the hands. I looked closer and yelled to Dave before he left the solarium.

I said, "Dave, wait a minute. Do you have reading glasses or a magnifying glass in your car?"

He said, "I have reading glasses right here, why?"

I said, "Can I borrow them I want to look at something."

He brought me over the glasses and I used them to magnify the palm side of one of the hands without actually touching it. Inside my head I screamed, "Oh my God, this thing has fingerprints!!

I said, "Dave, come over here and look at this. I need to know that I am really seeing this. I think this thing has fingerprints."

I could see the creepiness come over Dave's face and I am sure it came over mine. He took the glasses back from me and put them on. Then he gingerly bent down and leaned his head toward the hand very slowly as though he was afraid the thing would grab him by the hair.

He stood back up, took off his glasses, and said, "This can't be real. This has to be a joke."

We both stood there for a moment looking at the thing and trying to come to terms with an inescapable conclusion. The only way this thing would have actual fingerprints is if it were a corpse.

I said to Dave, "I have to call for a medical examiner. I need someone to look at this thing and tell me whether it's a corpse."

Dave said, "I agree. I think we need to treat this like a crime scene until we find out."

At that time, I put the request over the air for a supervisor, the detectives, and a medical examiner.

While all this was happening, Artie was not a blip on my radar. I had forgotten all about him. Suddenly I heard him on the radio. He was on his way back with a spare car and he told the dispatcher to stand by on the request for the supervisor, detectives, and the medical examiner (ME). I looked at Dave and he looked at me. We both decided not to do anything until Artie got there. We reasoned that he must know something we don't. After all, this is his sector.

When Artie got there he told us that he would take over responsibility for the assignment. He said Dave and I should just go back on patrol and he would handle everything.

I said, "Artie, I am not going anywhere without an explanation. Is this a corpse or not?"

He said, "Yes and no. It is a human body, but it has been taxidermied."

Then he told us the wildest story I had ever heard at that point in my career. Apparently, we were standing in the McCoy house. The original Mr. James McCoy was an extremely wealthy financier who not only survived the 1929 crash, but also anticipated it. During the 1930s, when everyone was going through a depression, Mr. McCoy had tons of cash. He bought works of art and jewels and property for pennies on the dollar. He had a son, Jeffrey McCoy who was a powerful judge during the mid 20th Century. Jeffrey McCoy was part of the original political machine that ran the County back in the day.

According to Artie, Jeffery McCoy managed to get some sort of legal waiver that allowed him to embalm/taxidermy/stuff his father and place him in the house at the table as though he were playing solitaire. The house we were in, according to Artie, had been legally designated a mausoleum. No one has lived there since the old man was placed into his card playing position some 30 years ago. I asked Artie how he knew all this. He said that he heard the story from Frank Deter, a cop who patrolled the Hamlet for 18 years until his retirement 15 years ago. Artie took his place.

Then an inconsistency hit me. If this guy has been visible through the solarium windows for 30 years, why didn't Mr. Avilla report it a long time ago? Why didn't someone else report it? Why today? Mr. Avilla remained behind at the McCoy house while his crew went on to their next customer. I told him he had to wait and speak with the detectives. After all, he was the impetus of all this.

I went outside for a moment to speak with him. He said that he took the business over just this week from the old gardener who passed away of a heart attack. My guess, which turned out to be correct, was that the old gardener was told it was a mannequin when he was hired and never questioned anything after that. Somehow, Mr. Avilla did not get the word. That day was his first time at the McCoy house. He came around the back of the house and saw a guy who looked like he died playing cards.

When I finished speaking with Mr. Avilla I turned my attention to Artie. I told Artie that I appreciated his offer to "take over the assignment" from me, but that I wanted to see it through to its completion, whatever that might be. I told him that I was re-requesting the supervisor, the medical examiner and the detectives because I was not convinced that the story he told me was true.

I said, "Artie, I know you believe the story is true, but I have a stuffed human being sitting here. He is not in a mausoleum. He is in a house. We have to confirm this story. Don't you think it is about time that *somebody* confirmed the story?"

Artie told me that I was going to open a can of worms and that I really didn't want to cross swords with these people. He said that they could have a profound influence on my career, positive or negative. He said if I just dropped this, he would speak to the right people about me and I could probably have my choice of assignments within the police department.

"Besides," he said, "Everything is on the up and up, so there is no harm and no foul."

I thanked him for his offer and his warning and I politely refused. Then I put over the request as I originally did before he told the dispatcher to stand by. The place was a crime scene until further notice and everyone but me had to leave the premises. That included Artie and Dave. Dave waited outside the solarium to secure the perimeter of the crime scene. Artie went back on patrol.

I began playing the waiting game. The medical examiner knew there was no urgency and so did the detectives. I needed a place to sit down and do some paperwork. We had determined earlier that the house did not have an alarm system, so I opened the door that led from the solarium into the house and went to find a table or desk or something. I began to believe the part of the story that said the place had not been lived in for 30 years. The dust in the place was thick on everything. I marveled at how much money one would have to spend to keep a place like this up with no one living here. Between the art work and the furniture, I thought I was in a museum.

I sat down in a chair at a hallway table that was in a position to allow me to watch the solarium through the open door. Then I started writing up my notes about what happened so far. After a while I called the Desk Officer to get the ETA on the ME and the Detectives. The Desk Officer called me back and told me it would be about another hour; that I should just sit tight and wait.

Boredom started to set in, so I decided to explore the house further. I asked Dave to guard the open door in the solarium. If anyone showed up, Dave would contact me by radio before allowing him or her access to the crime scene. Then I started to venture about. At one point I went upstairs to the second floor and poked around. I opened each door I passed and poked my head in to take a look and check things out. I had decided that if someone questioned my nosiness, I could justify my roaming around the house by saying that I was searching for more bodies. Sounds bogus right? Wrong!

I opened the door to a room that looked back on the rear of the property and freaked. There was a woman sitting in a chair with her back to me. She was in front of the window facing the woods that were behind the house.

I knew I wasn't going to get an answer, but I asked anyway. "Hello? Police, are you ok?"

There was no answer and no movement. As I entered the room I dreaded having to look another one of these things in the face. I gave the woman a wide berth as I circled to look at her from the front. She was also in her seventies and she was stuffed too. She was sitting there staring out the window with knitting needles in her hands. There was some uncompleted knitting project in her lap. I imagined that they set her up with the unfinished knitting she was doing when she died.

This day had now reached the top of both my surreal and bizarre list. I continued searching the second floor and then the third floor. I found no more bodies. God only knows what might be in the cellar and I wasn't going down there. I would leave that to whoever came to assist me. When I got on the radio and told the dispatcher to notify my Desk Officer that I discovered a second body, I suddenly became a priority. The first person to show up was Artie.

I asked him, "Did you know that they stuffed grandma too? She's upstairs. You wanna go look?"

He said, "No," and just shook his head in disbelief.

He seemed legitimately surprised at the discovery of the second body and I think he finally realized that something had to be done. Sergeant Jake McDonald arrived next. Jake and I had been friends since the Police Academy. He was in my academy class and we had been study partners. I helped him through the Use of Force test after he failed it the first time around. I was very happy when he made Sergeant. He was a good, pragmatic supervisor and I was glad when he showed up.

I briefed Jake on what was happening up to that point.

When I was finished he asked, "So did you eventually check the basement?"

I said, "No Jake, I didn't check the basement and I am not going to check the basement."

He said, "What do you mean? Go down and check the basement for more bodies."

I said emphatically, "I am not going down into the basement! There is probably a whole family stuffed down there and I am not dealing with it. Have someone else go into the basement. I have had enough warped, bizarre shit for one day."

Jake looked surprised by my indignation for just a moment, as did Dave and Artie who were standing there listening to Jake and I talk. Then Jake glanced at my chest full of medals, looked at my face, and started to smile. It was a wry and sarcastic smile. He reached out to my uniform and plucked something off my shirt. I looked at his hand and I did not see anything between his fingers. He withdrew his hand from my shirt and looked at his fingers as though he were holding something that came off my uniform. Then he blew at his fingers, released this imaginary thing into the air and began to pretend to follow it with his eyes as it floated through the air. He turned and looked toward Dave and Artie who were watching him also.

Then he turned back to me and through a laugh he said, "Look at that guys. It's a chicken feather. Mike is growing chicken feathers."

I said 'Fuck you Jake."

Then they all burst out laughing and Jake continued, "Don't worry Mike, I get it. You're afraid to go into the basement aren't you? You're afraid the *zombies* are going to get you. Aren't you? You're a little fraidy-scared cop."

Artie and Dave were laughing out loud now along with the Sergeant.

I started to whine a little. I said, "You know what Jake? Go take a look at this thing. Tell me if it doesn't freak you out and then tell me if you would want to run into more of them down in the cellar? I am telling you, there's probably a whole family of them down there and I'm not dealing with it."

He continued to laugh as Dave and Artie led him into the solarium to check out Mr. McCoy. I followed them. I could see the creepiness come over Jake as he looked at the wrinkles in the skin and the facial features and the glass eyes staring down at the table and the fingerprints.

I said to him, "Go ahead, touch the face. See what it feels like."

Jake said, "I'm not touching that thing," and I knew he understood where I was coming from.

He paused to think a moment and then he said, "Dave, go check out the cellar."

I breathed a sigh of relief and Artie started laughing loudly.

Dave said, "Why me? Its Mike's call and its Artie's sector – and I don't like zombies either"

Then Jake said, "Artie, go back up Dave and don't let the zombies get him."

That's when I started laughing.

I called out to them as they started walking toward the basement door, "Yea, go see if you can find any aunts or uncles or nieces or nephews. Oh, and don't worry, they only come alive after midnight."

It turned out that there were no more bodies in the cellar or the rest of the house. The lady upstairs was James McCoy's wife, Claudia. Her son, Judge Jeffrey McCoy, had her stuffed the same way he did his dad. As the investigation progressed, we discovered that Judge McCoy was also a partner in Lentz, McCoy, and Lederer. The three men owned this very powerful and influential law firm in New York. Judge McCoy passed away two years prior to this incident.

The house and the rest of the estate passed to his son Mark McCoy. Mark was a medical doctor who lived with his family in Connecticut. Mark's mother (Judge McCoy's wife) had passed away years ago. She was buried normally, as was the judge himself. The law firm was managing Judge McCoy's estate. Mark was aware of what his father did to Mark's grandparents and was in a quandary as to what to do about it. For the time being he just let things go on as they always had. He did not account for a change in gardeners. Well, Pandora's Box was now open and there was no putting the secret back in. Or so I thought.

It was amazing how fast things began to move. By the end of the business day, the police department received an order from a judge that prohibited us from disturbing the bodies and ordered us to vacate the premises. The injunction also gagged us against revealing the situation to anyone. It claimed that doing so would cause the house to become a curiosity and the gawkers would "disturb the sanctity of their resting place."

The judge who signed the order determined that all the legal issues surrounding the embalming/taxidermy and display of the bodies were in order. I would occasionally drive by the place every now and then, but I never went into the backyard after that. As far as I know, Mr. James McCoy still sits over his game of solitaire and Mrs. Claudia McCoy still holds her knitting to this day. The cops who are assigned to the Hamlet continue to remain flexible in their morality and ethics in order to accommodate situations like the real McCoys. Life never ceases to amaze me.

CHAPTER 21
TRAFFIC JAMS

In traffic court, like any other court in the United States, you are innocent until proven guilty. However, the circumstances involved in traffic offenses are different from most other offenses. In 96% of traffic court cases the evidence is completely testimonial evidence. The cop says you were speeding, you say you weren't. The cop says you rolled passed the Stop Sign, you say your wheels stopped turning.

Accordingly, if the court did not accept the police officer's word as proof beyond a reasonable doubt, 96% of the time no one would get convicted of traffic offenses. Sure, there are some drivers who might behave ethically without enforcement. There are other drivers who will obey the vehicle and traffic law out of the fear of becoming involved in an accident. However, the overwhelming body of evidence clearly shows that the number of motor vehicle accidents skyrockets when enforcement drops. Obviously, without the fear that they will be convicted, drivers would have little incentive to obey the vehicle and traffic law.

Since the courts *do* accept the officer's word as proof beyond a reasonable doubt, it becomes the defendant's job, or the defendant's lawyer's job, to introduce reasonable doubt. This can seem to some people like you are guilty until proven innocent. Judges are aware of the defendant's vulnerability in traffic court cases. The first way they help defendants is by insuring that the officer is not mistaken. In the case of a speeding ticket for instance, the judge will make sure the prosecution shows that the radar unit was operating properly and that the officer is proficient in its use.

The judges are also very concerned that the officer has no personal grudge against the defendant. The fact that a ticket is written to the new boyfriend of the officer's old girlfriend might cause reasonable doubt in a judge's mind. Lastly, the officer must not have a quota.

Quotas have been illegal in New York State for the past 40 years. Back in the day, the judges and the legislature realized that allowing police managers to impose quotas for tickets was tantamount to putting a bounty on the citizenry. Quotas are corruption prone. A quota tempts a police officer to write tickets that the officer otherwise might not write. Some officers might give in to that temptation if their performance rating depended on it. Judges must be able to conduct traffic trials without the fear that the officer has any reason to lie. That is the only way the judge can have faith in the officer's testimony and accept it beyond a reasonable doubt.

In fact, a traffic court judge once said to me, "As I am listening to both sides testify I seek to answer this question, 'Is there any reason for the officer to lie about what happened?'"

In today's world, if the police managers tried to impose a quota, the police unions would jump on them with both feet. Society has told the police to go out and enforce the vehicle and traffic law. Ethically then, society should believe the police when the officers describe the circumstances of a violation they observed. Additionally, police officers like the idea that they can simply tell the truth and they will be believed. They like the idea that their jobs, or even their assignments within the police department, do not depend on writing a quota of tickets.

I just shake my head when I hear drivers say something to the effect of, "I guess you need to make your quota this month." It is amazing how out of touch those people are. Sometimes I would like to say, "Sorry to disillusion you, but we have not had quotas for 40 years. You got this ticket because you deserved it ... asshole," but I just let it go. I can certainly walk in their shoes. Getting caught is not fun. The problem is that some people who get caught committing traffic infractions blame the officer for catching them. Instead of taking personal responsibility for their behavior, they try to get back at the officer.

Their revenge usually takes the form of false accusations. It is for this reason that I welcomed the introduction of audio and video recording equipment into the VTL enforcement arena. Unfortunately, so far my police department will not adopt the use of recording equipment. The official reason is that the initial cost of the equipment, the maintenance of the equipment, the legal record keeping and the lack of support by the courts, make the technology cost prohibitive.

Without a recording of the exchange between the officer and the motorist, the person making the accusation against the officer can say just about anything without any fear of consequences. The motorist could accuse an officer of soliciting sex in return for not writing the ticket, or accuse the officer of soliciting money in return for not writing the ticket. In turn, unless the accusation is completely absurd, the officer cannot possibly prove that the motorist is lying about what happened. The police cannot force people to take polygraph (lie detector) tests. Even if we did, the courts have ruled that the results of polygraph tests are not admissible as evidence.

Judges know that every time a police officer stops a car for a traffic infraction he or she risks false accusations. Nothing positive happens for police officers when they stop cars for traffic infractions. In fact, it is against the law in New York State for police officers to benefit in any way from writing tickets. They write moving violation tickets because doing so protects life and property. When the judges combine these facts with the lack of quotas, judges can be very confident in the officer's testimony about the event. After all, as the judge said, "Is there any reason for the officer to lie about the incident?" Still, there are always some defendants who will say and do anything to get out of a traffic ticket.

One day, my supervisor assigned me to do several hours of traffic enforcement in the vicinity of a school located in our precinct. The school administration, as well as the local residents, had complained that vehicles were speeding though the 20 mph school zone. I don't particularly like to do car stops. Car stops are inherently dangerous for police officers. Most of the time when a police officer first makes the decision to stop a vehicle, he or she has no way of knowing if the vehicle contains some little old ladies from Pascedena, or a car full of armed thugs. The officer is focused on what the driver just did with the car to violate the VTL. Only when the vehicle is real close does the officer focus on the occupants. Not that it should make a difference. Writing moving violation tickets is a significant part of our job. It goes a long way toward protecting life and property and like everything else that is important, I have learned to do it well.

I am trained and certified to use many types of radar and laser speed measuring devices. Still, my weapon of choice for this task is called the KR-10. It was first manufactured in 1965 and the technology still functions perfectly some 50 years later. It is an ancient weapon. Proficiency in its use requires practice and training. However, just like the Light Saber, in the hands of the Jedi Radar Master it is the only tool required. Every now and then I like to joke with younger officers about how they can keep their lasers and their phasers. The force is with me. I prefer this simple yet deadly accurate enforcement tool.

The KR-10 is a two-piece K-band radar unit that can be attached to the police car. The antenna, which detects the vehicle's speed, is attached to the window. The Base Station, which digests the radar readings and shows the vehicle's speed in the form of LED lights, is placed on the dashboard of the police car. It affords the officer the option of hands free operation and permits him or her to conduct a type of car stop called a "Step-Out."

The Step-Out is a much safer way of stopping cars than chasing speeding vehicles with a police car. Chases sometimes result in the officer becoming involved in an accident. Sometimes, the vehicle being chased becomes involved in an accident. Other times, innocent drivers bump into things as they rush to get out of the way of the police car. Remember, the police car is pushing its way through traffic with its lights and siren on trying to catch up to the speeder.

When an officer conducts a Step-Out car stop, the police car is stationary. The officer steps out into the roadway, raises his or her hands into a "Stop" position, and stops traffic. Then the officer directs the offending vehicle to the curb and starts the traffic moving again. In my 30 years of policing I have heard of many accidents that occurred during chases. I have been involved in two of them. However, it is rare for an officer to be hit while conducting a Step-Out car stop.

There is good reason for this. The operator of the vehicle being pulled over only has three choices. Choice one, the driver can stop for you and follow your directions to the curb. Choice two, the driver can drive around you and keep on going. Since the law-abiding vehicles have all stopped at the officer's direction, there are no vehicles between the officer and the subject vehicle that just sped past you. You jump in the police car, put it in gear, and the ensuing chase is reasonably safe. If the driver actually tries to run you over, you simply "step out" of the way. Since the other cars have stopped for you, you can chase the car down on a wide-open road and put the driver in jail for a long, long time.

When police officers set up to do speed enforcement they choose a vantage point from which they can see the vehicles passing the speed limit sign. Then the officer tests the radar unit for accuracy using whatever method the manufacturer of that particular unit prescribes. The process is called calibration. In the case of a school zone, the officer also verifies that school is open at that particular time. Most judges do not like to rule on cases where the offender is driving less than 10 mph over the limit. On this particular day, I made the arbitrary decision not to stop vehicles unless I estimated that their speed was more than 20 mph over the speed limit.

I attached the radar antenna to the side of the police car and pointed it down the road. Then I placed the base station on the dashboard of the car so that I could stand outside the car, look through the windshield, and read the speeds of the vehicles coming at me. I had already written several speeding tickets when I looked down the road and saw another car coming toward me at a relatively high rate of speed. I estimated the speed to be 45 mph. When I glanced at the radar unit, the radar unit verified that the vehicle was actually going 47 mph. The car was traveling faster than my estimate.

The radar beam on the KR-10 can reach out to 1000 feet. That is more than the length of three football fields. When I made the decision to stop that car it was still too far away for me to identify the type of vehicle, the plate number, or who was driving. All I saw was a dark colored SUV coming toward me. Another benefit of doing step-outs is that you never lose sight of the vehicle. Often during chases, vehicles try to evade the police by turning on to side streets and hiding if they can. It was not until the car was about 100 feet away and slowing down for me that I was able to see the driver for the first time. It wasn't until the SUV was about 50 feet away that I could finally read the plate. The driver was a male, white, about 36 years old.

    I directed the SUV to the curb and then started traffic moving again. For my own safety I chose to approach the car from the passenger side and tapped on the window with my hand.

    When the driver lowered the window I went into my standard spiel. "Good morning sir. My radar was tracking you at 47 mph and the speed limit here in the school zone is only 20. I need to examine your driver's license."

    The driver took his wallet from his back pocket and gave me his license.

    As he was doing so he said, "You must be mistaken. I wasn't speeding."

    I did not respond to what he said.

    When he handed me his license I said, "Thank you, and please show me proof that this vehicle is insured."

    The driver opened the glove box and took out a letter from his insurance company. I examined it and verified the vehicle was currently insured.

    He then iterated, "Maybe you got me confused with someone else. I am telling you, I wasn't speeding."

    I made eye contact with the driver and said, "I understand what you just told me. Thank you. Please remain where you are. I will be with you shortly."

    I walked back to the police car, sat down and began to write the ticket. The courts have ruled that a police officer can take up to 20 minutes to write a ticket. This is primarily because the courts want us to conduct computer checks on the driver and the vehicle. For a myriad of reasons, this takes time. We are required to reasonably determine whether the operator's license is valid, whether the car is properly registered, and whether or not the vehicle has been stolen. In this case, I completed the process in less than seven minutes.

I walked back to the SUV and said, "All right sir. There is an instruction form here that explains how to handle everything. You can go now."

As I began to walk away the driver said, "Excuse me. Why did you give me a ticket? I told you I was not speeding. I was not going more than 20 mph."

I took the three steps back until I was again standing right outside the front passenger window of the car.

There was a short pause and then the driver said with exasperation, "You know what? I want to see your radar. You show me where I was going 47 mph."

Rather than get into an argument over what he expected to 'see', I said, "Sir, we obviously differ over the facts and you are not going to examine my radar."

Then I continued with the party line, "The courts ruled long ago that issues like this are not to be dealt with at this time. Your next legal move is to plead not guilty to the ticket. When we are in court and I am under oath in front of a judge, you can conduct any examination the court will allow. I will also try to answer any question you have about this process, but not out here in the street."

The driver became indignant and said, "Why can't we deal with this now? Do you have something better to do? Do you have something to hide?"

I responded, "Sir, I am going to go back to stopping speeders now and you need to get on your way. You can bring all of this stuff up in court."

Again, I began to walk away from the SUV, but the driver called out, "I'll leave in a few minutes. I want to read this instruction form to make sure I don't have any other questions."

I walked back to the SUV. I leaned down and looked into the car from the passenger side.

I looked the driver in the eyes and said, "Sir, you can pull your car up about 50 feet and read anything you want for as long as you want. I am going to be pulling another car over very shortly and I will need this space to do so. I am now ordering you to move your vehicle from this location ... right now!"

He said, "You chose to pull me over here. I will leave when I feel I have all my questions answered."

I responded, "Really! I am going to give you until I need that spot to rethink your decision. If you are still here when I stop the next speeder, I am going to let that car go. Then I am going to lock you up for refusing to obey my lawful order to move your vehicle. I am also going to charge you with Obstructing Governmental Administration. After that, I will move your car myself when I impound it for safekeeping. You are about to go from a couple of pieces of paper to thousands of dollars in legal fees"

That said, I walked back to my position in front of the police car and began to look for speeders again. As soon as I stepped out to stop another car, he put his car in gear and drove off. It is important to note that throughout this entire incident the driver never moved from the driver's seat.

The next time I saw the driver of the SUV was when I went to court.

I knew I was in for trouble when the prosecutor came over to me and said, "Officer Rudolph, I think we have a problem. I just offered this guy an equipment violation as a plea bargain and he said 'No'. It would have only been a $75.00 fine and no points."

I asked the prosecutor, "Does he know that the fine for his speed is $280.00 plus three points?"

The prosecutor nodded yes and then said, "The guy told me that if I did not dismiss the case, he was going to expose you in court."

I asked, "Expose me in court? Expose what?"

She continued, "The guy says you cursed at him and that you assaulted him by pushing him down in the street. He said that when he threatened to report you, you told him that if he ever said a word you would have your cop friends go after him and his family."

I knew that the prosecutor wasn't kidding, but I couldn't help asking her, "Are you serious?"

She said, "I kid you not. What do you want to do?"

I stood there thinking about all of the aggravation I was about to face and I took a deep breath. I could see the asshole staring at us from the rear of the reception area. I am sure he knew what we were discussing. I don't see how my face would not have revealed how shocked I was by what I was being told.

I thought for about 10 seconds and then I said to the prosecutor, "Look, this thing is going to wind up at Internal Affairs one way or the other. Let's go to trial. There is nothing special about this case except a lying piece of shit defendant."

The prosecutor nodded in agreement and she set up the trial for that afternoon.

Before the trial, the prosecutor told the judge about the defendant's complaints. She also told the judge that the defendant refused a plea bargain and instead sought a quid-pro-quo (you do for me and I'll do for you) prior to going to trial. Apparently, the prosecutor, like me, also learned that whoever gets to mom first gets believed.

The judge told the prosecutor, "We need to cross all our T's and dot all our I's on this one. These charges against the officer will stand or fall in another arena. I want this trial to be about whether or not the defendant is guilty of speeding. I will tolerate no drama in my courtroom."

The prosecution always presents its case first. My testimony depicted the circumstances of the case exactly as they occurred. However, I ended my testimony with the issuance of the ticket. I did not bring up what was said after I handed him the ticket. As far as I was concerned, what happened after the issuance of the ticket was not relevant to the case.

When I was finished testifying, the prosecutor asked me, "Officer have you ever met this defendant prior to your encounter over this issue?"

I responded, "No ma'am. I do not recall ever meeting him before this incident."

Then the judge said to the defendant, "You may now cross examine the officer. This means that you may ask him questions and I will determine if those questions are appropriate. You may not make statements. You will have the opportunity to take the stand and tell your side of the story after the officer leaves the witness stand. Do you understand?"

The defendant said, "Yes judge."

Then the judge said, "All right then, begin."

The defendant asked, "Do you always tell people to go fuck themselves when they ask to see your radar?"

I responded quickly to the accusation, "I never told you to go fuck yourself."

Just as I finished saying that the prosecutor jumped up and said, "I object Your Honor. This question has nothing to do with whether or not the defendant committed the offense."

The judge said, "Sustained!"

Then the defendant asked, "Is it proper police procedure for you to push people to the ground when they ask you for your name and badge number?"

This time I hesitated before answering to give the prosecutor the chance to object again, but instead the judge spoke out.

He said, "Sir, you obviously have some complaints to make against this officer, but this trial is not the forum for those complaints. Please confine your questions to issues that challenge the assertion that you were speeding 47 mph through a 20 mph school zone. You may make your complaint to the police department after you leave here, if you have not already done so."

The defendant said, "I am sorry judge, but when this cop threatened to have his friends hurt me and my family I knew I had to tell someone. I thought this would be the place to start."

The judge said, "Sir, I repeat, do you have any questions for this officer that have to do with what happened before the ticket was written?"

The defendant thought for a moment and then said, "No sir."

The judge then said, "Officer, you may step down now."

The judge told the defendant that it was the defendant's turn to testify, if he wanted to take the stand. The judge warned the defendant that his testimony must be limited to those issues leading up to the issuance of the ticket, not what happened afterward. The defendant took the stand and testified that he was doing 20 mph, never more than that. He said that he saw me on the side of the road when he entered the school zone and that I frightened him when I "jumped out into traffic like a crazy person."

When he was finished, the prosecutor had the opportunity to cross-examine the defendant.

She asked, "Sir, how do you know you were only doing 20 mph? Were you watching your speedometer the entire time through the school zone?"

The defendant said, "Yes, I never took my eyes off it."

The prosecutor then asked, "Sir, you already testified that you were watching the officer from the time you entered the school zone. You said that you saw him 'jump' out into the roadway to stop traffic. If you were watching your speedometer all that time, how could you see these things?"

The defendant hesitated for a moment and then said, "I am quite capable of doing both."

The prosecutor responded with, "No more questions Your Honor."

The judge told the defendant to step down and return to his seat. Then the judge took about one minute to recap the testimony he just heard.

After that, he said, "I have considered the evidence presented in this case, I find you guilty of speeding 47 mph in a 20 mph school zone."

He gave the defendant the maximum sentence of $280.00 fine and three insurance points.

The defendant stood up and loudly demanded, "I want it on the record what this officer did to me. I want him arrested for pushing me and for threatening my family and me. I want him punished for cursing at me."

The judge told the defendant, "Sir, I will tolerate no more from you. I told you that you had to press your complaint with the police department. Now leave this room immediately or I will have the officer take you into custody, which I am sure he would be happy to do."

The guy actually did make a complaint against me that landed in Internal Affairs. He continued to insist that I cursed at him, pushed him to the ground, and threatened him and his family. After interviewing him, Internal Affairs referred the case back to the precinct. A patrol Sergeant was assigned to handle it. He did a canvass of the area where the incident took place to try to find any witnesses to what the defendant described as a "loud scene." Since the event never occurred, obviously no witnesses were found. The defendant could not *provide* the Sergeant with witnesses either. Apparently he could not convince anyone to conspire with him in making his false report.

The case against me was eventually closed as "Undetermined." It was undetermined because I could not prove the defendant was lying. If we could have proven that the defendant was lying, the case would have been closed as "Unfounded" and the defendant might have been arrested for a crime called Falsely Reporting an Incident.

When you are falsely accused of something it stays with you for a long time. I tried to put a positive spin on this incident by remembering that the accusations could have been much more serious. Since the department and the court treated me fairly, I did not let the incident stop me from doing VTL enforcement. It is still the best way to achieve accident reduction and protect life and property.

I have always looked at false accusations as one of the costs of doing business. Thankfully, the police department does also. However, when I heard the defendant's suggestion I thought it was a good idea. I gave all my "cop friends" his name, address, and plate number. After all, it is only fair that they should be aware of the need to protect themselves from false accusations should they happen to run into him driving around town one day. Payback's a bitch, isn't it?

CHAPTER 22
TRIED BY TWELVE OR CARRIED BY SIX

When I was in high school the passing grade was 65%. When I went to college, people with scholarships had to maintain a GPA of 3.0. That is about a B, or 80%. The passing grade for the courses recruits take in the Police Academy is 75%, except for one. That course is called The Use of Force. The passing grade for the Use of Force course is 100%. On top of that, the police department likes to play baseball. Three strikes and you're out. You get three chances to take the Use of Force test. If you fail the third time, they wash you out of the Academy. How do you like that for pressure?

When you think about it though, it makes a lot of sense. Do you really want a police officer on the street who gets the use of force wrong 25% of the time? I don't think so. I know I would not like to find myself in that 25%. Allowing someone to become a police officer with less than 100% knowledge of the use of force also creates an ethical problem for police management and society at large. If you say it is passable to use force incorrectly a certain percentage of the time, then you really can't blame the cop when he or she gets it wrong once in a while. To do so would be unethical.

One of the things we teach in the Use of Force course is the escalation of force. Through the evolutionary process of court decisions, society's expectation is that a police officer handling a situation will proceed through an escalation of force. In that way, the officer will use the minimum amount of force necessary to achieve a lawful goal. However, there is clear acknowledgment by the courts that the police may always use whatever force proves to be necessary to accomplish that lawful goal. In other words, the police can always use a little more force than the antagonist in order to resolve the problem.

Let's use an arrest as an example. The first level of force is verbal. The officer says, "You are under arrest. Turn around and put your hands behind your back." The criminal responds, "No way man, I didn't do anything wrong." The officer may then proceed to physical force. He or she may use his or her hands to try and make the criminal comply with the verbal command.

The criminal may choose to resist the arrest. He or she may pull away from the officer, or run, or adopt a posture that lets the officer know that the criminal is willing to fight if the officer touches the criminal. Although we are trained in certain defensive martial arts, like Jiu-Jitsu, we are not martial artists. If a person chooses to physically resist the arrest or adopts a menacing posture, the officer is under no obligation to wrestle with that person. Line of duty injuries cost the various municipalities too much money. By legislation and court decisions, the officer is encouraged to go to the next level of force which is a non-lethal weapon.

Non-lethal weapons include the use of a baton, chemical sprays such as mace or pepper spray, or a tazer device. If the baton is used, the officer tries to aim for a part of the criminal's body that will not result in a serious physical injury. Chemical sprays are designed to force criminals to close their eyes. People are much easier to manipulate into handcuffs when they are disoriented by their inability to see. The Taser is a type of device that discharges electricity into the subject and renders him or her physically compliant. The non-lethal weapon of choice is made by considering all of the facts and circumstances. Certain physical environments can limit the officer's ability to use certain non-lethal weapons.

The escalation of force sounds clean and neat, but sometimes things escalate so fast that it is hard to see the progression of force. For instance, after saying "No way man, I didn't do anything wrong" the person being arrested might produce a weapon, and start heading toward the officer.

In situations like that, officers may not have the time, or the safe location, to respond to this kind of threat with non-lethal weapons. It has been well documented that people who have been shot several times still manage to close the distance between themselves and the officers and attack the officers with whatever weapon they may be holding at the time. In cases like that, the cop will check off physical force and non-lethal force in a microsecond. The officer may then shoot the person to keep him or herself from being stabbed.

Article 35 of the New York State Penal Law deals with this issue. It states that if a person being arrested causes the officer to reasonably believe that the person being arrested is about to use some form of deadly force to resist the arrest, the officer is empowered to use deadly force against that person. Deadly force is any force, depending how it is used, that is readily capable of producing death, or a serious physical injury.

The Use of Force test consists of three parts. There is a written portion where the recruit is tested on his or her knowledge of the laws and court decisions that inform the use of force. The second portion of the test is a video examination in which the recruits watch reenactments of use of force decisions that police officers have made in the past. The recruit is then expected to determine if the use of force was appropriate or inappropriate and explain why.

The third component of the test is a giant video game called the Firearms Training Simulator (FATS). It consists of an IMAX type of life-size surround screen on which a computer projects shoot or don't shoot scenarios. The recruit is armed with a regulation weight and size service weapon that is loaded with high tech blanks. When the recruit fires his or her weapon, the computer records both the number of shots and where the shots went.

There is a small cadre of instructors who teach the Use of Force course. They are particularly skilled in differentiated learning techniques. If a recruit fails the test the first time, they put their heads together and create a tutoring program that is tailored to that recruit's particular learning style. Care is taken to make sure that the tutoring program does not give the recruit any special testing accommodations. The real world does not come with special testing accommodations. It is in the real world that the officer will be applying what he or she has learned in the Use of Force course.

You would think, after the intense vetting process to weed out power trippers, bigots, adrenaline junkies and cowards, and after the rigors of the Use of Force course, that no innocent people would ever be shot. Yet every now and then you will hear, through one form of media or another that a police officer has shot an innocent person. Thankfully, it does not happen often, but it does happen occasionally so we decided to study the problem.

What the law enforcement community discovered was that there are two situations in which an innocent person is more likely to get shot than any other situation. Oddly enough, what leads up to the innocent person getting shot is ultimately under the control of the person who gets shot.

On the day that I present this block of instruction I enter the classroom wearing a business suit and carrying a gym bag. I put the gym bag on the desk and stare out at a sea of faces. A Police Academy class usually consists of about 30 recruit police officers dressed in gray uniforms and, unlike the other courses they take; they are paying 100% attention. This block of instruction is part of the Use of Force course. They know their careers and maybe even their lives depend on learning what I am teaching this day.

After the standard introductions and teacher/student housekeeping chores I say, "I am sure you all realize what will happen to you if you shoot an innocent person, but I am going to tell you again because it bears repeating. First of all, if you liked being a cop, kiss the job good-bye. You will be probably be looking for another way to support yourself and your loved ones. Secondly, if you own a house, you might kiss that goodbye too. You will get sued and the court will put a lien on your house. The court will also take whatever else you own that has value. Then they will garnish your future wages from whatever job you may get. All of this will be to pay for the earning potential of the person whose life you took. Finally, you will most likely stand trial for homicide."

"With all this in mind, how many of you, because you are afraid of shooting an innocent person, have already made the decision that you are not going to fire your weapon until you see the bad guy's gun?"

A number of people will always raise their hands. I tell one of them to stand up and come to the front of the classroom. I open my bag of tricks on the desk and take out two cap guns. I give one to the recruit and I tuck the other cap gun into my waistband behind my back.

Then, like a movie director, I say, "OK, here's the scene. You are the cop. I am the guy who fits the description of the guy who just stuck up the 7/11 and shot the clerk in the face with a small caliber handgun."

As I am saying that I take the gun from the small of my back, show it to the class, and place it back again.

I continue, "You see me on the street. You draw your weapon, point it at me and say, "Police – Don't Move!" (All of which the courts have ruled to be reasonable and necessary police procedure.) But remember, we are playing by your rules. You cannot shoot me until you see my gun. OK, whenever you're ready"

I start walking across the front of the classroom like I was minding my own business.

At some point the recruit calls out, "Police – Don't Move."

I stop, turn toward the recruit, and very slowly put my hand behind my back. I get a nice firm grip on the gun. The recruit is focused on my arm, waiting to see the gun. I pull it from behind my back and BANG! I shoot the recruit before he or she can pull the trigger. The recruit is standing there, with the gun pointed at me, finger on the trigger, focused on my arm, and I shoot him or her *before* the recruit can pull the trigger.

Invariably, either the recruit of someone else in the class says, "Wow, you're fast."

When they do, I respond, "No, I'm not. I do not practice this. The fact is that action is approximately ¾ of a second faster than the fastest reaction. It takes a minimum of ¾ of a second for your eyes to send a picture of the threat to your brain, for your brain to send a message to your hand, and for your muscles to contract making your finger pull the trigger. Now let's try it again and see if you can be faster this time."

We try it again.

The recruit calls out, "Police – Don't Move."

Again, I take my time reaching behind my back. This time I grab my wallet from my back pocket. Just as I am bringing my arm to the front – BOOM! The recruit shoots me.

I say, "Well that's nice. You just shot an innocent man trying to show you his identification. Remember, we are playing by your rules. You cannot shoot until you see the gun. Now let's try it again."

Again, the recruit calls out, "Police – Don't Move!"

This time I get a firm grip on the gun again and BANG! I kill the recruit again. About 75% of the time the recruit will cheat and shoot me back, but it doesn't matter. The point is made. I shot first and from a distance that would make it very hard to miss. He or she is dead and everybody in the class knows it.

Over 200 years worth of dead law enforcement officers has shown us that if we wait to see the gun, we get shot. I am sure some of you have seen those old cowboy movies and TV shows where the good guy takes the moral high ground and lets the bad guy reach for his gun first. I doubt that anything like that ever really happened. If it did, the only way the good guy survived the encounter was if the "bad" guy was also a "bad" shot. No one in his or her right mind would be a police officer if he or she had to wait to see the gun. Still, society does need some of us to be police officers and to protect life and property, so the courts threw us a bone.

The courts ruled that it you identify yourself by saying "POLICE," and you tell the person what to do so they don't get shot, "DON'T MOVE," and you are pointing your gun at them (the universal symbol for this is very serious), and they still put their hands where you can't see them, you can shoot that person.

The reason the courts ruled that you can shoot that person, is because the alternative, which is to ask the police officer to stand there and get shot, is an unreasonable thing to ask a police officer to do.

The courts ruled that the police cannot shoot a person if the person runs from them. The courts also ruled that the police cannot shoot a person if they do something like scratch their head. It is all about the person putting their hands where the officer cannot see their hands, and who controls where their hands go? They do.

The second situation where innocent people are more likely to get shot is somewhat similar to the first. I make a different recruit stand up and come to the front of the room. I give the recruit the cap gun and leave mine in my bag of tricks.

Then I say, "You have the same kind of situation. You are the cop and I am the guy who fits the description of the guy who shot the 7/11 clerk. You see me and say, "Police – Don't Move." OK, whenever you are ready."

This time when the recruit says "Police – Don't Move," I turn and face him or her. I raise my hands on either side of my body to about shoulder height. Some would call it the universal sign of surrender. Then, with some quickness of step, I walk right toward the recruit. Try to keep in mind, that from the time the recruit says Police-Don't' Move to the time I start to kill him or her is no more than three seconds. It goes much slower when I explain it.

As I walk toward him or her, the recruit's brain senses danger and he or she starts saying things like, "halt" or "keep your distance" or "stop or I'll shoot." The variance in commands is based on the fact that we don't teach standard verbal commands after "Police-Don't Move." However, we do teach police officers to respond to "Police – Don't Move" with "Police – Don't Shoot."

As I get closer, the recruit is thinking, "Well I can't retreat. I am a cop and I am supposed to arrest this person. I can't shoot him because then everyone watching will say 'Oh look at that trigger happy cop. He just shot someone with their hands in the air trying to surrender.'"

Before the recruit can solve his or her problem, I get close enough to reach out with my left hand, grab the barrel of the gun, and push it toward the ceiling. The recruit usually pulls the trigger, but because action is so much faster than reaction, the barrel is pointed at the ceiling when the cap goes off. The recruit's brain is now screaming "Oh My God He Grabbed My Gun!" and the recruit focuses all of his or her attention on that fact.

At the same time I am grabbing the gun with my left hand, I reach out with my right hand and flick the recruit in the throat with my fingers. That flick represents my fist punching the recruit in the throat and crushing his or her windpipe. It is easy to do because the recruit has focused all attention on the gun. Now all I have to do is keep the barrel pointed away from me. Certainly, the recruit tries to pull the gun out of my hand, but it only takes seconds in a real situation for the throat to swell and for the cop to start to choke. As the cop releases his or her grip on the gun, the bad guy can take it and blow the cop's brains out with it.

In the real world, I would have killed this cop and I did not have a weapon to start with. More importantly, I am not Jackie Chan. It took no special practice to do it. Prison guards observe inmates actually *practicing* this kind of stuff all the time. That is part of another great misnomer – Correctional Facility. The only thing that gets corrected is the criminals' sloppy habits. That way, when the inmate gets out, he or she is less likely to get caught next time and more likely to hurt police officers.

Again, no one in their right mind would be a police officer if they had to put up with what just happened to this recruit. So once again the courts threw us a bone. They ruled that if we do the "Police – Don't Move" thing with our gun drawn and someone gets in our personal space where they can assault us we can shoot them. Why? The reason is because the alternative, which is to stand there and be murdered with one of our own weapons, is an unreasonable thing to ask a police officer to do. Just like in the other situation, the person we confront is in control of whether he or she gets in our personal space.

Make no mistake, even though it may be a righteous shooting resulting from the situations I just described, we will still get sued and we will most likely stand trial. However, with some decent witnesses, the right political wind, and some reasonable people on the jury, it might not be a career-ending event.

When I am finished with my demonstration there is usually someone in the class who disbelievingly asks, "How often does something like that really happen?" If no one asks the question, I bring up the issue myself. I tell the class that it happens more often than you might think and then I tell them this story.

I pulled a guy over for running a Stop Sign one day. He committed the violation while I was right behind him in my police car. I was thinking that the guy was either oblivious to me being behind him in the big old well marked police car, or he was pulling my tail for some sinister reason.

I knew full well that there are some people who have committed suicide by cop. They are usually armed to insure that the police will shoot them, and sometimes they like to take the cop with them on their trip into the great beyond. There have been other situations in which gang recruits make their bones by shooting cops. Getting pulled over is a sure way to get a shot at one. I was hoping the motorist was just oblivious, but I was also on guard.

I pulled my car in behind his in a standard car stop configuration. I opened my door and stepped into the street. Before I could move any further, the driver opened his door and came rushing back at me looking left and right as he approached. He was walking toward me at a very quick pace and when he put his hand behind his back I expected him to draw a gun and blow me away.

I screamed, "Police-Don't Move," drew my weapon and took aim at him, but I didn't shoot.

When he finally realized that he was in the kill zone, he was right at my car door, wallet in hand, and staring at the business end of my 40 caliber Sig. I had taken two steps back to put some distance between us and I started giving him verbal commands to not move, and to put his hands way above his head. I then circled around him and patted him down quickly for weapons before I holstered up. The adrenalin was rushing through my body and I started screaming at him.

"What the hell is wrong with you? Why would you do something like that? Everything you did made me think you were about to attack me. Don't you ever rush at a police officer like that again and for God's sake keep your hands where the cop can see them."

When I am finished with that story, I tell the recruits of another situation. I had pulled a car over for speeding. As I was asking the driver for his license, he quickly reached right under the driver's seat for something. I expect people to travel with their wallets in their pockets. I have seen them carrying their wallets in their coats, their hand bags, and even putting their wallets in their center console or glove box. Under the seat is where bad guys often keep their guns. When the driver reached under the seat without warning, my adrenaline spiked, but my reaction to his action was naturally too slow. When he pulled his wallet from under his seat and turned toward me I had not even cleared my gun from its holster. If he wanted to shoot me, I was dead.

Recruits come to understand that they will be facing dilemmas like these on a regular basis. They need to think about all of the ramifications. Whether they choose to shoot, or not shoot, they will live or die with the consequences. During one of my presentations of this material a recruit, who happened to be a former police officer from another department, asked me why I didn't shoot the first guy. He reminded me and informed the class of the oldest law enforcement axiom.

"It is better to be tried by twelve, than to be carried by six," he said.

I told him and the class that I didn't shoot for two reasons. First, I honestly was worried about the consequences I would face if I shot this guy who was definitely stupid, but most likely innocent. However, there is a second reason why I rolled the dice instead of shooting him. The second reason is that the motorist certainly would have considered my shooting him to be very unethical. The recruits look quite puzzled when I say that, so I tell the recruits to think about this. When ordinary citizens are stopped for traffic infractions, they do not expect that the person who has sworn to protect them is going to kill them.

Again, some motorists might be stupid, but most of the time they are not dangerous. Truly, police officers are between a rock and a hard place with this shoot/don't shoot stuff. Fortunately for everyone involved, most of us make the correct choices. Considering the number of interactions between the police and the public, unfortunate incidents are few and far between. The best-case scenario is not to be tried by twelve, or to be carried by six. A good day for a police officer is when everyone goes home in one piece.

CHAPTER 23
A DIPLOMATIC FAUX PAS

When people learn about my career in law enforcement they often ask me why I resigned from the City police, after several years of service, and became a stockbroker. I almost always say that I was looking to see what a "normal" job was like. The truth is that I resigned because I committed a diplomatic faux pas. I am not the first cop to commit a diplomatic faux pas, but I guess mine was worse than most. The first one I heard of was a situation where two cops stopped a guy for DUI in the Bronx. His wife was also in the car. He claimed to be a diplomat and showed the officers some documents in a foreign language. The guy claimed to be immune to arrest.

The cops, who had only a vague understanding of diplomatic immunity, ignored what they thought was a lame attempt to deceive them. They arrested the guy, cuffed him, and brought him in for processing. About three quarters of the way through the arrest processing procedure the Desk Officer got a call from the Police Commissioner's office. The wife had called her embassy, the embassy called the State Department, and the State Department called the Commissioner's Office. The officers were told that the guy they arrested had diplomatic immunity from arrests of this nature. They were ordered to release him immediately.

The incident was the impetus for a City wide training program so that every police officer would know what to do in the future. The Department did not want any more diplomatic faux pas. Every police officer in service was sent to the training. The training was also added to the Police Academy curriculum for new recruits. It is valuable training. Let's face it. The United Nations is in New York. There is no other city in the world with as many diplomats running around.

The training consisted of a brief history of diplomatic immunity. Then it described the status of the situation today. The Police Department also laid out a step-by-step process for us to follow whenever we encounter someone who claims to be a diplomat. Appropriately, they addressed officer safety first. Even full diplomatic immunity does not trump a police officer's constitutional right to protect his or her own life, or the life of someone else.

Once officer safety has been reasonably assured, the officer may detain the individual at the location where that person was stopped until the truth of his or her diplomatic status has been established. This is to be done with no handcuffs, assuming the subject's cooperation of course. The officer must immediately notify his or her supervisor that the officer has someone who claims to be a diplomat. The supervisor then follows the process required to verify the information with the State Department. If it turns out that the individual is not to be detained, the officers must immediately release him or her.

Although diplomatic immunity has been around for centuries, it was not standardized for most of its history. This caused many problems and misunderstandings. Each country negotiated separate agreements with other countries. The terms of the immunity often varied from agreement to agreement. The Vienna Convention on Diplomatic Relations of 1961 standardized diplomatic immunity for all countries that are members of the United Nations.

There are various levels of immunity granted to foreign officials, but the status of "Diplomatic Agent" is what has become known as full diplomatic immunity. Those designated as Diplomatic Agents may not be arrested or detained for any reason whatsoever. Their premises and vehicles may not be searched. They may not be subpoenaed as witnesses and they may not be prosecuted. They may be issued traffic tickets, but they are not required to appear in court to answer those tickets.

Obviously, diplomatic immunity is important. Here's a hypothetical example. Suppose you are a diplomat and you are sent to a country where the tree huggers make the laws. They have a law that says that the punishment for hurting a tree is death. Your kid decides to climb a tree in that country and inadvertently breaks a branch. You would not want your child to be punished by that country's law. Diplomatic immunity calls for your child to be punished according to the laws of his or her own country that apply to such transgressions.

Most of the information I obtained about Foday Limba came from interviews investigators conducted with some of his countrymen who knew him. Some of them were Sierra Leone ex-patriots. I did my own research to learn about the regime that ruled that country at the time of my diplomatic faux pas.

Foday Limba was the son of a warlord in Sierra Leone. He joined his father's forces as a soldier when he became a man. According to tribal tradition, that would be at about age 14. By age 17, he had developed a taste for blood and for brutally raping women. Whenever his father's forces conquered an enemy village, the surviving men of the losing side were tortured and executed. Their women were gang raped, tortured, and then either executed or enslaved. Foday literally developed a taste for blood. Another of his tribal traditions called for him to eat of the heart and brain of his enemy. That way he would acquire both the physical strength of his enemy, as well as his enemy's cunning in battle. Although why they would want the characteristics of someone they just defeated still baffles me.

Foday's father was on the winning side in a civil war.
Another warlord
became president, but as part of the deal Foday's dad became Minister of Defense. When there were no more tribes to conquer, Foday set about killing his father's political enemies and raping whatever woman he wanted without any fear of consequences.

The international community actually decided to recognize this new government in Sierra Leone. I am sure it had nothing to do with the fact that the country was rich in Titanium, Diamonds, and Gold. Soon after, their delegation took its place at the United Nations, which of course, is in New York. Accordingly, the U.S. Government recognized them diplomatically and with that came the various levels of diplomatic immunity.

Foday was sent to New York to attend Columbia University. As the son of the Defense Minister of Sierra Leone he was designated a Diplomatic Agent by his government. He was given full diplomatic immunity. This meant that no matter what crime he committed his only punishment would be deportation to his own country and revocation of his visa. He was 21 when he started college in New York.

Foday was cool for the first six months. As soon as he got comfortable with life here in America, he decided to take a female college student out on a date. His idea of a date was to take her to dinner and then take her back to her dorm room and rape her. When she opened her door and kissed him goodnight, he pushed her inside and closed the door. First he beat her and choked her into submission. Then he stripped her from the waist down, held her face down on her bed and forced his penis into her rectum. Foday tried to muffle her screams of pain by putting his hand over her mouth, but other students in the dorm heard her screaming and called 911.

Back in Sierra Leone what Foday did would have wound up being the woman's fault. According to both his religion and his culture, the woman is responsible for the attack unless there are at least two male witnesses who will testify that she was forced. In his culture, a woman's father, brother, or husband, is responsible for making sure she does not "entice" men into having their way with her. Foday brought his morality and this kind of ethic with him to America.

By the time the campus security people and the City police got there Foday had completed his brutal act and was on his way out the door. He claimed that it was no more than consensual rough sex. He said the woman knows he is the son of a wealthy diplomat. He said she was claiming rape because he refused her attempt to extort money from him. Some years later, I had a conversation with the detective who conducted the rape investigation. The detective said that during the interview, Foday told him that he (Foday) liked it when his penis split a woman's anus open. He said the profuse bleeding enhanced his pleasure.

Yea, Foday was a very warped individual. However, he had full diplomatic immunity, so in accordance with international law, he had his visa revoked and was sent back to Sierra Leone to face "punishment" according to their laws. There was no justice for the victim.

Two years later, Foday had become Major Foday Limba of the Sierra Leone army. His father appointed him security attaché to the country's delegation to the United

Nations. The U.S. again issued him a visa and in his new role he was again designated a Diplomatic Agent.

Bob and I had been partners in Anti-Crime for almost two years. We both liked working in plain clothes with unmarked cars. It is incredible how many arrests you can make that way. Even though you are still pretty easy to spot, people just commit offenses right in front of you. It is also the best way to sneak up on bad guys, particularly if they are either too arrogant or too dumb to notice. Before coming to my precinct in Queens, Bob worked Anti-Crime in both Manhattan and the Bronx. He was always telling me stories about his adventures there, so when Manhattan North needed volunteers for a task force we went for it. It was going to be Mike and Bob's excellent adventure in Manhattan.

The task force was after a guy who had raped four women in Washington Heights and Harlem. Each woman was found bent over and duct taped to an object like a desk, or a bench. They were all assaulted anally and they all had lacerations and internal injuries. The perpetrator was a male, in his 20's, with no distinguishing characteristics except what was described as an "African" accent. Based on the victims' descriptions of the attacker, the task force had a composite sketch of what the rapist looked like. We had no idea if it was accurate or not.

We were working a midnight-to-eight shift on the task force one day when we got a call to meet a cab driver near Amsterdam Avenue and West 125th Street. The call came over at about 0030 hours. When we got there, the cab driver said he picked up a man and a woman down around the theatre district about 20 minutes ago.

He said, "The guy leaned into the cab before the woman got in. He handed me two crisp one hundred dollar bills. Then he told me to stop when he said so and to keep my mouth shut after that. I took the money, but I didn't quite understand what the guy was talking about. The guy gave me an address off West 125th Street. As I pulled up to the address, I noticed that the building was a warehouse of some sort, no name on the building and right next to it was an alley that led down the side of the building."

"The male passenger said to the woman, 'Get out with me'. The woman replied, 'No! There's no bar here.' Suddenly, the guy grabbed the girl around the neck and began to pull her out of the cab by her head. As he was doing it, he said to me, 'Go. Just go and forget about us.' I said to myself, fuck him. I'll take his 200 and still call the police. I watched him start to drag the woman by her head down the alley. Then I drove to a pay phone and called 911"

Bob said to the driver, "Take us to where you dropped them off."

We jumped in the unmarked car and followed the cab driver to the building. It was only about a block and a half away. We already had all the information on the driver that we needed so we cut him loose. I got on the radio and I told Central where we were and what we had. There was another Anti-Crime team working on the task force that night. They were working closer to midtown, but I knew they would be coming to assist us once they heard the call.

I rushed to get out of the car and Bob said, "Wait. Let me get the crowbar out of the trunk. We might need it to get inside."

I started down the alley, gun drawn, and listening intently for anything that would lead us to them. Bob caught up to me very quickly. About 30 feet off the main road, I started to hear the woman's muffled screams. Bob heard them too. We hastened our pace down the alley and found a locked door. We could hear the screaming and crying coming from inside. I stood back while Bob quickly forced the door open with the crowbar. Then he set it down next to the door as quietly as he could and drew his revolver.

That part of the building was a storage facility for appliances like refrigerators, washing machines, and dryers. We only found out much later that the government of Sierra Leone had leased it. All of the appliances were due to be shipped to that country. We had turned our flashlights off when we opened the door. Neither of us wanted some bad guy to start shooting toward the lights. We looked over the expanse of the room. It was dimly lit by the light coming from an office that was off the main storage area. The office was only 20 feet from where we were standing. The screams and crying were coming from in there. We rushed quickly into the office.

The guy had the woman bent over a desk. Her arms and legs were duct taped to it. She was naked from the waist down and the guy was standing there savagely raping her from behind. She was screaming, out of her mind with pain, and she was bleeding from her rectum.

Without any warning I hit him from behind as hard as I could with my revolver across the right side of his head. The cylinder of the revolver opened a gash on the side of his face, but it did not immediately dislodge him from the woman. When he didn't react immediately, I hit him a second time, again as hard as I could. I hit him so hard I almost dropped my gun. After the second hit, he separated from the woman and turned toward me. I hit him a third time. This time, across the left side of his face. The last smack drove him to his knees and he put both of his hands up to protect his head. His hands were empty.

I screamed out, "Police – Don't Move! Keep your hands on you head. You move and I'll kill you."

The guy was kneeling with his pants around his ankles and he was bleeding from where my gun split his skin on both sides of his head. He was wearing a white dress shirt and a tie, which were quickly being stained with his own blood. Other than that, he seemed perfectly fine.

Bob ran to the woman and began to help her. He holstered up, took out his knife, and cut her bonds. I was standing there with my gun trained on the guy. The guy started to move, so I kicked him in the chest and knocked him on to his back. I did it to distract him from doing whatever it was he was about to do. He struggled to sit up and he leaned against a file cabinet. I was focusing on his hands to make sure he did not have a weapon, or try to reach for one that might be somewhere nearby.

I screamed, "You move again and I'll shoot you, you prick." Keep your hands on your head and don't move."

Bob told Central exactly where we were. He said we caught a guy in the middle of a rape. He said we needed detectives and crime scene, but most of all we needed an ambulance for the victim. Just as Bob was finishing with the radio, the guy started to talk. He was still panting from his strenuous activity and from me hitting him and kicking him in the chest.

He said, in broken English, "I am a diplomat with the United Nations. I want to go to my consulate."

Bob had already begun to help the woman. He was sitting on the floor with her. He covered her lower torso with some of her clothing. Then he used some of her other clothing to put direct pressure against her injuries in an effort to quell the bleeding. Bob heard what the guy said and he looked at me. I had seen that look before. When you have a steady partner, you begin to read each other's non-verbal communication. I knew that if Bob was not otherwise occupied, he would be beating this guy to within an inch of his life right now. The look he gave me told me that there was no way we should let him get away with this, even if he really was a diplomat.

I started thinking and that often gets me into trouble. I thought, if this guy actually is a diplomat then the window of opportunity to achieve some sort of justice for this woman was closing. Once others arrived, there would be nothing I could do, that I could also get away with. I knew the other Anti-Crime team would be here in a few minutes. They were from Manhattan North and neither Bob nor I knew them. That meant we could not really trust them to keep their mouths shut if we did anything against the rules.

This was quite a dilemma for me. It was one of those situations where two ethics (societal expectations) conflict with each other. The ethical thing to do from the government's perspective would be to adhere to the training on how to handle diplomats. This, of course, would result in no justice for the woman who was raped.

On the other hand, I don't think any female citizen of the United States would expect that the police and her own government would aid this man in getting away with savagely raping her. Since citizens rely on the police and the government in general to protect them, I can't imagine anything more *unethical* from her perspective. Imagine, "Oh, he's a diplomat? I guess then it is OK for him to rape me." Not likely.

Some police officers would have been happy to take refuge in the Department's ethic. They could say, "I did what the law and my supervisors expected me to do. I behaved ethically." This would require the officer to dehumanize the victim and refrain from applying the "Golden Rule." Would they do the same if it were their mother being raped? I don't think so.

It is a good way to protect your psyche from the traumatic assault to your senses that has just taken place. It is the perfect excuse for someone who does not want to put his or her career at risk. It is also the same rationalization used by the Nazi guards to justify their involvement in the holocaust. I would have nothing of it.

The victim's head was facing away from me as Bob was holding her. She could not see me, or her attacker, at that moment. I figured that I only had seconds to do something. Then the rapist began to speak again. This time he barked at us and there was arrogance and contempt in his voice.

He said, "I am a Diplomatic Agent of Sierra Leone. I am entitled to diplomatic immunity. You cannot arrest me. You will call your State Department immediately or face the consequences."

I said to myself, I can't believe this guy is actually giving us orders and threatening us. I speculated that maybe he thought we were merely functionaries. When I was in the academy there was a defensive tactics instructor we used to call the Tasmanian Devil. Physically, he was built just like his cartoon character namesake. Also, like his namesake, he was always full of energy, and itching to do battle. One day, while my class was waiting for a guest speaker to arrive, he decided to engage the class in conversation to pass the time.

He said, "I have a philosophical question for you people. What is the worst crime a person can commit?"

After saying "no" to many suggestions, he said, "The worst crime a person can commit is Contempt of Cop. You are not going to find it in any law book. However, I have seen murderers treated better by the police than a minor violator who also commits Contempt of Cop."

The fact that this rapist tried to assert authority over Bob and I, after committing such a horrific act, made my blood boil. I don't think the guy was aware of it, but besides committing Contempt of Cop, he was also disregarding Real Fact of Life # 2 and Real Fact of Life # 4 … at the same time! "Face the consequences," he said. OK. I focused, and then I fired two rounds from my revolver point blank into his chest. The medical examiner later said that the first shot shattered his sternum. The second one penetrated his heart. He died in a few seconds staring at me with the most surprised look on his face.

The situation was off the map. I was calmer than I thought I would be. The look of surprise on the rapist's face made me think about what another cop, Ronnie Souder, once said to a dying perpetrator. "I want you to see who is sending you to hell." I did not feel as passionate or spiritual about it as Ronnie did, but I did have a satisfying sense of justice at that moment.

The woman screamed from the sound of the gun and Bob held her head to his chest. Bob looked at the guy, watched him die, and then he looked at me. His expression was blank. I guess my solution to the problem surprised even a salty old dog like Bob.

I turned to Bob and said, "I told him not to move. He reached for something behind his back."

Bob nodded in agreement with what would later become my justification for shooting the rapist.

He said, "I saw him do it. He moved his right hand down from his head and reached behind his back."

I nodded that we were on the same page about what the guy did and which hand he used. We also agreed concerning a few other essential details to keep our stories consistent. Doing so out loud also served to plant those facts and circumstances in the mind of the victim. She did not see anything, but she was sure to be interviewed about it. If she said she saw what we saw, all the better.

Then, while still holding her, Bob said to the woman, "Don't worry. He's dead now. He will never hurt you, or anyone else, ever again."

She was sobbing into Bob's chest. A few minutes later we heard the words, "Police – Don't Move." The other Anti-Crime team had arrived. They were standing outside the building next to the door. They arrived well after I shot the rapist and they heard me talking on the radio letting Central know that we had shot the perpetrator. They saw our silhouettes moving around in the office and they wanted to make sure we were the good guys before they entered the building. In unison, Bob and I called back, "Police – Don't Shoot." Then they asked if we were OK and we said yes. Soon after that, the ambulance arrived and so did the rest of the cavalry.

I assume that some of you reading this believe that I should be punished for what I did. I am hoping that there are also some of you who would give me absolution for what I did. For those of you who might absolve me, I need to remind you that I did not know who this guy was when I decided to shoot him. I suspected that he might have been our rapist, but I did not know that for sure. He might have just been a completely different rapist. I certainly did not know that he was as warped an individual as he turned out to be. His history, both here and in Sierra Leone, was not known to me. It was not a factor in my decision to shoot him.

The point is that my decision to kill him was based on what was happening at that time. I am familiar with Romans 12:19, "Vengeance is mine. I will repay, says the Lord." My maker may very well hold me accountable for what I did. However, I knew what Diplomatic Agent meant. I went through the training. I was not going to let the same system that would allow this animal to get away with this, to punish me for ending the nightmare they created.

I saw no other way that this woman was going to get justice and I acted to remedy that. I also acted to stop him from doing this to anyone in the future. It was in accordance with my morality, which obviously was in conflict with one, but not both, of the applicable ethics.

This was not an act of vengeance. This was a reckoning. I soon came to learn that for this individual the reckoning was long overdue. Well, I was about to "face the consequences" for my decision. In addition to the usual scrutiny that a police involved shooting receives, the F.B.I. and the U.S. State Department were going to want to know what happened. The federal government would have a huge influence on the outcome.

In New York, a Grand Jury is composed of 23 U.S. citizens. Its purpose is to decide if the person being investigated for a felony crime should be indicted. If 12 of those 23 people believe that the individual accused probably did it (probable cause), the person gets indicted and has to stand trial. The prosecuting attorney (Assistant District Attorney or ADA) controls the Grand Jury. The prosecutor can call witnesses and introduce evidence before any of those witnesses, or pieces of evidence, have been deemed admissible by the courts. The defendant may tell the Grand Jury his or her side of the story. However, the accused must do so without an attorney present to give him or her any advice, or to object to any part of the proceedings. Because of this, defense attorneys have a saying that goes, "A good prosecutor can get a Grand Jury to indict a ham sandwich."

This all means that it was very, very important for me to convince the prosecutor that I acted out of fear for my life. When I learned that the person prosecuting my case was a woman, I felt that was in my favor. Her name was Ania Sawicki. By the time I had my interview with Ms. Sawicki, she had already learned of Foday's history as a brutal torturer and rapist, both here and in Sierra Leone. When I explained how the shooting occurred, I was humble. I expressed regret that he forced me to shoot him by reaching behind his back, after I told him not to move. I explained that I acted in accordance with Department guidelines for people who claim to be diplomats. I had not cuffed him.

As the investigation into the shooting progressed, I learned that when Foday's father, Minister Limba, was told that his son was killed he wanted me dead. He demanded that the State Department turn me over to him so that I could be sent to Sierra Leone to receive a "fair trial" for what I did. He threatened to take Americans in Sierra Leone hostage if the State Department did not comply with his demand. I also heard that some his personal guards, who were supposedly skilled at such things, volunteered to "hunt me" on the streets of New York and bring my skin to him as a prize.

Unfortunately, I would not put it passed the State Department to try to turn me over to Sierra Leone if the political wind was blowing in that direction. I prayed that U.S. interests in that country's titanium, diamonds, and gold, were not so great as to tempt them to consider such a thing. No paranoia here.

The other thing I was worried about was that the State Department was in a position to really help the prosecutor's career. They could offer her a federal judgeship, or some other career-enhancing situation. Something like that might make it advantageous for the prosecutor to throw me to the wolves in front of the Grand Jury. I had no way of knowing if the prosecutor was of the ilk that would be tempted by such things.

The State Department explained to the President of Sierra Leone that I would face due process here in the United States. The State Department assured him that retaliation against U.S. citizens, or other westerners, in Sierra Leone would be met with nothing short of a military response. They reminded the President of what Foday had done and they implored the President to control Minister Limba for the good of all concerned.

There had been a small amount of news coverage immediately following the shooting, but not much. The government of Sierra Leone apparently agreed because everything got quiet as I proceeded through the investigation of the shooting. However, I waited for the other shoe to drop. I knew this was not over.

The day before my case was to go before the Grand Jury, Ms. Sawicki called for a meeting in her office. On my side there was my attorney, my union rep, and me. On their side, there was the ADA, a Lieutenant from Internal Affairs, an FBI guy, and a gentleman from the State Department named George Cutrone.

When I entered the room, the ADA greeted me quite cordially. She said she was glad to see me again, but I was wary. We all sat down in chairs she had gathered around her desk. She made all the introductions. She was about to explain the reason for the meeting when the State Department guy interrupted.

He said, "If no one objects, I would like to speak with Officer Rudolph alone for a few minutes. Is there somewhere we can go that we will not be disturbed?"

The ADA said, "Of course,"

My attorney objected to a private meeting without him present, but I told my attorney that I wanted to hear what the man had to say. Then the ADA got up, and led us two doors down a corridor into a small, unoccupied office. Mr. Cutrone closed the door behind her as she left. He motioned for me to sit down in a chair. He sat opposite to me. The scene felt very informal.

As soon as we sat down I said, "Before we begin talking, I wanted to say thank you for whatever you people did to keep the media coverage of this to a minimum. I could just see those idiots in the press providing assassins from Sierra Leone with a roadmap to my house, if you know what I mean."

He responded, "Well, believe me when I tell you, it was in everyone's interest to keep this from becoming a media circus. We didn't need your *diplomatic faux pas* to become a public spectacle and the government of Sierra Leone did not want Foday's history to become public at all."

I said, 'Well thank you anyway."

Cutrone said, "Listen, please call me George."

I said, "Sure, George. I'm Mike."

We shook hands.

Then he said, "Mike, if our conversation does not go well, I will deny everything we are about to discuss. Do you understand?"

I nodded.

"First of all," he said, "I want to tell you that *I* think you were completely justified in shooting Major Limba. He was a despicable human being and based on his history, he could just as easily have had a weapon behind his back. He had no respect for his diplomatic immunity. He used it like a get out of jail free card. I am incensed by what he did to that woman and the other woman at Columbia a few years back."

I was impressed and a little relieved that he was aware of Foday's history and suitably appalled by his behavior.

I said, "I appreciate you saying so. It is often hard to tell where people are coming from sometimes. It can make a person quite paranoid."

He smiled at my comment and continued, "Let me tell you what is going on right now. Major Foday Limba had a following back in Sierra Leone. Those followers are whipping up anti American and anti-western sentiments in that country. They are waiting for the outcome of your Grand Jury hearing. The people in Sierra Leone are used to swift justice. When they hear the words "Grand Jury," they think your punishment will be forthcoming. If you are not punished in a way that satisfies them, they are going to start attacking westerners in Sierra Leone. Most of those people are missionaries and humanitarian aid workers. I have brokered a deal with the Sierra Leone government that would stop that from happening, but the deal won't fly without your cooperation."

I nodded, and he continued.

"Minister Limba has flown in to New York to take his son's body home. I have met with him. After some arm twisting from his own president, Minister Limba is willing to say *publically* that he wants no revenge against westerners for the *accidental* death of his son. I understand that privately he is very angry."

I interrupted and said, "Yea, I got the word he wants me skinned and he has guys willing to do it."

George responded, "Well, that's neither here nor there. The President of Sierra Leone and Minister Limba have assured me that they can stop any violence from occurring. To some degree they fear our "big stick," and our ability to freeze their assets, but they also need to save face. What they want in return is to be able to tell their people that you were fired and disgraced for making such a grave error in judgment."

I was blown away by what he was telling me. This came completely out of left field. I didn't know what to say, or how to react. I never imagined that my shooting of Foday would somehow be connected with innocent people being butchered. I never dreamed that what happened in that warehouse would wind up costing some people their loved ones.

The situation was very heavy. When I dropped the hammer on Foday, I knew I would have to face a Grand Jury. I thought I might even have to face a jury of my peers. I felt confident that with my testimony, Bob's testimony, the victim's testimony, and Foday's history, I would eventually weather the storm. However, I have to say that I never envisioned developments like these when I made my decision to pull the trigger.

The more I thought about it, the more I realized that although I did not anticipate this eventuality, I was still glad I shot Foday Limba. I started to get self-righteous. I thought to myself, this man was doing wicked things. Someone needed to stop him. Then I thought about the loss of life all around and I felt the weight of the situation again.

I decided to embrace George's plan. I reflected that maybe it was part of a penance I have to do. However, I decided to try to steer the Karma in a direction that would best suit me. I thought for a short minute and I came up with three issues that would be deal breakers for me. I made sure to maintain eye contact with George as I spoke. I wanted to watch his eye responses carefully to get a feel for his veracity as we conversed.

I said, "George, I don't care what you tell the government of Sierra Leone and I don't care what they tell their people. If I go along with this, my record with the City police has to show that I resigned from the Department for personal reasons. It cannot show that I was fired or left with any issues. I have taken entrance exams for two other police departments in this area. I am considering making the jump to another PD. This deal must not jeopardize that.

He thought for a moment and said, "OK, that's do-able. We can express publicly that you have been dismissed, but your records will actually show that you resigned for personal reasons with no prejudice."

I continued, "Also, I need a way to make a living until one of these police departments calls me. I need you to use whatever super powers the State Department has to find me a job. It has to pay as much as I am making now."

He thought about that for a few seconds and then said, "Agreed. We can do that. Is that it?"

I said, "One final thing. I have to be issued a carry permit. If they actually send people to assassinate me, I want to be armed and able to defend myself."

He asked, "Aren't you being a little paranoid now?"

I responded, "It's a deal breaker George."

He said, "Well, when you people separate from the Department don't you automatically get a carry permit?"

I said, "It's only automatic for retirees."

He said, "OK. I can make sure that happens. Are we done?"

I said, "Yes, but what about the Grand Jury and Internal Affairs?"

He said, "The assistant district attorney will present the evidence in such a way that the Grand Jury will not vote to indict you. Internal Affairs will handle this any way that we and the District Attorney want them to."

I said, "OK then. You have a deal."

He said, "Good," and he reached out to shake my hand. I took his hand and he placed his other hand over mine.

Then he said, "Oh, there's just one more thing."

I looked at him with dagger eyes and he knew I was suspicious.

He smiled at the classic sneakiness of his own behavior and said, "Minister Limba wants to meet with you. He wants you to tell him, face-to-face, why you were forced to shoot his son."

I hesitated in order to evaluate the ramifications and then I said, "OK. I'll meet with him if that what it is going to take to close the deal and make this go away."

George said, "Good. Then I'll make the arrangements for you to go to the embassy."

I said, "Wo-wo-wo-wo-wo! He wants to meet with me in the Sierra Leone embassy?"

George said, "Yea, is that a problem?"

I motioned with my hands in a Zen move to keep myself from getting angry with what I perceived was George's convenient stupidity.

Then I said, "George. It is my understanding that the embassy is actually foreign soil and that we can't go in there for any reason unless we are invited. Am I correct about that?"

He said, "Yea, but you are going to be invited. I still don't see the problem?"

I became incredulous and asked, "You don't see the *problem*?? The *problem* is George that once I go in that place, this guy can do whatever he wants to me and no one is going to help me. Everyone in the embassy has diplomatic immunity, don't they?"

George said skeptically, "Do you really think your life is in danger?"

I started to raise my voice out of frustration with him.

I said, "Are you kidding me? This guy's a goddam warlord for Christ's sake. He kills his political enemies. He's still got one foot in the jungle."

He still looked unconvinced.

I continued, "George, if I go into the Sierra Leone embassy the first thing that is going to happen is that I am going to disappear. Minister Limba is going to tell you some bullshit about how I left through some back door and you are not going to do anything about it. Then he is going to torture me to death. After that, he is going to chop me up and ship me to Sierra Leone in so many diplomatic pouches. Then he's going to put my head on a stake and feed the rest of me to the crocodiles. I am not going into the Sierra Leone embassy, George."

George was smiling and he actually chuckled at my angst and my description of what I thought Foday's father would do to me.

He said, "Mike, you have to meet with him. It is part of the deal. The deal will fall apart if you don't meet with him."

I said, "Fine George, I will be happy to meet with Minister Limba. I will meet him right here, in the ADA's office on my turf, not in the embassy on his turf. My mother did not raise a stupid son."

Again, George started to smile at my remarks and the high level of what he perceived as my paranoia. Then he shook his head.

He said, "I don't know if they are going to go for it."

I responded in a very calm and metered voice, "George, if the only thing he wants to do is talk with me, this will not be a problem. If he insists I meet with him in an environment where he can do whatever he likes to me without consequences, then he doesn't just want to talk."

George nodded his head. It was hard to escape my logic. He told me to go back into the ADA's office and to wait for him there. He needed to make some phone calls. When I re-entered Ms. Sawicki's office, all conversation stopped. Everyone looked at me.

I said to my attorney, "He told me to wait here. He had to make a phone call."

We all just sat there looking at each other, saying nothing. A couple of minutes later, George came back into the room.

He said to the ADA, "I think we may have resolved this."

She had a look on her face that told me that she was privy to what the State Department was proposing. Then George looked at my attorney, my union rep, and finally at me.

He said, "I don't think there is any reason for you to stay any longer. Ms. Sawicki will contact you."

My attorney looked at the ADA and said, "I assume there will still be a presentation to the Grand Jury tomorrow? My client still intends to testify."

The ADA looked at George and then told my attorney, "I'll call you later and we'll talk."

The next day, Bob and I testified before the Grand Jury. The prosecutor presented her case and the Grand Jury voted not to Indict me. Afterward, my attorney said that he would make sure that Mr. Cutrone fulfilled all the commitments that he made to me.

George turned out to be a standup guy. He called me personally after the Grand Jury made its decision and told me what happened with Minister Limba. He said that he told the father, in so many diplomatic terms, that I was not comfortable meeting at the embassy because it was foreign soil. George also told him that I would be more than happy to have the meeting in the district attorney's office, or some other location that was mutually agreeable. Just not at the Sierra Leone embassy. George said that the father smiled knowingly, thought for a moment, and then he said that the meeting would no longer be necessary.

I was silent on the phone. I was biting my tongue and fighting back the urge to say "I told you so," but I didn't have to.

George said, "Apparently Minister Limba may have had a hidden agenda after all."

I said, "So, do I get an apology?"

He said, "That's as close as you are going to get."

I responded, "No problem George."

The State Department fulfilled its side of the bargain. I got to resign for personal reasons. They found me a position in a broker training program with a firm on Wall Street. Most important to me, I got my carry permit. If Mr. Limba decided to send his assassins after me, I would be armed and the fight would take place on the streets of New York ... my turf.

At the time this incident occurred there was no such thing as DNA testing. We could not match Foday to the other four rapes in that way. Putting a dead guy in a line up to be identified by the victims was truly comical. The idea reminded me of *Weekend at Bernie's*. Even a photo pack identification was not do-able because we had no pictures of Foday while he was alive. The State Department refused to give us a picture of Foday from their records and Sierra Leone refused our request for a photo. The upshot is that Foday was never actually linked to the other four rapes. However, after Foday died, the rapes stopped. I guess I must have capped the right guy.

CHAPTER 24
END GAME

I began writing this book about six months before September 11, 2001. I cried when the towers came down. Oh, I cried for the people who loved and lost, but I also cried out of anger and frustration. You see, we were right and the ostriches were wrong. I cried because all those people who died paid for the inaction of the very people they elected to insure their safety. Most of all, I cried because I knew those responsible for the debacle would escape punishment for their selfish and unethical behavior. I knew the entire world would never be the same again because of what those officials failed to do.

For lack of a better explanation, September 11, 2001 gave me writer's block. I put this book away and immersed myself in homeland security. With the cooperation of some pragmatic and dedicated police administrators, I have been allowed to make my contribution to preventing another Ground Zero. So far - so good. I took my book out of mothballs as the tenth anniversary was approaching and finally finished it.

My career in law enforcement is winding down. These days, experience and treachery are what I use to compensate for the loss of youth and strength. Not that I am falling apart, I just can't do some police functions with the same intensity that I used to have. I acknowledge that I am beatable, but I am still quite formidable.

The thought of retirement frightens me. I know some cops who could not wait to retire and start phase two of their lives. I actually love what I do. In fact, being a police officer is not what I do. It is what I am. This poses a huge problem for me as my body betrays me and voluntary or forced retirement approaches.

I decided that this book should be part of the process I undertake to transition from being the hammer most of the time, to being the nail most of the time. As a police officer, I *choose* to step aside for a lot of people. However, there are very few people that I *have* to step aside for. I don't remember ever saying, "There is never a cop around when you need one." I just get pissed off and do something about whatever it happens to be. Also, being a police officer has allowed me to intervene and help a lot of people. I have changed many people's lives for the better and that is the coolest part of being a cop.

I was at a retirement party a while back and the retiree was waxing philosophical.

He said, "Mike, we are like shepherds watching over the flock, but even shepherds have to retire sometime."

I said, "Kevin, I see what you mean, but I tend to think we are more like sheep dogs patrolling the edges of the flock. That's how Plato described the Guardian Class in "The Republic," I kind of buy into that."

Then Kevin asked, "When are you going to retire? Are you even thinking about it?"

I said, "No way man. They say a cop's dick shrinks two inches when he retires. You think I want to walk around with a puny 10 inch dick?"

Kevin started laughing and said, "Yea, in your dreams."

I started laughing at my own joke and finally I said, "Seriously? I don't think I am ready yet. I think I'll wait for a good career-ending event."

Then we both laughed again because I always used to tell him that I would rather go out with a bang than with a whimper.

Kevin glanced around and said, "Look at this. All these young sheep dogs come to honor this old sheep dog. It really is nice to pass the torch."

I asked him, "So would you do it again if you could?"

He chuckled and said, "Yea, sure I would. It's been a great life. How about you? You were a stockbroker before this right? Would you choose to be a cop again knowing what you know now?"

I said, "Kevin, if I had it to do over again, I would ask for another 30 years." We tapped our glasses and finished our beer.

The party was a daytime affair that Kevin's wife held in their backyard. I had a beer or two, but I stayed sober because I knew I would be driving. Around four o'clock in the afternoon I said my goodbyes and my wife and I got into the car to drive home.

The neighborhood was beautiful. The streets were winding and the single-family homes were situated on large pieces of property. We just meandered along the road out of Kevin's development looking left and right at the landscaping and commenting to each other on how well the homes were appointed.

Then something caught my eye in the rear view mirror. I saw this black car coming up on me fast. The speed limit was 30 mph. I was doing about 20, so I pulled my car a little closer to the right side of the road and glanced left to make sure the guy had enough room to pass me easily. He did.

Suddenly he blew his horn. I looked in the mirror and the guy was riding my ass. There was no more than six feet between my car and his. My wife turned to look at the guy and I checked to make sure he had enough room to pass. The Titanic could have passed me on the left. Then he blew his horn at us again.

She turned to me and said, "Let it go. We're having such a nice afternoon, just let it go."

I said, "Honey, if he gets away with this, he is going to do it to other people. Do you want him to do this to someone who is in no position to do anything about it?"

I could tell by the look on her face that I made her feel guilty with my last remark. She cares a lot about other people. She's not selfish. All she wanted was for us to have a peaceful day. I appreciated that.

I looked her in the eyes and said to her, "OK then. We'll play baseball."

She knew what I meant. He had blown his horn at me twice. That was strike one and strike two. If he just passed me and drove off, I would let it go. After strike three, he was out. It took about another 20 seconds for the asshole to blow his horn the third time.

I jammed on my brakes, threw the car in park and jumped out. The guy stopped short just before hitting me. I took out my shield and ID and with my left hand I held it prominently in front of me so the driver would know I was a cop. The car was a brand new black Mercedes S Class and the driver was a male, white, about 22 years old. A 22 year old was driving a car worth about $85,000.00.

Car thieves don't draw attention to themselves, so I reasoned that he had to be a celebrity, a drug dealer, or someone's arrogant little prick son. Then, a semi-paranoid possibility came to me. This tactic has been used in the past to assassinate law enforcement officers and other people as well. The harassment causes the victim to get angry and react without thinking. It draws the victim out of the car. Before the person knows what is happening, he or she is gunned down in the street. There I was, standing like a target in the street.

I was carrying my service weapon tucked into the front right side of my pants. My shirt covered it. As the years went by I stopped wearing a holster when I was off duty. Holsters make a prominent bulge under whatever clothes you happen to be wearing. Also, I liked the idea that my gun was on the anterior portion of my body. That way no one could sneak up behind me and try to pull it out. As I got close to his car, the driver suddenly reached his right arm toward the glove box.

I yelled, "POLICE – DON'T MOVE!" and drew my gun at the same time. Then I pointed it at him and yelled, "PUT YOUR HANDS ON THE STEERING WHEEL! PUT YOUR HANDS ON THE WHEEL WHERE I CAN SEE THEM!" The driver complied and I walked passed his door and took a position just behind his left shoulder.

While still covering him with my gun I asked, "What's in the glove box?"

He said, "Nothing."

I said, "If there is nothing in the glove box why were you reaching for it?"

He said, "There's just my cell phone."

I said, "I want to you reach over and open the glove box. Then put your hand back on the steering wheel. Do it slowly, because if you reach into the glove box I'm gonna shoot you."

He reached over slowly, opened the box, and then he put his hand back on the steering wheel. I looked into the box and there was a car book, some papers, and a cell phone, nothing else.

I put my gun back into my pants and asked the driver, "What the hell was that all about? Why did you tailgate me and start blowing your horn at me?"

He said, "You were going so slowly."

I said, "Going too slowly? There is no minimum speed limit on this road and I was not impeding you in any way. I was pulled all the way to the right. You had plenty of room to pass me. Why didn't you just pass me instead of harassing me like that?"

He didn't have an answer, so after a moment I requested his license and the paperwork on the car. It turned out that he was indeed driving daddy's car.

Just at that moment, three marked police cars came driving up to us with their lights on and stopped. My wife and I had an understanding that if I ever got involved in something, drawing my gun would be her signal to call 911. Apparently, she did. She gave them a great description of me, of the situation, and of the person and the car I had stopped. Still, I held my shield up high as two uniformed officers and a Sergeant approached. I wanted them to understand clearly that I was a police officer. I stepped away from the Mercedes and told the cops and the Sergeant what was going on. The Sergeant said that she makes it a habit to roll on any calls that involve off duty cops.

She said, "I don't make it my habit to get involved unless I am needed, but whenever the call involves someone who is off duty, eventually a supervisor winds up getting called."

Just as she finished speaking, Junior called out to us. He said, "Excuse me. I would like one of you to call one of your supervisors please. I want to talk to a supervisor."

The Sergeant just looked at me and rolled her eyes. It was one of those "see what I mean" looks. She walked over to the Mercedes and said, "I am a supervisor. What can I do for you?"

Junior told the Sergeant that he wanted my name and badge number. He said I had no right to point a gun at him and that I threatened to shoot him just because he blew his horn at me.

The Sergeant said, "Well I understand you did something that frightened the officer just before he drew his weapon. Do you remember what that was?"

Junior said, "I didn't do anything to frighten him. All I did was try to get my cell phone."

The Sergeant said, "And where was your cell phone? "

Junior responded, "In the glove box."

The Sergeant informed Junior that police officers have been shot by people who suddenly pull guns out of their glove boxes. She told him that if I had reason to suspect that my life was in danger, I could point a gun at whomever I thought was threatening me. She told him that it had nothing to do with him blowing his horn.

The Sergeant said to Junior, "When I drove up, the officer did not have his gun out. Did the officer put his gun away after he saw that you had no weapon?"

Junior said, "Yes, but he never should have pointed it at me to start with."

The Sergeant repeated that there was nothing illegal about what I did, but that Junior was entitled to make a complaint if he wanted to. Junior told the Sergeant that he would consult with his lawyer first. The Sergeant was smiling when she walked back to me and told me what Junior said.

"I am guessing that the kid is going to tell his daddy on you and that he will be making a complaint against you," she said.

I shrugged my shoulders and said, "Yea, what's new? God forbid he should actually take responsibility for causing this problem to begin with. This guy really needs a serious attitude adjustment."

One of the cops then said with a smile, "Well, attitude adjustments are what we do."

Then, with emphasis he said, "We are Attitude Adjustment Coordinators. Do you want to lock him up? That'll adjust his attitude."

I could see by the looks on their faces that processing a stupid arrest like this was not how they expected to spend their day. Still, they were willing to do it for a fellow officer and I appreciated that.

I said, "You know what guys? I'm just gonna write him a couple of tickets. I'll burn him for the unnecessary use of his horn and following too closely. I'll put it in front of a judge that way."

The Sergeant said, "Good choice. That sounds about right. Listen, I have a funny feeling that after daddy and his lawyer talk to him, the kid's story is going to change. I know what he told me and I know what I told him. When you find out what supervisor in your command gets assigned to investigate this have him or her call me." The two cops seemed happy at my choice of solutions also.

As I handed Junior his tickets he asked, "Is your name and number on here?"

I said, "Oh yes. I printed them very clearly for you so you will know exactly who to complain about."

Junior said, "I'll see *you* in court."

I responded, "Oh, I hope so. I am looking forward to telling this story to the judge."

I couldn't help but smile and shake my head at the thought of this guy rubbing shoulders with the unwashed masses at traffic court. I felt sure he would send daddy's lawyer to handle everything.

As I turned to walk away I said, again with a smile, "You now have my permission to leave. Drive safely young man."

He saw me smiling and steam started to come out of his ears. I walked over to the other cops and told them that he was really pissed off. I told them to get ready for him to peel some rubber as he leaves. The other officer, who hadn't said anything up to that point said, "Good, then I'll burn him for an unsafe start, or maybe lock him up for reckless driving."

The Sergeant said, "Don't forget to call me when the complaint comes in."

I thanked her again.

The "Attitude Adjustment Coordinator" said, "Nice meeting you brother," as he walked away.

At that point we all walked back to our cars. Junior was smart enough to drive away slowly. I guess he wasn't a complete idiot after all. I put my car in gear and resumed our leisurely drive out of the development.

When I first got out of the car my wife watched what was happening through the rear window. However, she could not hear what the driver and I said to each other. She also wasn't sure how the matter was resolved. My wife knew enough not to distract me while the situation was percolating, but now it was over.

She asked, "So tell me what went on back there?"

In an exasperated voice I said, "What went on back there was an idiot kid! I *know* I was not that stupid when I was his age. Can you imagine that? Blowing your horn at people like that when all you have to do is drive around them? It's just plain mean."

She nodded and said, "I agree."

Then I continued. "He completely disregarded Real Fact of Life # 1."

Before I could say anything else, she interrupted me and said, "Wait a minute. Now, which one is that? Is that the one with the herbivores and the carnivores, or is that the one where I get to save the furry little dog and let Hitler drown?"

She had this phony look of confusion on her face and just a hint of a smile. Every now and then she enjoys yanking my chain. She is forced to listen to me pontificate whenever another event in the world around us reinforces the validity and reliability of one of the Real Facts of Life. I know she knows them all by heart.

I just smiled at her sarcasm and said, "It's the one with the herbivores and the carnivores, smart ass, and if you don't mind, I do have a point to make."

She said, "Well by all means, make your point."

I said, "My point is, that the kid had no idea who was in this car. For all he knew I could have been some nut with a gun."

She turned slightly in her seat, faced me and said, "*Could* have been? You *could* have been some nut with a gun?"

I glanced at her over my right shoulder and I started to get defensive. I was about to say, "Excuse me?" Instead I bit my tongue and with a smile I gave her a "please stop breaking my balls" look. Then she reached across the car with her left hand and gently patted the back of my neck.

"Don't worry Mike," she said. "You just do whatever you have to do. I've got your back."

I smiled at her and said, "Thank you Honey."

Then I started thinking. Retirement is going to be worse than I thought.